D0260740

CINEMA ON THE PERIPHERY

Contemporary Irish and Spanish Film

CONN HOLOHAN

Foreword by
ROSA GONZÁLEZ

IRISH ACADEMIC PRESS
DUBLIN • PORTLAND, OR

First published in 2010 by Irish Academic Press

2 Brookside
Dundrum Road
Dublin 14, Ireland

920 NE 58th Avenue, Suite 300
Portland, Oregon,
97213-3786, USA

© 2010 by Conn Holohan

www.iap.ie

British Library Cataloguing in Publication Data
An entry can be found on request

978 0 7165 3022 0 (cloth)
978 0 7165 3023 7 (paper)

Library of Congress Cataloging-in-Publication Data
An entry can be found on request

Printed by MPG Books Group, King's Lynn & Bodmin

Contents

Acknowledgements

This book grew out of my doctoral thesis, and I am therefore indebted to many people who have aided and supported me throughout the long process of producing it. My thanks to the Centre for Media Research at Ulster University, Coleraine, which provided me with the funding and opportunity to pursue this research project. Thanks especially to Martin McLoone and Niamh Thornton for their invaluable support and advice throughout its duration, and to John Hill for his early guidance and for giving me the chance to pursue the research project that inspired me. Thanks also to all the other staff and research students at Coleraine who provided direction and motivation along the way, in particular Maire Messenger Davis and Robert Porter. Not forgetting Ciara and Niamh for putting me up and putting up with me.

I would also like to thank those I have worked with at Trinity College Dublin who have encouraged and advised me in the process of adapting from thesis into book, in particular Barnaby Taylor and Ruth Barton. Thanks also to the Centre for Film Studies, UCD, for the Teaching Fellowship which enabled me to pursue that process. Thanks to the staff at the Irish Film Archive for all their help, and to Lisa Hyde at Irish Academic Press who has always been available to provide support and suggestions.

All efforts have been made to establish copyright for images used in this book.

A special thank you to Claire for her love and support throughout, to Shane for the late-night sounding boards, and especially to my parents, who have supported and encouraged me in more ways than I can ever thank them for.

Conn Holohan
September 2009

List of Illustrations

Foreword

The current context of globalisation has no doubt added weight to the commercial imperative faced by cinema since its inception. The search for box-office returns and transnational marketability has progressively pushed film industries, particularly medium and small sized ones like those of Spain and Ireland, towards standardisation of their cinematic output. The co-option into the mechanisms of mainstream global culture (sometimes carried out at the expense of originality, experimentation and political engagement) doesn't necessarily result into a homogenised monoculture. Whilst global consumerism leads to an increasing number of people buying a narrower range of cultural products and watching a narrower range of films, thankfully it does not preclude local allegiance and the expression of national specificity. The pull between global demands and local concerns is auspiciously balanced out by the so-called glocalisation and its sensible motto 'think global, act local'.

Although our postmodern age no longer abides by the aesthetics of mimetic authenticity (and its notion that art holds up a mirror to reality), probably few people would refute the notion that cinema acts as a 'window' on the time and place that produces it. Indeed, given the significant role currently played by visual imagery in the discursive field of identity politics, fiction film can be considered one of the main 'cultural proxies' or conduits by which communities define themselves and their surroundings, and communicate them across the globe. The starting point of Conn Holohan's timely analysis of contemporary Irish and Spanish cinema is precisely a firm belief in the existence of nationally specific cultural markers in the filmographies of these two European countries. His personal contribution lies in perceptively identifying a number of historical experiences and of social and economic conditions shared by Ireland and Spain, and in convincingly tracing parallelisms in the representational strategies that a sizable number of contemporary films have resorted to in order to engage with the new realities of their respective processes of modernisation and to articulate them cinematically.

Material connections and empathetic bonds between Ireland and Spain are both ancient and deep, ranging from common myths of origin and medieval trading relations to religious affinity, geopolitical interests and cultural exchanges. On the Spanish side there is a longstanding interest in Irish literature and culture as witnessed by the translation into Spanish of the work of most Irish authors and the popularity of Irish music, both traditional and modern (U2's choice of Barcelona as the venue to kick off its 2009 world tour being a recent example). At the academic level, there is a thriving interdisciplinary Spanish Association for Irish Studies (AEDEI) and an ever growing corpus of scholarly publications.

Irish knowledge and interest in Spain and its culture has been mostly channelled through tourism. Still, besides the popular holiday in the sun Irish people can avail of a very large supply of reading material in English, for Spanish culture has been extremely well served by Hispanophiles from the Anglophone world under the auspices of the energetic Association of Hispanists of Great Britain & Ireland and the Anglo-Catalan Society, both founded in the 1950s, to which was added the networking group of gender and women's studies WISPS (Women in Spanish, Portuguese and Latin American Studies) in 1999. These dedicated researchers have produced some excellent work and filled a much-needed critical gap during the prolonged and rigidly censored Francoist dictatorship. The frequent trips many Spaniards made to Perpignan (southern France) during that period would often combine a visit to the cinema to watch X-rated films then forbidden in Spain, such as Bertolucci's *Last Tango in Paris* (1972) and *Emmanuelle* (Just Jaeckin 1974), with a call to bookshops in order to buy copies of Gerald Brennan's 1943 *The Spanish Labyrinth: an account of the social and political background of the Civil War* and Hugh Thomas' 1961 *The Spanish Civil War*, the first two volumes published, in Spanish translation, by the publishing house Ruedo Ibérico, set up in Paris by the Spanish anarchist José Martínez in 1962. Ruedo Ibérico later published The *Nationalistic Repression of Granada in 1936 and the Death of Federico García Lorca* (1971) by Irish author Ian Gibson, who has since settled in Spain and written on authors García Lorca and Camilo José Cela and on surrealist painter Salvador Dalí.

Like Spanish history and literature, Spanish cinema has equally been the object of thorough and theoretically sophisticated analysis by outsiders. Since Peter Besas attempted the first history of the country's cinematography from its beginnings in *Behind the Spanish Lens: Spanish*

Cinema under Fascism and Democracy (1985), the film production of the following decades has been mapped among others by Marsha Kinder (1993), Jordan and Morgan-Tamosunas (1998) and Thomas Deveny (1999), the new millennium bringing an increasing number of studies focusing on gender issues such as *Stars and Masculinities in Spanish Cinema: from Banderas to Bardem* (Christopher Perriam 2003), *Gender and Spanish Cinema* (Ed. Steven Marsh and Parvati Nair 2004) or *Live Flesh: the Male Body in Contemporary Spanish Cinema* (Santiago Fouz-Hernandez and Alfredo Martinez-Expósito 2007).

Notwithstanding this wealth of publications in the Anglophone world, and despite the interest shown by Irish audiences in the films of Almodóvar and Amenábar, to this date there was no sustained analysis of the filmographies of Ireland and Spain from a comparative perspective. *Cinema on the Periphery: Contemporary Irish and Spanish Cinema* is thus a ground-breaking initiative. And a daring one for, on the surface, the divergences between the two countries and their film industries would seem to outweigh the similarities.

To begin with, and as might be expected from the substantially larger size and population of Spain, the film production of this country far exceeds that of Ireland. Thus, over the period 1970-2008 approximately 4,000 feature films and 5,000 shorts were made in Spain compared to some 200 feature films and 500 shorts in Ireland where, given that indigenous filmmaking did not really take off until the last two decades, the number of films made in the last 15 years trebled that of the previous 25 years. This late development would have several consequences, a significant one being that insofar as Irish filmmakers found a repository of representations of Ireland and the Irish coming from an outsider's perspective (and tending to mark Ireland as exotic), they faced the opposite options of either drawing on the international signifiers of Irishness – consequently running the risk of perpetuating stereotypical images – or 'writing back' by providing correctives to the received images. For their part, Spanish filmmakers (whose work comes close to 20 percent of the quota of films annually released in Spain) have been much more actively involved in the construction of their country's cinematic identity.

Still, a substantial number of connections can be found in the social and cinematic cultures of Ireland and Spain. These range from incidental concurrences like the fact that both countries have been holding film festivals since the 1950's [San Sebastian (1953), Valladolid or Seminci (1956), Cork (1956)], that they are currently the most enthusiastic cinema-goers in Europe (respectively occupying the top and second positions in the annual frequency of visits to the cinema), or that the Academy Awards won around the same time by *The Crying Game* (1993) and *Belle Epoque* (Fernando Trueba 1994) spurred international interest in Irish and Spanish cinema, to the more significant circumstance that, after spending the majority of the twentieth century as inward looking, conservative societies on the cultural and economic periphery of Europe, in the last decades of the twentieth century both countries not only embarked on a parallel national process of modernisation (and a corresponding recasting of identities), but they also underwent a distinct revitalization of their cinematic production.

In a shrewd analysis that never loses the reader in unnecessary detail, the present book usefully draws on the existence of these shared conditions in order to focus on how the changes undergone by Ireland and Spain have transformed the cultural imaginary of the two countries and have inflected their cinema. Eschewing both an exhaustive analysis of the filmographies of Spain and Ireland, and judgmental pronouncements aimed at establishing a canon, Conn Holohan focuses instead on the deep structure underlying the iconography and narratives of Irish and Spanish cinema. Combining learning with readability, Holohan offers insightful readings of the representational strategies used by some sixty contemporary films through the prism of gender, sexual identity, urban/rural space, and the relationship between past and present, thus providing a useful framework for approaching the thriving filmographies of both countries.

Rosa González
University of Barcelona
July 2009

Introduction

The implicit assumption in any discussion of national cinemas is that the national origin of a film marks it in some way that can be considered unique. This assumption has proved a problematic one when discussing an art form which is shaped to a large extent by the commercial dictates of the global film industry. In addition to the problem of deciding which films should be considered part of any particular national cinema, given the international character of many film productions, there is the difficulty of ascertaining which aspects of those films considered reflect specifically national concerns. The necessity of appealing to local and international audiences as well as the demands of narrative structure and genre all contribute to the thematic and visual strategies adopted by a film. Nevertheless the nation continues to be invoked by critics and theorists as a means of categorising films. When discussing national cinemas, the tendency has been to focus on a particular body of critically acclaimed films, such as the Italian neo realist films of the 1940s and 1950s, or to concentrate on what Metta Hjort refers to as 'themes of nation',[1] which can be elicited from the study of a group of films with a shared national origin. The term 'elicited' is crucial here, as it implies a conscious critical engagement with a body of films in order to establish connections both between the films themselves and with the wider social and cultural context from which they emerge. It is this latter approach that will be adopted by this book, eschewing the focus on any fixed canon of texts in order to explore the ways in which nationally specific cultural concerns can be traced to a wide range of contemporary Irish and Spanish films.

The dominant critical frameworks for interpreting Irish national cinema have focused on its relationship to Irish romantic nationalism and the continuing legacy of Ireland's historical relationship to Britain on the national imagination. Thus, the few films that were produced in Ireland up until the 1970s, as well as the British and American films which were produced about Ireland, tended to reinforce the romanticised, ruralist image of Ireland that was promoted within official Irish culture but which was also a reminder of the colonial mindset that conceived of Ireland as an exoticised 'other'. This produced a dominant set of representational strategies including the focus on landscape as an expression of character and the elision of the city from the Irish cinematic identity. A central component of these representations was the opposition between tradition and modernity, with the latter tending to be viewed negatively as a foreign corruption of traditionally Irish ways of life. This view began to change with the wave of oppositional filmmaking that emerged in the 1970s and 1980s and which challenged the cultural orthodoxies of Irish Catholic nationalism. These films explored issues such as discrimination, clerical abuse and the social and cultural suffocation experienced by many within an Ireland dominated by the twin ideologies of Catholicism and nationalism. This critical engagement with Irish national culture decreased in the Irish cinema of the 1990s, as a wave of films emerged for whom the concerns of traditional culture simply no longer seemed relevant. These films often display a celebratory attitude towards the modernised, youthful culture they depict which makes the forces of tradition, if they appear at all, seem little more than an anachronism.

Critical histories of Spanish cinema tend to begin with the relatively small number of films made under the 46-year reign of Franco which were in some way critical of his regime. Although numerically inferior, these films have received far more critical attention than the folkloric comedies and melodramas that made up the majority of the cinematic output at the time. As the Francoist regime began to liberalise slightly in the 1960s and 1970s, there was greater possibility for such oppositional cinema to be made and in the years immediately following his demise there was a wave of films which addressed the legacy of Francoism as well as the social and cultural problems facing a newly democratic Spain. However, moving into the 1980s this form of politically engaged cinema declined and a new wave of filmmakers and artists emerged, amongst them Pedro Almodóvar, who declared the irrelevance of Franco and the past to their work. As in Ireland, the 1990s saw a shift towards producing films within international genres, such as the romantic comedy or thriller, and away from the specifically national concerns of earlier filmmakers.

This rejection of the symbols and concerns of traditional culture open up recent Irish and Spanish films to the accusation (or commendation) that they lack national specificity. As stated, many such films operate within internationally recognisable genres and, as such, can be seen as merely localised versions of an international product, the Irish- or Spanish-ness of which stretches no further than their cast, crew and setting. However to take such a view is to reinforce a binary outlook that continues to equate national culture with tradition and a narrow concern with the nation. In such an outlook the increasingly global interactions which shape modern life become viewed in terms of either cultural loss or, alternatively, as an escape from the repressive isolationism of traditionalist national culture. Neither of these views adequately addresses the complexity of the relationship between tradition and modernity, between the national past and the transnational cultural and economic interactions of the present.

This book will address the interactions between the national and the transnational through a comparative analysis of contemporary Irish and Spanish cinema. Firstly establishing certain shared historical conditions within both countries, it will trace the effects of these conditions in contemporary cinematic representations. By establishing specific idiosyncratic features shared by Irish and Spanish films, this book will illustrate the ways in which those films which apparently reflect a homogenised global modernity are in fact marked by a specifically national process of modernisation. Critical discussion of national cinemas can often tend towards the myopic, being more concerned with what sets a particular nation apart rather than the connections which can usefully be drawn between different cinematic cultures. By taking a comparative approach, this work seeks to sidestep this problem, observing in both Irish and Spanish cinemas evidence of a problematic relationship to the pan-European experience of twentieth-century modernisation.

Both Ireland and Spain spent the majority of the twentieth century on the cultural and economic periphery of Europe, sharing inward-looking, conservative cultures which were dominated by the Catholic Church and the ruralist prejudices of strongly nationalist political regimes. This caused both countries to engage with the process of modernisation somewhat uncertainly as the inevitable need for economic modernisation was often coupled with an anti-modernising rhetoric and an attempt by the dominant cultural forces within each country to prevent social and cultural change. Whilst in the case of Ireland the reason for this uncertainty can be traced to the legacy of colonisation and the particular form of national culture which it generated, for Spain, itself a former colonial power, this is clearly not the case. Therefore this book takes these shared cultural features as its starting point and, while tracing their differing historical geneses in each country, is more centrally concerned with their ongoing effects on the cultural relationship to modernity within each, especially in the latter part of the twentieth century when both Ireland and Spain experienced rapid social, economic and cultural change. In such a way we can mark the representations of modernity that occur within contemporary Irish and Spanish cinema as distinctive and explore the interactions between national culture and transnational economic and cultural forces which shape the cinematic depictions of modern life.

The key theme running through this book is the relationship between social and cultural power and the interpretative frameworks of Irish and Spanish cinema. It argues that the decline in influence of Catholic nationalist ideologies within both societies has produced a level of cultural uncertainty, especially around issues of power and authority. Prior to the accelerated social and cultural change which has occurred in both countries since the 1960s, the cultural power of the Catholic Church and a nationalist cultural orthodoxy provided the dominant frameworks for the production and interpretation of a national imagery. However, the sudden decline in the cultural authority possessed by these frameworks has left something of a vacuum within Irish and Spanish culture. This book will trace the roots of this vacuum as well as exploring its effects on the representational strategies of contemporary Irish and Spanish cinema, specifically in relation to gender, sexual identity and urban and rural space. It will outline both the negative effects of this cultural vacuum, such as the unwillingness to critically engage with the economic and social forces which continue to structure national life and an occasionally uncritical embrace of modernity, as well as the cultural opportunities which it provides, including the possibility of a critical re-engagement with the national past which opens it up as a potentially radical force in Irish and Spanish society.

The focus of this book will be the detailed textual analysis of a selection of films produced in Ireland and Spain between 1992 and 2006. The beginning of this period, although inevitably arbitrary to some degree, coincides with the change of government in Ireland which led to the inauguration of the second Irish Film Board, an event which was responsible for the surge of film production in Ireland through the 1990s and beyond. Furthermore, 1992 was the year of both the Barcelona Olympics and the Seville World Expo, key events in Spain's narrative of modernisation. This year also marked the 500th anniversary of 1492 and the beginning of the Spanish conquests, an occurrence which provoked a re-engagement with the national past and a re-evaluation of Spain's colonial heritage. This period is further chosen as one in which the political engagement of Irish and Spanish cinema is generally thought to have declined in comparison to previous periods. However, through a politicised reading of these films, they will be reinscribed into a debate on national identity and its relevance within the increasingly globalised culture of contemporary life.

Whilst textual analysis will be central to this work, readings of films will be contextualised through reference to social, cultural and political developments within Ireland and Spain as well as the cinematic histories of each country. The choice of films analysed is guided by the desire to illustrate specific points about Irish and Spanish cinematic culture. However, these films are held to be representative of more general trends which can be distinguished across a wider range of films. In order to critically engage with the selected film texts, a range of theoretical approaches will be utilised, from Michel Foucault's analyses of the operations of power to the theories of space developed by writers such as Henri Lefebvre and Michel de Certeau. Although a prior awareness of these theoretical areas may be useful to the reader, the concepts employed are intended to give particular insights into aspects of the films discussed. As such, the intention is not to offer a comprehensive introduction to any of the theories that inform the readings in the book, but merely to explain why the specific ideas used are useful for our purposes.

A point that must be made at this stage is that this book does not directly deal with the position of Northern Ireland or the Spanish regions. The Irish films which are discussed all emerge from the Irish Republic and do not, for the most part, address the ongoing political situation within the North. The political and cultural conflicts within Northern Ireland are a direct consequence of the historical relationship between Britain and Ireland and are therefore an implicit presence within any study of Irish national culture. However, this book takes Irish culture as its object of study at a moment when it appears to have left behind the concerns of nationalism in order to embrace a cosmopolitan, modern identity. Although this dynamic may also be in evidence within Northern Irish culture, the possibility of adopting such an identity is clearly problematised by the continuing power of nationalism and unionism to structure political and cultural discourse. Therefore, addressing the full complexity of this issue is beyond the scope of this book. Also beyond its scope is a consideration of the regional disparities which are undoubtedly evident in Spain's process of modernisation. Substantial cultural differences exist between the different regions in Spain and, indeed, even applying the description Spanish to films which emerge from Catalonia or the Basque country is problematic. Nevertheless, what these regions shared historically was the repressive force of a monolithic Francoist culture, and it is in their shared reaction to this culture that useful comparisons to Ireland's own historical experience can be made.

Chapter 1 of this book will briefly sketch the historical development of cinema in Ireland and Spain, as well as examining further the social and cultural connections between the two countries. In the process, it will establish more clearly the benefits of approaching the cinematic output of the countries from a comparative perspective. The subsequent chapters will then take particular themes, representational strategies or narrative structures which recur in both Irish and Spanish cinema, situating the genesis of these recurrent tropes in the social and cultural contexts from which they emerge. Chapter 2 will look at the representation of power, and in particular patriarchal authority, in Irish and Spanish cinema. Chapter 3 will examine the ways in which images of femininity have changed in recent films, arguing that these films are often characterised by a sexualisation of all human relations. Chapter 4 will address the growing visibility of the city in Irish and Spanish film, situating these urban images in relation to both a transnational cosmopolitanism and specifically national histories of cultural representation. Finally, chapter 5 will turn its attention to the ways in which history has been addressed in the films of Ireland and Spain, arguing that it has frequently been approached in a reductive manner which narrowly equates the past with tradition and repression. Against this, the chapter will offer three case studies of films which, through their own critical engagement with the past, open up ways of reimagining history as a radical force in contemporary culture.

The Comparative Approach

THE DEVELOPMENT OF A NATIONAL CINEMA

Up until the 1980s the story of Irish film production was largely that of the failure to develop a viable production infrastructure within the country. With very few exceptions, such as *The Dawn* (1936), a War of Independence drama produced by the Killarney cinema owner Tom Cooper in the 1930s, films made in Ireland up until the 1970s had been the product of foreign finance and expertise. From 1910 until 1912 the US production company Kalem Films produced a number of silent films set in Ireland, frequently depicting Irish nationalism in a favourable light and contrasting the oppression and poverty of Ireland with the opportunities available in America.[2] Although the establishment of the Film Company of Ireland in 1916 did offer hope of a genuinely indigenous cinema developing within the country, the antipathy felt towards the cinematic medium by successive Irish governments allied with Ireland's fragile post-independence economy prevented this from occurring, and it was only in the 1970s that the first tentative steps towards a national cinema were taken.

Despite the censorious approach to the medium by the Irish government, with approximately three thousand films being banned by the censor in the first forty years of the office's existence,[3] cinema-going remained a hugely popular pastime in Ireland. Nevertheless, there was little appetite within the Irish government to encourage native film production. As Lance Pettitt states, 'the dominant cultural view saw cinema not only as a carrier of values that were corruptive and antithetical to those promoted by the state but that cinema itself was an agent of unwelcome modernity'.[4] This attitude is illustrated by the dáil debates over the 1923 Censorship of Films Bill, in which one Cumann na nGaedheal TD described the censorship office as an agency which would 'help to realise our Gaelic traditions'.[5] Given this attitude to the cinematic medium amongst the politicians and clergy of independent Ireland, it is little surprise that Irish filmmaking took so long to develop. Although a series of government-funded documentaries were produced through the 1940s and 1950s, reaching their pinnacle in the nationalist histories of *Mise Éire* (George Morrison, 1959) and *Saoirse?* (George Morrison, 1961), it was only when Ardmore Studios was set up with government subvention in 1958 that a serious attempt to develop an indigenous film industry was made. However, as Lance Pettitt points out, 'the studio became fairly quickly a hireable facility monopolised by British and US studios as a production space'[6] and failed to support the development of a native film culture.

In the absence of indigenous attempts to engage with Irish themes and history on celluloid, it fell to foreign directors such as John Ford and Robert Flaherty to construct an on-screen vision of Ireland and its people. However, the representational strategies and themes of these films were frequently tailored towards non-Irish audiences. For example, Ford's *The Informer* (1935), which reworks Liam O'Flaherty's story of an informer in the Irish War of Independence into a 'failed emigration narrative',[7] was undoubtedly designed to appeal to an audience of Irish-American emigrants. The 1930s to the 1960s saw British and American production companies draw on Irish material; putting on screen IRA stories such as *Shake Hands with the Devil* (Michael Anderson, 1959) and *Odd Man Out* (Carol Reed, 1947), whimsical comedies such as *The Luck of the Irish* (Donovan Pedelty, 1935) and stories of emigrant return such as *Kathleen Manourveen* (Norman Lee, 1937). Two films of this period which were widely seen and highly influential on subsequent Irish film culture were) Robert Flaherty's *Man of Aran* (1934) and John Ford's *The Quiet Man* (1952), each of which offered highly romanticised, if quite divergent, images of Irish life. That such seminal films within Irish national cinema were in fact foreign productions is symptomatic of Ireland's relationship to film for much of the twentieth century. It was only in the 1970s that a body of indigenous films developed, the concern of which was frequently to challenge the dominant cinematic depictions of Ireland, as well as addressing the social and cultural failings of the Irish state.

Kevin Rockett describes the challenges to the cultural establishment posed by these films thus:

> a more complex notion of the past was examined; the family became a location of instability and fragmentation; sexuality was examined if albeit obliquely and hesitantly; repressive Catholic education was relived on the screen; the use of landscape as an idealised backdrop for Irish Arcadian beauty was partly discarded; working-class experience made its appearance for the first time; experiments in film form challenged narrative's traditional supremacy.[8]

This quotation gives an idea of the scale of cultural change which these films set out to provoke, at the heart of which was the central conflict between the suffocating traditionalism of the previous fifty years and the modernising forces which began to emerge in the 1960s and 1970s. The family, the fundamental institution of the state according to the Irish constitution, was frequently the locus of attacks which exposed the hypocrisy of much of the 'Irish Ireland' rhetoric of the previous years. Martin McLoone describes the 'dysfunctional families' and 'perverse family groupings' of these films as 'metaphors for the sickness of the nation itself'.[9] Central to this attack on the family as a site of oppression were feminist filmmakers such as Pat Murphy and Margo Harkin. Harkin's *Hush-a-Bye Baby* (1989) was also pointed in its criticism of a Catholic discourse on sexuality which was inherently patriarchal and debilitating for women. Many of these films reveal the anger felt at the dominance of Irish politics and culture by the narrow concerns of Irish nationalism, and they can be seen as the cinematic contribution to the wider revisionist approach to Irish history occurring at the time. Although little seen, they provided an impetus for the nascent Irish film industry, which received a timely boost in 1982 with the setting up of the first Irish Film Board to fund local production. Although the first film board was relatively short-lived, its successor, established in 1993, would be responsible for the vast increase in Irish film production through the 1990s.

Unlike the Irish political establishment, which viewed cinema as a corrupting foreign art form, Franco's regime recognised the value of cinema as a way of disseminating its own vision of Spain and encouraged the production of suitable films through a system of subsidies. CIFESA, the Spanish production company founded in 1932, had split into nationalist and Republican camps during the civil war. However, from 1939 it associated itself with the interests of the Francoist regime. The favoured genre of the regime was the historical epic, focusing on Spain's imperial past and emphasising past glories. Films such as *Alba de América* (*Dawn of America*, Juan de Orduña, 1951) and *¡Harka!* (Carlos Arévalo, 1941) emphasised national unity and patriotic sentiments and were 'imbued with conservative forms of Catholic ethics'.[10] As well as influencing the direction of domestic film production, Franco's administration sought to control the images that audiences were exposed to from abroad through censorship. Films were cut and also altered in the dubbing process, sometimes to the extent that the plot itself was dramatically transformed. However, as in Ireland, where a similarly censorious approach was taken to film, the continued popularity of foreign films shows the failure of the regime to completely impose its culture on the people.[11]

Despite the substantial numbers of films produced within Spain in the early years of Francoism, the suffocating atmosphere of cultural nationalism had impeded the development of the medium as an art form. In 1955 the First National Film Congress was held in Salamanca, an event which brought together both right- and left-wing filmmakers to discuss the state of cinema within Spain. At this event Juan Antonio Bardem declared that 'after 60 years of films, Spanish cinema is politically ineffective, socially false, intellectually worthless, aesthetically non-existent, and industrially crippled'.[12] Bardem would go on to direct some of the most important oppositional films of the Francoist era. He and his fellow filmmakers were greatly influenced by the Italian neo-realist style, which they felt was the only way to counter the 'falsities' of Francoist cinema. However, perhaps paradoxically, the first important neo-realist film to be produced in Spain, *Surcos* (*Furrows*,1950), was directed by the Falangist (the Spanish fascist party of the 1930s and 1940s) José Antonio Nieves Conde. Although the film did explore the social problems associated with poverty and enforced urbanisation, within it 'the moral restoration of the patriarchal family (rather than the political solution of urban problems in the barrio) becomes the primary "popular objective"'.[13] Thus, the narrative concerns a peasant family who move to the city and face the harsh realities of unemployment as well as, in the world of the film, the moral corruption which is an inevitable danger of city life. The film resolves its narrative by restoring the authority of the family patriarch, which had been undermined in the urban environment, and returning the family to their rural origins, thereby ignoring the social and economic reasons for their move to the city in the first place. This deflection of political issues to the domestic arena of melodrama was a common feature of both Francoist and oppositional cinema. This can be seen as a continuation of the long history of melodrama in Spanish popular traditions, from Cervantes to the plays of Federico García Lorca. However, displacing political issues to the domestic arena also permitted oppositional filmmakers to make oblique criticisms of the regime which could not have been explicitly made in the censorious atmosphere of Francoist Spain.

With filmmakers such as Bardem, whose *Muerte de un ciclista* (*Death of a Cyclist*) won the International Critics Award at Cannes in 1955, and Luis García Berlanga, who won special mention at Cannes in 1952 for his satire *Bienvenido Mr Marshall* (*Welcome Mr Marshall*), Spanish film began to make an impact outside of Spain itself. Whilst

1. Victor Erice's *Spirit of the Beehive*

Luis Buñuel had left Spain in the aftermath of the civil war, the increased cultural openness of the 1960s led to his return in order to make *Viridiana* (1961), which won the Palme d'Or but was banned in Spain on the grounds of blasphemy. The 1960s also saw the emergence of Carlos Saura, who would go on to be one of Spain's most innovative filmmakers over the next three decades, critically exploring many aspects of Spanish national identity. In 1973 one of the most celebrated films to come out of Spain, *El espíritu de la colmena* (*The Spirit of the Beehive*), was directed by Víctor Erice. This abstract reworking of the Frankenstein story filtered the cultural stasis of Francoist Spain through an experimentalist approach to film form. The muted criticism of Spanish society contained within these films must be read out of the occasionally oblique symbolism which they contain as the oppressive cultural atmosphere of the totalitarian state in which they were produced greatly limited the filmmakers working within it. Nevertheless, despite the limitations placed upon its subject matter, the level of film production in Spain far exceeded that in Ireland during the same period. Indeed, those films which were made in Ireland during the period were, as argued above, almost exclusively foreign productions. Therefore, unlike later Irish filmmakers who were forced to respond to a set of representations which came from an outsider's perspective and marked Ireland as exotic, Spanish filmmakers were much more actively involved in the construction of Spain's cinematic identity.

IRISH AND SPANISH CINEMA INTO THE 1990s

As stated, the establishment of the second Irish Film Board in 1993, along with a tax incentive scheme designed to attract filmmakers to Ireland, has seen a significant increase in the number of films produced in the country since that time.

However, the difficulties faced by contemporary Irish filmmakers are highlighted by Ruth Barton's discussion of one such film, *About Adam* (2000), directed by Gerry Stembridge. The film is a romantic comedy set in an affluent Dublin, unrecognisable from prior cinematic depictions, which is marked by conspicuous consumption, sexual liberalism and a confident cosmopolitanism. Although lacking any traditional markers of Irish identity, Stembridge claims that the film's vision of Irish modernity has a specific resonance within the national context, asserting that such a representation 'would have an entirely different emphasis in Ireland than elsewhere; here it has more to say about issues like guilt, the secular society and the liberal agenda'.[14] Thus for Stembridge, far from indicating a loss of national specificity, his film addresses a set of concerns that are specifically Irish. However, as Barton points out, the response of the *Sight and Sound* film critic to the film is telling. His review suggests that, in an attempt to appeal to an international market, the filmmakers had strained out any sense of a distinctive local identity. As these contrasting responses imply, the concern of Irish filmmakers to represent contemporary Irish experience on screen may not coincide with the expectations of international film audiences as to what constitutes an Irish film. Barton describes the film as illustrative of 'a culturally specific desire not to be culturally specific'.[15] However it takes a particularly sensitive reading of the film to inscribe it within such a nationally specific discourse and the danger is that, along with much other recent Irish cinema, it may be all too easily incorporated into a bland cosmopolitanism that dissolves national specificity into a culture of global consumerism.

The desire of contemporary filmmakers to avoid those themes that may be considered specifically Irish is perhaps understandable. As Gibbons argues, considerations of landscape and violence have 'informed the representation of Ireland to such an extent that any new departure in cinema which addresses itself to one of these themes, even in a sustained critical manner, runs the risk of being appropriated back into the very tradition which it is opposing'.[16] The explicit concern of Irish filmmakers to escape the straitjacket of a film culture defined in national terms is evident in the declaration of Geraldine Creed, director of *The Sun, the Moon and the Stars* (1996), that 'there are personal politics as well as social politics. Not everyone is talking about 1916 and the fucking formation of the state and the mother figure in the household'.[17] Indeed Pettitt locates in films such as *The Sun, the Moon and the Stars* and *Snakes and Ladders* (Trish McAdam, 1996) a concern to offer more diverse representations of Irish life than had hitherto been witnessed on the big screen.[18] Thus the 1990s has seen an increased focus on issues of gender, sexuality and the marginalised of Irish society, even if those issues have frequently been addressed through the formal and generic strategies of mainstream, international cinema.

McLoone discusses the shift away from the nation as the organising category for experience in generational terms. He describes how the first wave of Irish filmmakers 'brooded' on a problematical Catholic nationalist past, while the younger generation of filmmakers 'feel they have inherited the world already from their traumatised parents and can breezily cast aside their neuroses and learn to live with an American popular culture that their emigrant ancestors helped to build in the first place'.[19] However, this apparently confident cosmopolitanism does not negate the effect of Irish national specificities on the way these filmmakers inhabit and perceive the world. For 'underneath the breezy surface', McLoone locates in the new wave of films an anxiety about this generation's relationship to their parents, which is dealt with by erasing the parental figures 'through parody or displacement'. This can be witnessed in the countless examples of incomplete families in recent Irish cinema, from the unmentioned father of *About Adam* to the idealised absent mother of *Breakfast on Pluto* (Neil Jordan, 2006). Indeed, McLoone outlines the preponderance of Oedipal narratives in the Irish films of the 1990s, seeing in it a crisis of paternity which finds its roots in Ireland's colonial past.[20] As will be explored more fully in chapter 2, this suggests that, far from being an irrelevance, the national past still has contemporary resonance and reminds us that 'even if these films are not politically engaged, they can be engaged with politically'.[21]

Recent Spanish cinema has also faced the charge that it lacks national specificity or the kind of political engagement that characterised earlier Spanish films. Indeed, for many of those who opposed Franco during his reign, this disenchantment set in during the 1980s, as the political idealism which had characterised oppositional politics and culture was replaced by a more apolitical youth culture which embraced the values of consumerism. Central to this was Madrid's *movida* movement, a group of artists, musicians and filmmakers, which included Pedro Almodóvar. This movement espoused 'a radical apoliticism and practised a kind of "cultural transvestism", trying on the range of different identities which suddenly became possible'.[22] Almodóvar epitomised this practice with his flamboyant films which mixed aspects of local and international film genres while radically recasting the iconography of Francoist Spain within a new sexualised setting. Also characteristic of the cultural moment was Almodóvar's insistence that Spain's Francoist past was an irrelevance to his films, that the political conflicts of history were of no importance in this newly cosmopolitan Spain. What is remarkable, however, is the extent to which Spanish national culture became generally identified with the youth culture of the *movida* in this period, revealing the degree to which Spanish national identity was open for reinterpretation at this time. As Mark Allinson points out, youth culture is usually counter-hegemonic and its accession to the mainstream in this moment revealed the need for the majority of Spanish society to reject all associations with its authoritarian Francoist past.[23]

It is this rejection of previous forms of cultural authority which will inform my readings of Spanish film since the 1990s. As suggested, these films are usually considered to be less explicitly political than those of the 1970s and 1980s and more easily incorporated into the international trends of entertainment cinema. One factor in this depoliticised approach has been the change in focus of government support for the film industry and the alteration of funding strategies in order to encourage private investment based on prospective box-office success. This has constituted a sizeable change from the government policy of the 1980s, which supported the development of 'quality' cinema that would engage in a serious manner with the concerns of Spanish national culture, an approach that failed to generate a sufficient number of successful films. Thus, it is the pastiche and irreverence of Almodóvar which has become the dominant influence on 1990s cinema, ironically as Almodóvar himself has moved towards more of a 'quality' aesthetic.

The 1990s saw the rise of several Spanish filmmakers to international prominence, such as Alejandro Amenábar, director of the English-language film *The Others* (2001), as well as a substantial increase in the number of films produced in Spain. These films often contain quite specific cultural references and, indeed, the *Torrente* series of films, which have been amongst the most successful Spanish films ever made, are at times incomprehensible to an audience which is unaware of the local humour. Nevertheless, the majority of films produced have been within internationally recognisable genres such as the thriller or, frequently, the sex comedy. With their youthful casts and sexualised plots, these films fit squarely into the parameters of a global entertainment cinema and, as such, seem a far cry from the *auteur* cinema of the past, which explored issues of identity and desire in a specifically national context.

However, it is important to remember that the playful aesthetic, which is evident in many of these films, can serve merely to conceal ongoing anxieties. Therefore, this book will critically engage with the confident (post-)modernity of recent Irish and Spanish films in order to reconnect them to the national political and cultural contexts from which they emerge. The approach which it takes is a comparative one, seeking similarities between Irish and Spanish cinema which mark both cultures as different within a global, or more specifically European, modernity. The aim is to develop a form of 'critical regionalism' that addresses the ways in which 'the local and the global interact in creative ways'.[24] This allows us to expand the terms of debate on recent Irish and Spanish cinema without naïvely rejecting the nation as an interpretative framework. A comparative approach allows us to consider how nationally specific cultural concerns continue to impact upon the films studied while situating these concerns within the international context of twentieth-century modernisation. The validity for adopting Ireland and Spain as points of comparison will be more fully explored below.

THE CATHOLIC CONNECTION

In *Behind the Spanish Lens*, Peter Besas' history of Spanish film from its inception until the 1980s, he writes that, in the films of Francoist Spain, 'a young woman's going abroad (unless it was to Catholic Ireland) was tantamount to eternal perdition and certain loss of chastity, both mental and physical.'.[25] This quotation is revealing, both of the level of insularism which characterised official Francoist culture, and for the cultural link which it creates between Spain and Ireland, both of which spent a large proportion of the twentieth century on the economic and cultural periphery of Europe. A key component of this link was the dominant position of the Catholic Church in both countries, which was both a powerful institution with close ties to the state and a popular belief system central to the social and cultural life of the nation.

The historical link between conservative Spanish nationalism and Catholicism is illustrated by a 1903 quotation from a Spanish Jesuit that 'Catholicism is so incorporated and connaturalized within [Spain's] very being, that it cannot cease to be Catholic without ceasing, first of all, to be a nation'.[26] Indeed, religion was an important unifying force throughout Spanish history, binding together often disparate regional factions in a common Christian identity in the battle to drive the Moors from Spain

between the ninth and the fourteenth centuries. Following the reconquest of Spain from the Moors, the regions were united through the
marriage of Isabel I of Castile and Fernando II of Aragon, and 'the identity of the united crown was perceived as being guaranteed through
religious unity'.[27] The degree to which religious faith and loyalty to the
crown were conflated was made clear by the Inquisition, which sought
to bring about the religious purification of the Iberian peninsula through
the use of force between the fifteenth and nineteenth centuries. From
1851 until the advent of the Second Republic in 1931, Catholicism
became the official state religion, with the Spanish government paying
the salaries of priests and the church greatly expanding its control over
education as well as other areas of life. The anti-clerical legislation
enacted by the first left-wing government of the Second Republic in the
1930s, and the hostile reaction which this brought from those on the
political right, illustrate the extent to which the church had become a
symbol of the conservative Spain of right-wing nationalism. Republican
violence against clerics during the civil war cemented the link between
Francoism and Catholicism, which would be central to the political and
cultural development of post-civil war Spain.

During Franco's reign Catholicism was the only religion to have legal
status. The church received financial aid from the government as well as
a range of other supports. A 1953 Concordat with the Vatican expanded
the privileges that it was accorded, such as granting the right of the
church to establish universities and giving it greater control over state
censorship. However, this tying together of church and state should not
be seen as the natural expression of Francoist values, but rather as an
instrumental policy of the Francoist regime, the aim of which was its
own legitimation. As Mike Richards argues, with regards to Franco's
approach to modernisation and industrialisation, 'the "moral force"
represented by the ideology of the Catholic Church was seen by the
regime as offering a way of disciplining the work-force by granting the
possibility of "redemption" through total obedience to authority'.[28] The
church was not just an expression of Spain's historical unity; it was
central to the Francoist attempt to implement modernisation without
any threatening consequences to the existing social order. In this
respect, the church occupied a similar position to that which it held
in Ireland, where it was central to the modernising process in the
aftermath of the Great Famine. This centrality persisted into post-independence Ireland where, just as in Francoist Spain, Catholicism offered
the ideological underpinning to the newly established regime. In Ireland
this was manifest in the direct influence exerted on government decision

makers by clergy and Catholic pressure groups, as well as in the everyday decisions made by civil servants and legislators who 'did not separate the job of governing from their own Catholic consciences'.[29] By situating the Catholic Church at the heart of the nation-building process, Ireland and Spain negotiated a unique path towards modernity within Western Europe. As Tom Inglis argues, it is not that Catholicism has prevented the evolution of a modern nation, but rather 'it is because the Irish [and by extension the Spanish] became the same as other westerners in and through the Catholic Church that they have remained different'.[30]

The Great Famine is posited by many commentators as an event that transformed the Catholic Church's position in Ireland, and the centrality of the church to Irish economic, social and cultural life dates, to a large part, from this time. The economic changes wrought by the famine, including the change in succession practices, whereby the eldest son inherited the entire family farm (thereby condemning the younger offspring to celibacy or emigration), and the rise to ascendancy of a tenant farmer class, saw a shift in social structures and attitudes. Vast numbers of the rural labouring class had either died or been forced to emigrate during the famine and thus the middle-class values of the tenant farmers came to dominate post-famine Ireland. Within the new social structure, conservative attitudes towards sexuality in particular became dominant, for reasons which will be elaborated in chapters 2 and 3, and the church became charged with ensuring the moral rectitude of Irish life. The shift in attitudes towards religion which occurred at this time are illustrated by the fact that previously, in the 1830s, mass-going in some rural areas was as low as 20 per cent.[31] However, the rise in influence of the Catholic Church from this time, shown by the substantial increase in clergy and church infrastructure over the following years, would see the decline of older forms of worship and behaviour, which did not conform to the strictures of Catholic spiritual and moral dogma. Thus, the post-famine turn to Catholicism was part of, and fundamental to, a wider process of modernisation in Irish social and economic life. Although crucial to Ireland's development as a prospective nation-state, this central role which the Catholic Church was granted within Irish society would have fundamental consequences for all facets of Irish life long into the next century.

The persistence of Catholic values in twentieth-century Ireland is illustrated by a 1962 survey of attitudes in the Dublin area, which showed a cross-class consensus about the right of the church to exert authority in the social, economic and political spheres. In the event of a church–state clash, 87 per cent of respondents said they would support the church, while 88 per cent said that the church was the greatest force for good in the country.[32] These figures indicate the extent to which the Catholic Church and the state had been intertwined in the decades since independence. The controlling ethos of this period is captured in the 1930s statement of Father John Hayes, founder of the Catholic community action group Muintir na Tíre, that 'Rural Ireland is real Ireland and rural Ireland is Ireland true to Christ.'[33] Although de Valera resisted demands to make Catholicism the state religion when drawing up the 1937 constitution, that document did recognise the 'special position' of the Catholic Church in the Irish Free State. Diarmaid Ferriter refers to 'the whole host of mediating structures through which Catholicism operated in Irish life', ranging from church campaigns against 'jazz' music to the institutional control it maintained over education to the activities of the Catholic social movement in combating social problems.[34]

Thus, it is a shared Catholic heritage, and the prominent role the Catholic Church has played in their development as nation-states, which most obviously suggest social and cultural connections between Ireland and Spain. Indeed, this book will argue that it is the sudden loss of what are labelled Catholic nationalist values that is crucial to understanding the representations of contemporary life which emerge from Irish and Spanish cinema. Catholic nationalism can be understood as the confluence of Catholic morality and nationalist ideology which underpinned the ruling regimes within Francoist Spain and post-independence Ireland and which impacted on all areas of political, social and cultural life. Although these values were not, of course, uncontested within either society, they were dominant in structuring the forms which each society took until at least the 1960s.

This leads us to a further shared characteristic of Ireland and Spain, which is the relatively rapid process of modernisation and urbanisation which both underwent from the 1960s. Up to this time both countries were characterised by a high level of church influence on moral and, occasionally, political issues, a protectionist approach to culture that viewed international cultural trends with suspicion, and an underdeveloped economy. However, in the time period since, both have become largely secular, culturally open and economically modern societies. It is one of the arguments of this book that the rapidity of that change has in itself affected Irish and Spanish society and culture. As Helen Graham and Jo Labanyi, writing in 1995, argued in relation to Spain, 'the accelerated change of the last two decades has obliged Spaniards to live in two different timeframes at once: to experience simultaneously what in the rest of Europe have been successive stages of development'.[35]

The impetus for much of the change that occurred in both Ireland and Spain was the abandonment of economic protectionism for a free-market approach that sought to encourage inward investment. In the case of Ireland, the first programme for economic expansion between 1960 and 1969 resulted in 350 new foreign companies locating in the country. The improved economic performance of the country at this time, 'although not very high by European standards',[36] was reflected in the fact that 1966 saw the population increase for the first time since the famine, while by 1971 the population had risen by 100,000.[37] This period saw increased educational opportunities and the beginnings of the development of a welfare state. Concomitantly, the relationship of the Irish state to the Catholic Church began to shift and in 1972 its special position in the Irish Constitution was abolished by referendum. At the same time the growth of television brought church spokesmen into the public domain, where their opinion was now open to challenge. Despite the continued importance of Catholicism in Irish life, as evidenced by the crowd of over one million people who attended the Pope's visit to Dublin in 1979, its institutional and moral hold over Irish life would steadily decline from this time until the present.

Similar to what occurred in Ireland, between 1962 and 1969 the Franco regime introduced what was known as the policy of *aperturismo*, the opening up of Spain both economically and culturally. Once again, Spain's economic boom was caused by an increase in foreign investment and the wider European boom that occurred at the time, which, as well as facilitating Spanish industrialisation, also ensured a massive rise in the number of tourists who could afford to visit Spain. However, this economic development also had social consequences and led to a much greater degree of foreign influence on Spanish society. Examples of this increased openness include the invitation to Luis Buñuel to return from exile to film *Viridiana* and the reappointment of the comparatively liberal García Escudero as general director of cinema. There was also increasing social unrest in this period with workers, students and even some priests attacking the restrictions of the regime. By the time of Franco's death in 1975, labour strikes had spread across the country, universities were sources of constant agitation, and the Basque terrorists ETA had assassinated his would-be successor. The move to democracy in 1977 and the 1978 Spanish constitution cemented the unprecedented changes which Spain experienced in this short period.

DIVERGENCES

Despite the shared trajectories outlined above, there are clearly significant differences in the historical experiences of Ireland and Spain, the
most obvious being their respective positions on the world stage. Spanish conquests in the New World from the fifteenth century established
Spain as one of the first colonial powers, while throughout the sixteenth,
seventeenth and eighteenth centuries Spain was at the heart of political
and military manoeuvrings in Europe. Spain's implication in wider
European affairs can be traced to the Spanish Civil War, which is often
seen as a rehearsal of the ideological conflicts that would characterise
World War II. Sixteenth-century Ireland, meanwhile, experienced
colonisation from the perspective of the vanquished, as Henry VIII's
reconquest of the country and the British plantations policy transformed
Ireland into an internal European colony. This disenfranchisement at
the hands of the British state engendered an Irish nationalism which,
although containing more inclusive and radical elements, towards the
end of the nineteenth century became increasingly associated with an
insular Catholic identity. In Spain, on the other hand, Catholicism was
associated not with the disenfranchised, but with the powerful forces
which controlled the country's resources, to the extent that one Cata-
lan writer in 1909 argued that the Catholic Church had associated
itself too closely with the protection of property rights.[38] The loss of
Spain's final colonies in Cuba, Puerto Rico and the Philippines in 1898
caused great introspection amongst the Spanish élite, many of whom
blamed the loss of empire on the influence of corrosive foreign models, such as the Enlightenment, and embraced a concept of Spanish
unity predicated upon a strong Catholic identity.[39] Therefore, although
the colonial circumstances of Ireland and Spain were vastly different,
the experience inculcated in both a regressive form of Catholic nationalism which defined itself in opposition to the modernisation and industrialisation of nineteenth- and twentieth-century Europe. It should be
noted that these ideologies were not totalising, and Spain did possess
an avant-garde tradition with close ties to European modernism, just as
Ireland possessed both a modernist tradition and a critical body of
work, such as Synge's *Playboy of the Western World*, which decon-
structed the rural romanticism of Irish nationalism. Nevertheless, it was
Catholic nationalism that was to become the dominant ethos of both
countries as the century progressed.

A further key difference between the two countries was the fact that
Francoist Spain became a totalitarian state, while Ireland managed the,

at times fraught, task of creating democracy from the devastation of civil war. If the fact that three-quarters of the 900 Irishmen who fought in the Spanish Civil War did so on the Nationalist side, while a pro-Franco meeting in Dublin attracted 40,000 to the streets, suggests a certain ideological sympathy with Francoism in Ireland, it should be remembered that much of this support was due to the perceived anti-clericalism of the Republican side rather than an embrace of fascism.[40] The one proto-fascist organisation that did develop in Ireland, the Blueshirt movement of the 1930s, was marked by divergences between the ideology of its leaders and the concerns of grass-roots members and was ultimately 'faced down' by the Irish government.[41]

Of course, the appellation 'fascist' can be only problematically applied to Francoism. Herbert Rutledge Southworth defines fascism as

> that manifestation of capitalism which made its appearance, within the geographical limits of Western and Central Europe and within the temporal limits of that period which began with the Russian Revolution and ended with the decolonisation struggles that followed the Second World War, in the form of a modern, highly or-ganised attempt to save the menaced capitalist structure in certain vulnerable countries through the subversion of the revolutionary élan of the workers, channelling this élan away from the class strug-gle and towards an enterprise of class collaboration, necessarily and inevitably debouching into an adventure of imperialist conquest.[42]

This narrowly defines fascism as 'an ephemeral solution to a capitalist crisis',[43] which, lacking the resources for imperialist conquest, Fran-coist Spain could not conform to. Although the Falange, a fascist organ-isation founded in 1933, was a vital element in the coalition of forces which formed the nationalist side in the Spanish Civil War, Southworth argues that they were not the victorious party in that war. Instead, he claims, the conservative elements who owned Spain's resources were the victors, and many of the ideological aims of the Falange were left unfulfilled.[44] Stanley Payne sees Francoist Spain as undergoing a process of defascistisation, begun by Franco as soon as it became clear that Hitler and Mussolini were going to lose World War II.[45] He divides this into three stages: the first between 1942 and 1947 when the Falange was replaced by the broader 'National Movement'; the second that took place between 1945 and 1957 when the regime occupied 'a kind of halfway house between the European fascist structures of the preced-ing generation and the resurgent new democracies'; and the post-1960

2. *The Quiet Man's* romanticised vision of rural Ireland

transformation of society following mass industrialisation. In the place of fascism, Catholicism became the dominant ideology of the state. Kinder describes the intertwining of both under Franco in her declaration that 'only in Spain was fascist ideology subordinated to and rewritten as traditional Catholic doctrine'.[46] Indeed Esteban argues that the collapse of fascism in the 1940s forced Franco to give power to Catholic politicians in order to create a new face for the regime.[47] Thus Catholicism provided a legitimising discourse for a totalitarian state which, although not fascist by strict definition, can nonetheless be usefully described in terms of the social, economic and political goals of fascism.

ROMANTICISM AND NATIONAL CULTURE

Although acknowledging the disparate historical experiences of Ireland and Spain, we can see above how, in the twentieth century, Catholicism became the guiding ethos for the political regimes of each. A further shared characteristic of the two countries is their experience of existing on the cultural fringe of Europe. Both countries have been depicted over the past centuries as spaces existing outside the shared Enlightenment values of Western Europe. In *Cinema and Ireland* (1988), Luke Gibbons associates cinematic representations of Ireland with the romantic sensibility which emerged in eighteenth-century Europe as a response to the perceived alienation caused by industrialisation. Representations of Ireland have been, he argues, 'enclosed within a circuit of myth and romanticism' tracing back to the Stage Irishman, who was a stock character in Victorian melodrama.[48] He argues that for a peripheral, underdeveloped country like Ireland, the predominance of romantic images associated with it had far-reaching consequences, as the country 'came to embody ... all the attributes of a vanished pre-industrial era'.[49] This representational trend is particularly accentuated in cultural products emerging from Britain, which stressed Ireland's underdeveloped status, frequently depicting the country as a precivilised space of nature. This must be seen in terms of Ireland's colonial relationship to Britain and a British colonial outlook that sought to elide any political explanation or responsibility for social conditions and revolutionary violence in Ireland. In place of historical analysis, British drama, literature and film dealing with Ireland posited 'a strange osmosis between climate and character',[50] finding the explanation for Irish behaviour in the turbulent weather and rugged, unkempt landscape. Equally, in *The Quiet Man* we witness an American fantasy of Ireland as a prelapsarian idyll, a space of escape from the ravages of industrialised modernity.

The irony of this point is that Irish cultural nationalists sought to claim the same premodern, rural identity for the nation that can be seen in such outsider images. For a means of understanding this apparent paradox we must look to postcolonial theory and the model of cultural development which it proposes. Many Irish cultural critics see parallels between Ireland's experience of direct British rule and the experience of colonised countries in Asia, South America and Africa. These writers have drawn on the work of postcolonial critics such as Frantz Fanon and Edward Said to show how such analogies can provide insight into Ireland's cultural and political development.

Central to the colonising experience was the denigration of the native culture by the coloniser, wherein the colonised was constructed as the negative 'other' to the positive cultural values of the imperial centre. Typically, the colonised native was seen as uncivilised, violent and existing in a pre-cultural state of nature. We can bear witness to this dynamic in the British representations of Ireland outlined above, which depicted the Irish as atavistic in their underdevelopment. Within the resistance to colonisation, however, these depictions were rejected and the validity and authenticity of the native culture asserted. This nationalist stage looks to 'a once scorned and perhaps abandoned identity'[51] as a means of establishing a distinct nation. The Irish cultural revival, which took place at the end of the nineteenth century, was just such an attempt to reassert a distinctive Irish nation with historical roots in a precolonial

3. Spain as exoticised 'other' in Carlos Saura's adaptation of *Carmen*

Gaelic society. However, the irony of this cultural process is that the model of nationality adopted by the colonised country tends to remain firmly within the parameters established by the imperial centre. Thus, Irish national identity was imagined within a restrictive dichotomy which was predicated on an opposition to all things British. The markers which distinguished Ireland from Britain – its Catholicism, its rural nature – were elevated to the status of national ideals, thereby ensuring a culture that was nationally distinct but unable to escape the legacy of the colonial mindset. Whereas Ireland's lack of industrial development was previously used by the British establishment to denote the country's backwardness, it was now asserted as an affirmation of the Irish nation's authenticity in the debased world of modernity. It is this model of national culture which would remain dominant in Ireland for much of the twentieth century and which accounts for the strange conformity of internal and external images of the country, both of which share a romanticising impulse which effaces complexity in favour of an essentialised vision of national life.

A similar dynamic is evident in both insider and outsider representations of Spanish culture and identity, despite its one-time status as an imperial power. In a 2002 article, José Colmeiro refers to a recent European poll which revealed that, after Don Quixote and Don Juan, Carmen was the fictional character most identified with Spain.[52] Mérimée's *Carmen* is an early example of the *españolada*, a genre of literature, and later film, which 'cultivated the exotic nature and the local colour of an underdeveloped part of Southern Europe'.[53] The *españolada* originated within French romanticism, for which Spain represented the possibility of a return to an idealised, premodern past, and was only later imported into Spanish culture. Colmeiro argues that Spain embodied qualities which the romantics were looking for: 'a rich cultural past, a preservation from modernity, a certain quaintness, and a heroic history'.[54] This mirrors the romantic appropriation of Ireland as a preindustrial space. However, just as in Ireland, the exoticised vision of Spain which came from outside the country was mirrored internally by a nationalist discourse which created its own essentialised national image, rooted in a romanticised vision of the past. In a quotation which could be quite easily appropriated to describe the relationship of Irish culture, and specifically Irish cinematic culture, to its own past, Marvin D'Lugo declares that

> Spaniards, having come under the spell of the foreign impostor impressions of Spain, find themselves seduced by this falsification of their own cultural past. The creative artist, bereft of any authentic tradition with which to identify, and situated within an artistic milieu he does not even discern as colonised by a specious foreign mentality toward Spain, only repeats the models of that fraudulent Spanishness in his own works and perceptions. [55]

By identifying with these exoticised qualities, Spain, like Ireland, became 'an internal other to European modernity'.[56] Again, this retreat into a mythologised past must be understood in relation to Spain's decline as a world power and the loss of its colonies. Balfour describes the essentialised vision of Spanishness promoted by the conservative establishment after 1898 as 'a flight from the dilemmas of modernization'.[57] Just like the cultural and economic protectionism of post-independence Ireland, Francoist policies can be seen as an attempt to control these dilemmas and secure the passage of an old social order into the new. However, the cultural cost of this was the refusal to engage with the complexities of modernity, preferring instead a retreat into an essentialised past that created an internal 'otherness', a discrepancy between the idealised vision and the lived experience of the nation.

It must be pointed out that this cannot be considered a totalising description of all cultural activity within Ireland and Spain. Bardem's *Bienvenido Mr Marshall* was a biting satire on the Spanish embrace of foreign clichés, depicting a small Spanish village's attempts to play up to Andalusian stereotypes in order to receive Marshall Aid from America. Their comic attempts to display to a foreign audience of American diplomats the signs of Spanishness which they expect to see, insightfully mirrors the dynamic which D'Lugo is discussing. Similarly in Ireland, *The Rocky Road to Dublin* (Peter Lennon, 1968) utilised avant-garde film form to expose those aspects of the Irish state which were suppressed by a celebratory nationalist rhetoric. Pettitt describes it as a film which 'hit the revolutionary spirit of the time',[58] and its use of *verité* techniques borrowed from French cinema suggests an engagement with an international cultural context. Nevertheless, the dominant cultural images of Ireland and Spain were those which retreated into an essentialised vision of the nation as premodern idyll. These images emerged from both the external discourses of colonialism and romanticism and an internal conservative nationalism. Despite the many political and cultural differences between Ireland and Spain outlined previously, this shared aversion to the consequences of modernity offers a point of convergence from which to conduct a comparative analysis of the respective national cinemas. It is to an elaboration of their particular relationship to modernisation and cultural change, as evidenced in some of the representational trends that can be traced historically through Irish and Spanish film, that this chapter will now turn.

PROBLEMATIC PATRIARCHY

Ruth Barton describes how 'the general thrust of filmmaking [in the Free State] was to eulogise the masculine ideals of the new Ireland'.[59] She gives as examples War of Independence films such as *Irish Destiny* (George Dewhurst, 1926) and *The Dawn*, which 'portray[ed] the war as a testing ground for honour and masculinity' while skipping over the 'already unmentionable Civil War'. In their celebratory attitude towards active masculinity and the nation-state, these films reflect the tendency of newly formed states to be 'paternalistic and autocratic'. In its epic vision of primal masculinity, *Man of Aran* could be considered the pinnacle of this representational trend. It is only later films such as *Korea* (Cathal Black, 1995), she claims, that 'filter their critique of cultural nationalism through a problematising of masculinity, even if ultimately they reassert its validity as a symbol of national identity'.[60] However, there was a countervailing tradition within Irish literature and drama which focused on 'the compromised or broken father [who] could provide no convincing image of authority'.[61] The image of the broken father expressed the disenfranchisement suffered by the colonised male, and is evident, for example, in the plays of Sean O'Casey and the work of James Joyce. This failure of the Irish male to fulfil the role assigned him by patriarchy is frequently depicted in film as a political and/or sexual impotency, a failure in both the public and the domestic sphere. One such example is James Mason's doomed IRA man in *Odd Man Out*, who is depicted through the film's narrative, visual strategy and indeed title as an outsider in the community, excluded from both the public sphere of politics and the possibility of domestic happiness by his inability to escape the 'curse' of violence. John Hill describes him as a character '[unable] to undertake positive action or control his own destiny'[62] and therefore at odds with the ideal of active masculinity which was evident in some of the earlier Irish films. This problematic masculinity is also evident in the 'pathological' IRA commandants of *Shake Hands with the Devil* and *A Terrible Beauty* (Tay Garnett, 1960), whose pathology Hill connects to sexual abnormality and repression.[63]

At the heart of this representational trend is the problematic interrelationship between the British monopoly of state power under colonisation, the legitimacy of the newly founded Irish state and the moral authority of the Catholic Church. In chapter 2 I will argue that the extended period in Ireland for which state power signified British power and colonisation, problematised the legitimisation of state power in post-independence Ireland. Kiberd writes that 'the leaders of the new state remained painfully uncertain of its legitimacy ... [generating] endless crises of self-legitimation, and with them a nervously patriarchal psychology'.[64] This uncertain legitimacy was also an effect of a divisive civil war, which ended with the defeated side refusing to acknowledge the institutions of the new state. In this context it was the Catholic Church which provided both a distinctive identity for the Irish nation and a means of legitimising the actions of the state, which by invoking the ideology of the church could provide a moral framework for its acts. However, the problematic consequences of situating the church above the state as a source of authority is reflected in the results of the survey cited above, which showed that 87 per cent of those surveyed would support the church in the event of a church–state clash. Chapter 2 will trace the effects of this problematic relationship to authority in recent Irish cinema and its representation of state and parental authority, both of which remain uncertain. The tendency within Irish cinema has been to represent authority as either repressive or, as signified by the countless number of absent fathers in Irish films, entirely lacking.

Spanish film shares with that of Ireland a tradition of representing fathers as either repressive patriarchs or absentees. In *Blood Cinema*, Kinder outlines the recurrent Oedipal narrative within Spanish cinema, highlighting the recurrence of idealised, yet absent fathers.[65] She connects this

cinematic trend to the wider political context of Francoism, and the disenfranchisement of Spanish males within a totalitarian state in which the
majority of them were denied access to political power or influence within
the public sphere. She links the preponderance of Oedipal narratives in
Spanish cinema to Girard's argument that the revival of the Oedipal narrative is caused by the weakening of the father's authority in western society, bringing him into direct conflict with the son.[66] Kinder claims that
'this weakening of the father occurred not only during the Francoist era
when Spaniards were infantilised but also in the post-Franco era when
the last model patriarch was deposed' (ibid.). Once again, this problematic relationship with authority is reflected in contemporary Spanish cinema in the prevalence of uncertain authority figures as well as in an
overstated 'hyper-masculinity', which connects to the Spanish *machismo*
tradition and is read by Timothy Mitchell (1990) in his analysis of Andalusian culture as a displacement of socio-political impotency to an overem-
phasised potency in the sexual sphere.[67]

Issues around masculinity have been central to many recent Irish
and Spanish films. Ging relates recent representations of masculinity
in Irish film to a wider questioning of male identity in a post-feminist
era.[68] She claims that whilst films of the 1980s and 1990s critiqued
traditional Irish masculinity, 'contemporary films express a more
universal and ambiguous portrait'[69] of Irish males. Indeed Barton claims
that 'questions of masculinity have returned as the pre-eminent discourse of Celtic-Tiger and post Celtic-Tiger Ireland', citing the recent
number of gangster films produced within Ireland as central to this
probing of male identity.[70] Similarly, Jordan and Morgan-Tamosunas
describe the exploration of masculinity in recent Spanish cinema as 'a
Spanish inflection of what some have called a "crisis in masculinity" in
contemporary society'.[71] This is evident in films such as *Jamón Jamón*
(*Ham, Ham,* Bigas Luna 1992), which parodies stereotypical Spanish
machismo, and the films of Almodóvar, in which patriarchy is often
critiqued through a focus on female characters. However, this book
will insist on connecting these contemporary representations back to
issues of national identity and a nationally specific attitude towards
authority, reinscribing them in the process into a politicised national
discourse which engages critically with modernity.

FEMALE IDENTITY AND THE OEDIPAL DRAMA

The inverse image of the weak father of Irish cultural representations is
the figure of the strong matriarch, which can be traced from the Irish

stage through to Mrs Brown, determined to get an education for her handicapped son in *My Left Foot* (Jim Sheridan, 1989). Barton describes the mother figure in Irish cultural representations as 'alternately and simultaneously, Mother Ireland and the Virgin Mary, devoted and a-sexual, her own desires subsumed into the maternal. At the same time, she dominates the domestic space, often dislodging the emasculated male as head of the family'.[72] This elevation of the matriarchal role can be read in both sociological and symbolic terms and finds its genesis, once again, in the experience of colonisation. Barton refers to 'the obsessively oedipal nature of Irish representation' (ibid.), which Kiberd links to the political disenfranchisement experienced by colonial subjects. He argues that, lacking any allegiance to the state or its institutions, the Irish were confined to the domestic sphere and therefore 'there could have been few experiences as intense as that of family life [in colonised Ireland]'.[73] Thus the family is the arena in which questions of power and nation have been frequently dramatised within Irish culture, and within that arena it is the mother who has been symbolically elevated to embody the nation.

However, this has not always been to positive effect for actual women in Irish society, whose own concerns have frequently been co-opted and concealed by the idealising discourse of nationalism. This is seen, for example, in *Anne Devlin* (Pat Murphy, 1984), the story of Robert Emmet's housekeeper who refused to inform on him when captured by the British authorities. Gibbons describes her recourse to silence, 'to the mute condition of her own body, as a site of resistance'.[74] The film, he claims 'points to a political project in which the silent bearers of history whether they be women or the labouring poor, cease to be instruments of social designs worked out by others ... but actively intervene in bringing about their own emancipation'.[75] However, this celebratory take on the film ignores that the freedom for which Anne Devlin was struggling was the freedom to be oppressed by a new patriarchal order. Despite the idealisation of women within nationalist rhetoric, independent Ireland would prove to be a restrictive space for women, and the challenge for future cinematic productions would be to develop a feminist discourse on its own terms. In this context, Gibbons sees the emergence of 'maternal narratives' in the late 1980s and early 1990s as a response to the reactionary shift in Irish culture of the 1980s, in which women's voices became silenced by the patriarchal discourses surrounding events such as the abortion referendum.[76] This silencing of female voices is a legacy of a nationalist ideology which subordinated issues of female disempowerment to an overarching discourse of national emancipation.

As Elizabeth Butler-Cullingford suggests, if female marginality is co-opted as a symbol of national marginality, then 'the price of insight into one injustice … may be blindness to a variety of others'.[77]

Mirroring this description of the symbolic family of Irish culture is Helen Graham's assertion that in Spain, 'the patriarchal family was seen as representing the corporate state in microcosm'.[78] However, as has been suggested already and will be expanded on in chapter 3, it was frequently the mother who stood in for the absent patriarch within that family. The negative consequences for these symbolic women who represented authority in a totalitarian society are captured by Kinder's assertion that 'no other national cinema contains so many matricides'.[79] Or as Lesley Heins Walker states, 'the mother in Spanish cinema often seems to have an extreme ideological burden: she comes to be figured as the agent par excellence of both political and psychic repression'.[80] Thus it is no surprise that in the Spanish Oedipal narrative a younger generation leaves behind the repressive past by expelling the mother figure, either symbolically or literally.

Paul Julian Smith traces the development of the family as an ideological space into post-Franco cinema, seeing it as a point of struggle 'between new subjectivities and older power structures'.[81] Furthermore, he outlines a shift from the family to the couple as the basic narrative and ideological unit of Spanish cinema, along with an abandonment of the virgin–whore dichotomy that structured traditional Spanish representations of women and upon which the image of the desexualised mother depended. This shift from the familial to the sexual as the basic relationship within Spanish film reflects a breakdown in the power structures which the family symbolised. Sexuality becomes the symbol of a modern, democratic Spain in which the strictures of Francoism are now an irrelevance. Similarly, recent Irish cinema has seen an explosion of diverse sexual identities on screen. Chapter 3 of this book seeks to connect this new sexualised national identity with prior representations, tracing the generational conflict of the Oedipal drama into the sexualised space of contemporary cinema. It explores the impact of this shift on the maternal figure, who has been deprived of the symbolic power conferred upon her by nationalist ideology. Finally, it asks if the celebratory sexual discourse of these films confronts the issues of disempowerment and discrimination that were ignored within nationalist discourse, or if these films merely replace the old body of national imagery with a new totalising vision predicated on an uncritical image of the nation as the site of progressive modernity.

THE CITY AND THE RURAL

D'Lugo describes the folkloric Spanish cinema of the 1930s and 1940s as one which 'imaged a sanitised, provincial world of pure spiritual and moral values, implicitly opposing the milieu of moral corruption, sexual promiscuity, and heretical foreign ideas that for the regime was synonymous with urban culture'.[82] The model of the Spanish nation constructed by Francoism was, D'Lugo states, as much conceived in opposition to 'the urban life-styles of Madrid and Barcelona' as 'the external otherness of foreign political ideologies and social customs'.[83] This view is echoed in a 1937 publication from the Francoist government press which declared 'we shall transform Spain into a country of small farmers',[84] an aim that was not entirely divorced from reality given that 46 per cent of workers in 1930 were employed in agriculture. The comparison with contemporary Ireland, and declarations such as Father Hayes' that 'rural Ireland is real Ireland', is immediately apparent. Of course, there was a certain hypocrisy in this attitude, and 'in spite of an enthusiasm for the peasant farmer as the "core of the race" ... the regime early saw that ... migration to the cities was a natural consequence of industrialisation'.[85] Nevertheless, the opposition between the corrupt city and the innocence of rural Spain continued to be a central image of Francoist Spain, not least because of its marketability to foreign audiences and tourists. Cinematically, the image of Spain as rural idyll is visualised in *españoladas* such as *Morena Clara* (*Clara, the Brunette,* Florián Rey, 1936) and *Nobleza baturra* (*Rustic Chivalry*, Juan de Orduña, 1965). This divide was also utilised by oppositional film-makers, who depicted the city as a 'refuge from the oppression of provincial life'.[86] Films such as Bardem's *Calle mayor* (*Main Street*,1956) 'appropriated the rural context for the elaboration of a critical discourse which established rural Spain as the spatial representation of stasis and repression'.[87]

Rockett gives an early example of the urban–rural opposition within Irish cinema in *When Love Came to Gavin Burke* (Fred O'Donovan, 1917), with its contrast between 'the hard-working small farmer, Gavin, and the alcoholic hotelier, and by extension, town resident and businessman'.[88] McLoone argues that an opposition between 'the traditional Gaelic purity of Ireland's western seaboard' and Dublin, 'the "strumpet city" that had prostituted itself to foreign cultural influence', was a central construct within Irish cultural nationalism.[89] This is reflected in *Man of Aran*'s 'ascetic nationalism', with its vision of 'an Ireland of frugal self-sufficiency',[90] as well as in the 'pre-industrial rural paradise'[91] of *The Quiet Man*. In contrast, *The Informer* depicts Dublin as 'a locus of decay ... policed by the embodiments of the colonial power'.[92] These contrasting representations set up a Manichean opposition, in which the rural came to stand for tradition and 'more human ways' while the city signified alienation, poverty and immorality.[93] This opposition gained such cultural currency within Ireland that even when the depiction of Ireland as a romanticised rural space was attacked by later filmmakers, the central urban–rural divide remained. McLoone links this with the failure to develop a tradition of social-realist film-making in Ireland and the relative absence of the urban from the screen, arguing that 'in a country like Ireland, so committed to a romantic rural identity, there was always the likelihood that to show urban reality was to confirm rural prejudice'.[94] It is the legacy of this anti-urban prejudice for contemporary representations of urban life that chapter 4 of this book will explore, arguing that the absence of the city from the national culture within Ireland and Spain has ensured that it remains a semantically open space, and relating the representational consequences of this to issues of cultural power and the interaction between national identity and global modernity.

If the city has become the quintessential space of modern life within Irish and Spanish cinema, the rural remains the means of signifying tradition and the national past. The final chapter in this book will explore the limitations of this representational strategy adopted by many Irish and Spanish films. It will go on to suggest alternative ways of engaging with history and the rural–urban divide through an analysis of three case studies; *La mala educación* (*Bad Education*, Pedro Almodóvar, 2004), *Breakfast on Pluto* (Neil Jordan, 2006) and *Soldados de Salamina* (*Soldiers of Salamis*, David Trueba, 2003]). It will examine how these films connect the past and the present in fundamentally different ways to those proposed by either nationalist ideology or the modernising narrative which replaced it within Ireland and Spain. In such a way this book will attempt to reinstate the nation and progressive forms of national identity as a position from which to engage politically with the forces of modernity. But first we turn to representations of judicial and paternal authority in recent Irish and Spanish films, finding in the images which occur an ongoing uncertainty regarding the legitimacy of these patriarchal institutions in contemporary society.

Power and Patriarchy

As outlined in Chapter One, social and political realities as well as cultural discourse within post-independence Ireland and Francoist Spain were heavily influenced by the dominant ideologies of Catholicism and nationalism. These ideologies were structured around a notion of social and symbolic power which was rooted in the unquestioned ideals of God and Country. They created a society and culture where judgement could be passed on individual conflicts or behaviour according to their adherence to these sacred truths. However, as Ireland and Spain experienced a move towards a modernised social and economic system, these central structuring ideologies began to lose their power. The cultural discourses which assigned value, meaning and power in relation to the sovereign concepts of God and nation began themselves to lose meaning. Conventional symbols of authority became open to challenge and the very concept of power became a problematic one, associated negatively as it was with the experience of colonisation and Francoism in Ireland and Spain respectively. Thus a crisis emerged in the cultural representation of power within contemporary Ireland and Spain; a power vacuum could be said to exist.

This crisis of authority in Irish and Spanish culture and society is most obviously and emblematically expressed as a crisis of patriarchal power, a failure of 'the father' to fulfil the role assigned to him by society. Within a society in which male values are dominant, the father figure becomes a key symbol of the perpetuation of those values, which he must in turn pass on to the son. Freud invokes the myth of Oedipus to describe the psychological process whereby the son learns to distance himself from the maternal bond and aspire towards the father's role in society. The working out of this Oedipal process is a key narrative structure within film and other cultural forms. However, in a culture where the values represented by the father have themselves become devalued, this process, and by extension this narrative structure, become problematic. The idea of a benevolent patriarchal authority which works to reproduce an agreed set of social values becomes unsustainable.

As suggested by this centrality of the father in discussing power and authority, the family is a key representational space within which issues of power can be negotiated. An analysis of the family structure within Irish and Spanish cinema allows us to relate issues of familial and sexual relations to wider social and cultural structures which operated historically in those countries. Recurrent motifs such as the absent or ineffective father and the dominant, castrating matriarch must be read in the context of the problematic relationship with patriarchal power which existed in these cultures. As a central symbol within the discourses of Catholicism and nationalism, the family was appropriated by both states as the paradigmatic institution upon which nationhood was built.

What this chapter seeks to explore is the effects on the family structure when the ideology of Catholic nationalism, which exalted it and which fixed its meaning, becomes devalued in contemporary society. Asserting that the family models which recur across Irish and Spanish cinema have their roots in historical experience yet also serve as a prism through which wider social dynamics are represented, I will argue that the effects of socio-cultural changes can be read in contemporary representations of family life. The recurrent figure of the dominant matriarch can only be understood in terms of the symbolic repertoire of Catholic nationalist ideology. Equally, the frequency with which fathers are represented as either absent or emasculated within Irish and Spanish films finds an explanation in the historical experiences of each country. If these iconic characters find meaning in relation to a Catholic nationalist discourse that has lost its cultural power within the shift to urban modernity, then it follows that this ideological shift will provoke corresponding representational changes. It is to the genesis of these symbolic figures and the changes which they have undergone within the process of modernisation that this chapter will now turn.

COLONISATION AND PATRIARCHY IN IRISH CULTURE

The absent father/dominating mother trope in Irish cinema has been linked by Martin McLoone to the necessity of delayed marriages in post-famine Ireland.[95] Tom Inglis describes how the change in succession practices at this time, whereby one son inherited the entire family farm rather than it being subdivided, necessitated the regulation of sexuality so as to ensure celibacy amongst those who were thus denied a means of supporting a family.[96] This was achieved, he claims, by elevating the Catholic Church to a position of centrality within a modernised social and economic formation, and placing its moral teachings at the heart of the socialising process. Central to the church's maintenance of this position of power was a strict control over all areas of sexual discourse. This in turn was achieved through an alliance between the mother, who policed sexuality in the domestic sphere, and the priest, who replaced the father as the site of the authoritarian super-ego.

This usurping of the role of the father could only have been realised in a context where patriarchy was already undermined. As Luke Gibbons argues, 'the anomaly colonial Ireland posed to an equation of nation and fatherland was that Irish men lacked the control of the public sphere that paternal authority required'.[97] Therefore, Ireland's status as a colonised country, and the disenfranchising effect of this status for the Irish male, can be seen as the conditions which engendered the figure of the dominant matriarch whose authority was conferred by the structuring presence of the Catholic Church.

Declan Kiberd claims that the experience of colonisation results in a 'fatherless society' as it falls to the young to revolt against the occupier, rendering the older generation ineffective bystanders.[98] Equally, a revolt by the son against his father is politically meaningless as the father has no power and it therefore has no social or political effect. Thus in the absence of outright rebellion, the revolutionary spirit of the younger generation 'sink[s] back into the curtailed squabble of family life'.[99] This helps to explain the recurrence and intensity of the Oedipal trope in Irish cinema as, barred from the public sphere, the frustration of Irish youth folded back in on itself and was unleashed within the domestic setting. Kiberd traces this motif through the work of O'Casey, Joyce and, most obviously and emblematically, in Synge's *Playboy of the Western World*, where Christy 'kills' his failure of a father.[100]

Concurrent with this discrediting of the father as a figure of authority came the investment of cultural power in the figure of the strong Irish mother. Richard Kearney traces an increase in the idealisation of women in religious and nationalist ideology as Ireland became more dispossessed.[101] As the Irish male was denied a political identity, Irish women were elevated in order to possess an identity in the realm of the imaginary. Women, Kearney claims, 'became as sexually intangible as the ideal of national sovereignty became politically intangible'.[102] Religious, gender and nationalist discourses were conflated to give what Angela Martin refers to as a 'direct mimetic correspondence extant among Irish women, Mary and Irish national identity'.[103] The connection between this symbolic elevation of woman to represent the nation and the experience of colonisation is evidenced by the fact that imagery of Ireland as Fatherland, '*an t-atherdha*', was previously used in bardic poetry up until the seventeenth century.[104]

Thus, as Gibbons describes on page 35 and in a process described repeatedly in studies of the colonial experience, Ireland, as a colonised country, became feminised or reimagined as feminine in the cultural/symbolic sphere. The Irish male suffered the marginalisation experienced by females within the colonising country, while the Irish female was doubly marginalised as both woman and native. However, this double marginalisation can also be seen as a position of potential power, as the domestic sphere which the colonised female inhabits is in fact the only sphere in which power can be assumed by the native. As stated, this sphere was very much in the control of the Irish mother, whose power was confirmed not by the father but by the priest. Inglis argues that the priest, through confession, had greater knowledge of a woman than her husband, with the consequence that the husband became alienated from his wife and tended to become submissive to the moral authority of wife and pulpit.[105] This illustrates how the coloniser's control of the public sphere and the Catholic Church's control over sexual discourse combined to render the Irish male politically and domestically impotent. It is this abasement of the Irish male which precipitated a crisis in the representation of patriarchal power and which created the 'broken fathers' of Irish film and literature.

However, as Kiberd declares, 'in Irish political and social life, matters did not unfold as in the texts of Wilde, Synge and Joyce, or as in the theories of Fanon and Memmi. Instead, the fathers had their revenge on the sons for daring to dream at all'.[106] Post-independence Ireland did not witness a generational shift in power, but rather saw the radical elements of the Irish revolution fade as the middle-class establishment seized control of the political and symbolic spheres, curtailing the impetuosity of youth. This shift is aptly captured in the decision of the Free State government to close down the illegal Dáil courts, which had been operating around the country since 1918, preferring instead to import the British judicial system wholesale into the newly founded Irish state. The conservative character of the Free State should not, perhaps, be surprising for, as Kiberd points out, although the nationalist revolutionaries seemed young, 'their muse was old'.[107]

Social, political and cultural life in post-independence Ireland was defined by a turn towards a prelapsarian, idealised Celtic culture which could remove the corruptive, modernising taints of the invader. However, this turn towards a distant and wholly imagined past can itself be seen as symptomatic of a continuing crisis of patriarchal power. Kiberd describes the elder Irish generation under English occupation as 'enthusiastic revivalists'[108] who lamented the heroes of the past as well as their own past conquests. Of course these heroic deeds could only exist in the past, as the contemporary political reality left them powerless to act. A continued reverence towards the past within independent Ireland can be read therefore as a persistent uncertainty about the legitimacy of the new political order, given the institutional connections between the old system of British rule and the Free State. As Fintan O'-Toole argues, in a post-colonial society there will inevitably be a problematic relationship with institutional power, 'a difficulty accepting that "the system" is now our system, rather than one to be subverted and undermined'.[109]

One means of legitimising the power of this political order was to situate the Catholic Church at the ideological base of the new Irish state. The church had been central to the modernising project which occurred in the aftermath of the famine and this was perhaps a logical extension of that role. Indeed, Inglis describes the Irish civilising process as essentially European in origin, the difference from other European nations being that 'by using different means to become civilised [i.e. the church], the Irish avoided becoming protestant and fully anglicised'.[110] Nevertheless, the particular process of modernisation which had occurred in post-famine Ireland was one which situated the priest as the moral and spiritual authority in the community to the detriment of the lay male, whose own social power was consequently undermined. By giving Catholic teachings such a central role in the process of nation-building, the new political order of independent Ireland subjugated its own authority to the ultimate authority of the Catholic Church. Even revolution could not raise the Irish male to the position of power enjoyed by his counterpart at the colonial centre.

This uncertainty around the nature and legitimacy of power also haunted the social and cultural practices of Francoist Spain. Although Franco presented himself as the ultimate patriarch, *el caudillo*, who embodied those eternal Spanish values, which had been corrupted by modernity, the legitimacy of his autocratic regime was forever troubled by its roots in violence. The Spanish Civil War was precipitated by a rejection of democracy, a military uprising against the elected Republican government, and the ensuing bloodshed and loss of life was an irremovable stain on Spain's national past. The historical fact of the civil war, in which families, towns and regions turned against each other, belied the subsequent Francoist rhetoric of national unity. The civil war revealed the destructive potential of power and the patriarchal values

which underpinned it, creating a society and culture in which these values were undermined, even as they were enshrined in the longest last-
ing European dictatorship of the twentieth century.

PATRIARCHY AND THE MYTH OF SACRIFICE IN SPANISH CULTURE

According to Virginia Higginbotham, in the three decades after the
Spanish Civil War there were only 45 films made which dealt with the
conflict, and of them only 21 actually showed combat scenes.[111] These
figures suggest the difficulty of representing an historical event which
tore apart the social and political fabric of the country, and in which,
including post-war reprisals, an estimated three to four hundred thousand people were shot on the Republican side alone.[112] Jesús González-
Requeña defines the presence of the civil war within Francoist cinema
as being governed by an economy of psychosis. He describes the civil
war as 'a radical absence ... that [was] present neither in an allusive or
metaphorical way', 'a black hole' that never acceded to the subject's
symbolic world.[113] It was a silence 'that perforate[d] or punctuate[d]
the text in a radically absent manner, leaving openings that extend[ed]
their effects throughout the entire textual fabric'.[114] Thus, although the
civil war was rarely depicted, its effects were everywhere felt in the
films produced within Francoist Spain, if only in the lengths to which
films went to avoid mentioning it. These effects included the impossibility of developing 'those cinematographic genres that pivot around a
phallic hero',[115] as the violence of the father was the very thing that
had to be repressed. The active, violent male, central to so many cinematic genres, became unrepresentable in a Spanish context, and the act
of violence was displaced into the sacrificial gesture, institutionalised
within a masochistic Catholic aesthetic.

   This inability, or refusal, to represent the violent acts which occurred
at the foundation of the Francoist state was not limited to cinema but
permeated through all Spanish cultural life. The fact that the Francoist
state's existence was founded upon the massacre of fellow Spaniards
was necessarily repressed in order for that state to claim legitimacy as the
naturalised embodiment of Spain's historical destiny and as representative of the whole of the Spanish people. The distinction between sacrificial violence and massacre made by Tzvetan Todorov and utilised by
Marsha Kinder in her discussion of Spanish cinema, is useful as a way
of understanding the relationship between violence and Francoism.[116]
The mode of operation of these forms of violence and their relation to
the social fabric are very different. Sacrifice, Todorov claims, 'testifies

to the power of the social fabric, to its mastery over the individual'.[117] Massacre, on the other hand, 'reveals the weakness of this same social fabric',[118] the inability of society to contain all forces within the social contract. For this reason, according to Todorov, '[massacre] should be performed in some remote place where the law is only vaguely acknowledged'. In this place 'the individual identity of the massacre victim is by definition irrelevant (otherwise his death would be a murder)'.[119]

Massacre, in the form of imperial violence, was central to the Fascist regimes of Italy and Germany, as the revolutionary potential of the working class was channelled outwards into imperialist conquest. Despite the fascist leanings of Francoism, however, Spain had little appetite for colonial adventure during World War II. In the aftermath of the civil war, Spain was not in a position to channel disaffection into imperial conquest. As Southworth evocatively surmises:

> The revolutionary élan of the working classes had not been subverted into preparation for a great adventure; it had been bled to death on the field of battle and against the patio walls in the grey Castilian morning and in the desolate marches to exile.[120]

It was this fact that Francoism needed to repress. Spain's massacre had not been against a de-individualised 'other' in a remote land. It had been against its own sons and daughters, their identities only too well known. Unlike Nazi Germany, there was no 'Jew' who could have responsibility for the nation's ills thrust upon him, but only those Spaniards who had strayed too far from the beliefs of the 'authentic Spain'. Violence had ceased to be a tool that could be used to conquer others, it had been turned by the Spanish upon themselves.

The reaction of the Francoist state to this was twofold. One was to exclude the defeated Republicans from its definition of Spain and Spanishness, thereby justifying the use of violence against them. This is exemplified in the language used in a 1959 speech by Franco in which he states: 'the struggle between Good and Evil never ends no matter how great the victory. Anti-Spain was routed but it is not dead'.[121] By labelling Republicans the 'Anti-Spain', he conversely equates Spanishness with Francoism. However, he also excludes a large proportion of the population from that definition and problematises the fantasy of national unity which is central to all nationalist movements.

Therefore, alongside this rhetoric of exclusion there was a celebration of sacrifice that sought to deny the violent exclusion which was inflicted by the civil war victors upon their enemies. By replacing images of massacre with those of sacrifice, the Francoist state sought to deny its complicity in the historical massacre which engendered it, and instead to claim the position normally reserved for the powerless and the defeated. Through adopting this rhetoric, the forces of Francoism sought to disavow the worst excesses of political power and violence which had been exercised in reality. This was aided by a Counter-Reformation, Catholic aesthetic which fetishised martyrs and which was the ideological accomplice of the Francoist state. As Marsha Kinder states, 'during Spain's neo-Catholic revival in the 1940s ... the baroque fetishisation of sacrificial death in the popular arts [helped] to empower both the religious orthodoxy of the Church and the absolute power of Franco'.[122] This motif occurs repeatedly in Nationalist civil war writings, in which 'the ordinary soldier became a crusader and martyr to God who did not "die" in battle but "fell" and went to the starry firmament'.[123] The ubiquity of this theme is illustrated by the fact that within a 1993 anthology of civil war poetry, all but one of the poems is a homage to a dead fighter.[124]

This celebration of sacrifice can be witnessed cinematically in the 1940s historical epics such as *Los últimos de Filipinas* (*Last Stand in the Philippines,* Antonio Román, 1945), in which violence against Spain's enemies was replaced by 'the glamorized deaths of individualized Fascist heroes'.[125] Even in such a triumphalist film as *Raza* (*Race,* José Luis Sáenz de Heredia, 1941), scripted by Franco himself, the glorified Nationalist characters are depicted not in victory, but achieving martyrdom at the hands of the Republican soldiers. Unlike the violence of massacre, in sacrifice 'the victim's identity is governed by strict rules ... his personal qualities [count]'.[126] The Nationalist soldier possesses the qualities necessary to die for Spain, and in these films it is his death rather than that of the Republican which is presented as the sacrifice upon which the nation is built. In this way the founding violence of the Francoist state becomes the purifying violence of sacrifice rather than the dehumanising committal of massacre.

The ultimate effect of this disavowal of the Francoist state's original generative violence is to problematise the representation of power and patriarchy within Spanish culture. Through the motif of noble sacrifice, the Francoist forces of patriarchy sought to occupy the absence that haunted Spanish social and cultural life, that of the fallen Republican soldier. Through this paradoxical attempt to inhabit an absent space, to actively claim a position of passivity, patriarchy became devalued as a structuring value system. When the authority invested in the figure of Franco himself declined over time, combined with the declining influence of

Catholicism, Spain was therefore left without the symbolic structures which could confer legitimacy upon authority.

REPRESENTING POWER

Stephen Tropicano describes the Oedipal conflicts within Spanish cinema as being characterised by an absent father, who is usually idealised; a patriarchal mother, who is both the object of the son's desire and the instrument of his repression; and an emotionally stunted child with patricidal tendencies which, in the absence of the father, must be displaced on to the mother.[127] To this configuration can also be added the figure of the repressive patriarch who occupies a conservative ideological role but whose authority is already undermined by his association with the problematic authority of Francoism. This must be read in the context of a post-civil war society wherein the memories and voices of a generation of defeated Republicans were literally erased by the victorious government forces. Thus the choice of patriarchal figure becomes that of the victorious, but reactionary, patriarch, or the absented but idealised father; the defeated Republican who is denied any presence in the public sphere.

The privileging of the father–son relationship can be seen in the Spanish version of film noir, *cine negro*. Unlike the wave of noir which emerged from Hollywood in the 1940s and 1950s, within this localised version, the focus is not on the erotic desire for a sexually liberated woman and its troubling consequences for male autonomy. Instead, as Kinder points out, 'most of the criminals become deviant because there is something wrong with their father: either he is a dead idol, impossible to equal, or too weak, or too strict'.[128] As argued above, this problematic relationship to patriarchy must be traced back to the experience of the civil war and the totalitarian state which emerged from it. Indeed, according to González-Requena, it is a crisis of paternity that is the founding condition for any civil war. Civil war is 'a war between brothers, between children of the same generation who share the same mother tongue but do not recognize any paternal world'.[129]

The specific model of paternity that was authorised in post-civil war Spain was, of course, a Francoist one which positioned Franco himself as the supreme patriarch. This patriarchal model frequently retreated into the past, to a time when Spain's colonial power enabled the expression of Spanish male prowess. However, even here, male violence was frequently displaced into sacrifice. Against this, in a climate of restrictive censorship, the oppositional forces of Spain could offer only absence.

Issues of authority were often displaced into melodrama, where they could be interrogated in a context which was not immediately political and could therefore escape the hand of the censor. Filmmakers such as Juan Antonio Bardem, Carlos Saura and Victor Erice subtly challenged Francoist patriarchal values with their charged, claustrophobic familial dramas. However, the Republican (or by extension anti-Francoist) male himself was effaced from the national cinema, as from public life generally, except in those occasional films set during the civil war such as *Posición avanzada* (*Advanced Position*, Pedro Lazaga, 1965) or *La orilla* (*The Border*, Luis Lucía, 1971), which represented events very much on Nationalist terms. Thus in the aftermath of Franco's decline and death there was no tradition of oppositional male representation which could be drawn upon as an alternative model of patriarchy, one which could confer legitimacy on new expressions of power in a new cultural and political reality.

Problematic representations of the male have, of course, been a central trope within Irish cinema also, the roots of which have been previously argued. Examples range from James Mason's doomed IRA man in *Odd Man Out* to Christy Brown's feckless alcoholic father in *My Left Foot*. The purpose of this chapter is to analyse representations of authority within recent Irish and Spanish film in the context of the problematic relationships to power outlined above. I will argue that power is always contested and contestable in the films analysed. Power cannot reside in a pre-existing set of hierarchical relationships, or be conferred by the unquestioned authority of church or state. Instead, power must be constantly claimed through action and is always provisional to the circumstances in which it is enforced. This makes the representation of the forces of state power such as the police problematic, as, in order for them to function as a signifier of legitimate power, a particular set of power relations must be accepted as themselves legitimate. Without the symbolic authority which structures the state's relationship to society hierarchically, state violence exists within the same sphere as criminal violence and must justify its own use according to the realities of everyday life instead of through reference to any symbolic institution. All power therefore becomes precarious. Within cinema, this contest for legitimacy is most visible within the crime film, as it is centrally concerned with the power of the law to sustain a fixed moral order, and it is therefore Irish and Spanish crime films that will primarily be referred to within this section.

INSTITUTIONS OF AUTHORITY

One of the most emblematic moments of undermined patriarchy within Spanish cinema is the spiked gazpacho scene in Pedro Almodóvar's *Mujeres al borde de un ataque de nervios* (*Women on the Verge of a Nervous Breakdown*, 1988). When the police come to question the main character Pepa (Carmen Maura) about her connection to Shiite terrorists, she offers them a glass of gazpacho, which she had previously laced with sleeping tablets in order to drug her ex-lover. The tone and demeanour of the two policemen is intimidating as they demand that Pepa explain herself. We see them march about her apartment, chests puffed out, attempting to assert their control over the situation. However, as the drugs kick in, their words become slurred, their actions uncertain, until, finally, they slump to the floor, their heads resting on each other's shoulders, and slide out of the camera shot unconscious. Gwynne Edwards describes it as 'a spectacle of authority completely undermined and made to look ridiculous'.[130] As parental, state, and indeed divine authority have been undermined within the move to modernity, the representation of authority becomes severely problematic. For, if the power to confer authority has become contested, then any authority portrayed is itself necessarily contested and provisional. There can be no assumption that the police uphold the moral order for there is no longer a central structuring belief system such as Catholicism which fixes that order in place. Thus, the police on screen are subjected to ridicule, represented as ineffective, or indeed noted mainly for their

4. Almodóvar's image of authority undermined

absence. Value systems are seen to be relative and must be justified within the terms of the world represented on screen, either through narrative resolution or by the characters themselves. There is no safe symbolic space wherein power is legitimated, but only the endless social reality where the forces of order and disorder must continuously struggle, and where, in fact, that very distinction is called into question.

Foucault describes a relationship of power as a mode of action that doesn't act directly on others (like violence) but 'acts upon their actions'.[131]

> It is a set of actions on possible actions, it incites, it induces, it seduces, it makes easier or more difficult; it releases or contrives, makes more probable or less; in the extreme it constrains or forbids absolutely, but it is always a way of acting upon one or more acting subjects by virtue of their acting or being capable of action.[132]

He describes a shift in the operation of power in the eighteenth and nineteenth centuries from a political practice that utilised displays of power as spectacle, such as through public executions, to the exercise of power through making its target more visible and audible. 'This enables the disciplinary power to be both absolutely indiscreet, since it is always everywhere and alert ... and absolutely "discreet", for it functions permanently and largely in silence.'[133] However, I would argue that the instability of power structures as depicted in Irish and Spanish cinema prevent this discreet mode of power from operating. To return to Foucault's configuration, power in these cinemas operates more as a direct mode of action on others, as violence does, than as a set of constraints upon others' actions. The operations of power become visible, and therefore contestable.

The precise operation of this mode of power is illustrated in an Irish context by a scene in *Ordinary Decent Criminal* (Thaddeus O'Sullivan, 2000) in which the police attempt to assert their power over the Irish gangster Michael Lynch (Kevin Spacey). We have seen the police repeatedly humiliated throughout the film as Lynch pulls off a series of crimes, despite being supposedly under their surveillance. In an effort to curtail his movements, the police finally decamp to the road in front of his house, where they proceed to flaunt their supposed upper hand over him. As Lynch and his wife (Linda Fiorentino) sit huddled inside the house, a police detective (Stephen Dillane) parked outside begins to taunt him over a loudspeaker, the sound inescapable within. We see the distress on Lynch and his wife's faces, and the smug satisfaction on the face of the policemen as finally they gain a measure of revenge for their humiliations. Through a self-conscious display of power, an invasion of Lynch's private space, the police assert their position as the embodiment of state power. However, this means of asserting their authority proves to be precarious, and we soon see the look of smug satisfaction on the detective's face turn to discomfort and then rage as Lynch and his wife turn the police's tactics back against them. By loudly simulating sexual intercourse they invade the public space in which the police operate and assert their own power from their domestic space. When state power ceases to be discreet it opens itself to attack, for when power acts with indiscretion, potential points of resistance become visible. In this example, the failure of the police to discreetly survey public space and regulate activity therein forces them to make a public display of their power, thereby revealing their own weakness. Ultimately the unwillingness of the criminal to recognise the legitimacy of police power leads to them operating in such a way that Lynch can claim of the police, 'we've dragged them down to our level, they're acting like criminals now'.

Similarly, in John Boorman's *The General* (1998), a dramatisation of the same true-life story as *Ordinary Decent Criminal*, the notion of the police as upholders of moral order is questioned from the very first scene. After seeing Martin Cahill (Brendan Gleeson) gunned down in broad daylight, immediately we cut to a scene of celebration within a crowded police room as one officer announces 'they got the general'. From the start, any suggestion that the police occupy a position of moral authority is refuted, and the film strongly suggests that they collude with the IRA in the murder of Cahill. This notion is supported by a short flashback montage at the start of the film which succinctly undermines the pillars of authority within Catholic Ireland. We have already seen a young Cahill evade the police successfully in a prior scene, and they are seen to take their revenge for their humiliation when the officer who does manage to catch him immediately starts to beat him. There is then a cut to a dormitory filled with young boys with their bottoms bared, being slapped by a priest, who does not however lay a hand on Martin. The reason for this becomes clear when the priest returns during the night and attempts to sexually molest him. However when he realises what is happening Martin hits the priest, who in turn begins to slap Martin. In this series of images we see a policeman, a priest and Cahill engaging in violence. There is no differentiation between the violence perpetrated by the criminal and that of the forces of state authority, and indeed the film positions us

to sympathise with Cahill. Thus the notion of legitimate force is undermined and the police are seen to operate within the same moral sphere
as Cahill, and are forced to compete for legitimacy within that sphere.

The impotence of the police is repeatedly emphasised in the face of
Cahill's ingenuity and general public distrust. At the start of the film we
see them driven out of the council flats where Cahill lives by an angry
mob which clearly does not accept their authority. Cahill himself frequently undermines their power, tricking the police into providing him
with an alibi after having committed a crime, incorporating their pre-
dicted response to a burglar alarm into an elaborate art theft, and leaving them stranded in the middle of the Wicklow mountains without
any petrol having led them on a wild goose chase in search of the stolen
paintings. Significantly, we see the stranded police car, isolated against
the expanse of wild landscape which engulfs it – the imagined space
of nationalist Ireland turned against those who are charged with maintaining the nation-state. An even more audacious subversion of the
institutions of power is shown when Cahill breaks into the law library
at night in order to study up on a point of law. We see him, torch in
hand, thumbing through the annals of legislature until he discovers a
technicality which he can exploit in his own court case; the rule of the
law is shown to be anything but unimpeachable.

Although the police may be incapable of asserting their authority in
The General, there is a force within the world of the film which, although in the main only alluded to, acts as a boundary to the limits of
behaviour and guarantees the dominance of a particular social and symbolic order. This force is the IRA, which acts in the film as the only
meaningful arbiter of behaviour, as it is the only institution which has
the means to assert its power. The threat of force which the IRA embodies is invoked by the police when one officer tells Cahill 'next time your
door is kicked you'll be fucking praying it's the police'. Yet the IRA
does not represent the forces of law and order, and the reliance of the
police on this external threat only illustrates their own lack of power.
The symbolic order that the IRA upholds is not predicated on a respect
for the integrity of the state, but on that of the nation. Thus it is only
when Cahill decides to sell his stolen paintings to the UVF that his behaviour exceeds the boundary of acceptability and his world begins to
crumble; it is this which, it is suggested, leads to his death.

The absence of a structuring value system and the subsequent moral
relativism which this engenders is poignantly captured in the descent of
John Voight's 'good policeman' Inspector Kenny. Portrayed as a man of
conscience and dedication to duty, he alone of the policemen does not

5.The descent of Jon Voight's 'good cop' in *The General*

celebrate Cahill's death in the opening scene, realising it is an empty victory for the forces of law and order. However, his frustration at his inability to apprehend Cahill, and at Cahill's rejection of the law as a legitimate arbiter of behaviour, ultimately drives Kenny to violence. Unable to get through to Cahill when they are alone in a police cell, he begins to beat him wildly until finally, slumped with Cahill on the floor of the cell, there is nothing left to tell them apart. 'You're getting to be like me,' Cahill tells him, 'trespass, harassment, intimidation, beating people up; you've had to come down to my level.' As he speaks, the camera slowly pulls back from him to reveal Kenny holding his face in his hands in the flickering darkness of the cell. 'That's right Martin,' he replies, 'you brought me down with you. I'm in the gutter as well.'

Although the descent of the good cop into the world of criminality is a narrative device within crime films stretching back to film noir, it is imbued with a particular significance within a culture that is experiencing the decline of moral certainties concomitant with the process of modernisation. This is illustrated by the comments Cahill goes on to make in the same scene, claiming that Kenny used to be a straight cop who knew right from wrong and 'always did what the priest told him'. Thus the figure of the priest as arbiter of behaviour is invoked by Cahill, immediately relating Kenny's belief in law and order to the particular ideology of the Catholic Church, which suppressed moral ambiguities for so long in Ireland. Cahill goes on to ask 'Did the church let you down, did it?', lamenting that 'nobody believes in nothing any more, except me'. The implication here is that, with the decline in belief in

Catholic ideology in Irish society, there is no longer any means of judg-ing right from wrong and therefore there are no standards of behaviour which the forces of law and order can or must adhere to. In this moral climate, Cahill's own system of belief is as valid as any other and can be credibly used to legitimise his behaviour. Kenny's reply only serves to confirm this analysis, asking, in the belief that Cahill's life was in danger from the IRA, 'Would it suit you Martin if it was my bullet?' He is left with no choice but to act according to the modes of behaviour of the criminal, and all he can do for Cahill now is perhaps offer him a more humane death.

Shifting to the Spanish context, this lack of distance between the police and the criminals is seen to recur within both comedic represen-tations and thrillers in Spanish cinema. Perhaps the most famous ex-ample of the former is *Torrente: el brazo tonto de la ley* (*Torrente: the Stupid Arm of the Law*, Santiago Segura, 1998), one of the highest grossing Spanish films of all time, which depicts a racist Madrid ex-cop who basks in his own vulgarity while espousing a mix of rabid nation-alism, misogyny and police brutality. He assembles a gang of misfits and outcasts in order to track down and infiltrate a drug-dealing gang. Whilst the force of law is upheld through the narrative resolution – in that the criminal gang is destroyed – its representative in the person of Torrente (Santiago Segura) is so compromised by his own activities – in-cluding drug-taking and racial abuse – that any notion of the law as representing a superior moral order is negated. Furthermore, through encouraging narrative identification with this character, the anarchic, self-serving relationship to the law which he embodies is celebrated by the film.

The almost casual assumption of police brutality and incompetence recurs repeatedly through Spanish cinema and serves to underline a general mistrust of the institutions of state power. *Dias contados* (*Run-ning Out of Time*, Imanol Uribe, 1994) tells the story of a group of Basque terrorists who travel to Madrid with the aim of blowing up a police station with a car bomb. Whilst in Madrid, one of the terrorists, Antonio (Carmelo Gómez) becomes involved with a young drug ad-dict, Charo (Ruth Gabriel), who is living in the flat next to his. In an early scene within the film, Charo and her flat mate are visited by the police, who proceed to verbally abuse them in front of Antonio. One of the officers tells Charo 'if you were my daughter I'd beat the hell out of you', at once equating state and domestic authority and also un-dermining both as representative of violent patriarchy. Even the police officer who initially seeks to sympathise with them responds to their

6. Rafa resorts to physical threats in *Dias contados*

rebuttal by declaring that they need a beating. Whilst Antonio calmly
tells the police that they need a search warrant to enter the flat, the
head officer Rafa (Karra Elejalde) calls him an imbecile. When Antonio
tells them that he is a press officer the police are clearly impressed and
swiftly leave the flat, Rafa shaking his hand as they go and warning him
against the two girls. What is noticeable about the scene is that it is Antonio, a terrorist, who acts with calm assurance and a knowledge of
legal procedure, and the police who are violent and hysterical. Furthermore, the extent to which they are impressed by Antonio's supposed
occupation suggests a hypocrisy between their mode of action in the
company of society's marginalised and their desired image in society at
large.

Both the terrorist and the police officer in *Dias contados* can be seen
in terms of the brutalisation of the public sphere, an inevitability in a situation in which social structures and established power relations have
disintegrated. The very existence of the terrorist group serves as a challenge to the legitimacy of state power, and the actions of the police in the
film, from the physical and verbal violence which they exert to their fear
of exposure by a member of the press, furthers the suggestion of illegitimate power in operation. As outlined above in relation to *The General*
and *Ordinary Decent Criminal*, without a stable set of power relations
which act as a discreet set of restraints upon behaviour, power must

always act directly upon its object; a mode of operation that inevitably debauches into violence. Like Antonio's terrorist acts, which depend on their visibility for impact, Rafa's pursuit of the drug dealer 'El Portugués' (Chacho Carreras) must ultimately abandon surveillance for direct confrontation in order to achieve any success. Having been apparently unsuccessful in linking 'El Portugués' directly to a large drug deal, the police resort to abducting him off the street and driving him into the countryside, away from the surveillance ironically personified in Antonio's *faux* press photographer. There Rafa forces him to kneel on the ground and points a gun to his head, demanding that he admits that he is scared. When 'El Portugués' does so on the brink of tears Rafa pulls the trigger, revealing the gun to be empty, before admitting 'we're all scared'. As in *The General*, the distinction between the mode of operation of the police and the criminal, and in this case terrorist, becomes blurred. Whilst Antonio carries out terrorist acts with impunity, shooting a police officer in the middle of a crowded Madrid street, the police are cowed by the presence of a supposed member of the press. It is they whose actions are regulated by an implied surveillance which they themselves seem powerless to implement over the criminals they pursue. Without the power to discreetly regulate behaviour, they are forced into a more direct mode of action, a display of force that acts directly and violently on their object of pursuit. However, this act of violence both displays and undermines the power of the police through its very visibility. For an act of violence is precarious; its power is quickly exhausted and it is open to retaliation. It reveals not only an arbitrary power which is nothing more than an expression of force, but also an equivalency between the subject and object of its expression which disciplinary power conceals. In *Dias contados* the aura of legitimate state power vanishes in the parallel trajectories of state and terrorist violence, and the distance between criminal and police officer is erased in Rafa's frank admission that, like 'El Portugués', 'we're all scared'.

The general absence of credible authority figures for a generation of young Spaniards is a central feature of *Tesis (Thesis*, Alejandro Amenábar, 1996). In this thriller Angela (Ana Torrent) and Chema (Fele Martínez), two young university students, investigate a snuff movie production ring which they inadvertently discover at the university. Having found her film professor dead of an asthma attack in a screening room, Angela removes the video which he was watching at the time. It shows a young woman, a former student at the university who disappeared two years previously, being savagely beaten to death by a masked man. This discovery leads Angela and Chema into a web of conspiracy and murder, stretching into the upper echelons of the university. The girl who was murdered is found to be one of several, all killed so as to produce these videos for monetary gain. The world represented by the perpetrators of these acts is one devoid of all values except the commercial. That one of these perpetrators is Angela's replacement film professor, who justifies his behaviour by claiming 'you give the public what it wants', implicates the university and the social and cultural authority which it represents in this loss of values. The devaluation of traditional forms of authority is furthered by the absence of the police from the film. It is only at a late stage of the film that Angela suggests bringing the evidence they have acquired to the police, a suggestion met with hostility by Chema. As it transpires, Angela's suggestion is not acted upon and it falls to Angela and Chema to resolve the situation by killing the perpetrators of the murders, despite the personal danger that this implies for themselves. The attitude to the police within the film is captured in an exchange between Angela and Chema in which she suggests that he is speaking like a policeman and he replies, 'don't insult me'. The absence of authority extends to the parental figures in the film. Chema's parents are entirely absent and he lives alone in a flat, while Angela's mother goes so far as to invite her potential killer to stay for lunch where, in Angela's words, he charms her family. She seems removed from her parents, incapable of confiding in them even after nearly being killed. The film suggests a fundamental breakdown in the relationship between the generations and a concomitant diminution of established social and cultural values, a dynamic which has been repeatedly teased out in the Oedipal dramas of Irish and Spanish cinema, as will be explored more fully below.

ABSENT FATHERS AND OEDIPAL DRAMAS

The Boy from Mercury (Martin Duffy, 1996) relates that most common of stories within Irish culture, the attempt of a young boy to deal with the effects of an absent or inadequate father. As a means of escaping his grief and loss after the death of his father, Harry Cronin (James Hickey) fantasises that he is not of this world, but has been sent from Mercury to research life amongst earthlings. Early in the film there is a series of images that conflate the figure of Harry's father with those images and institutions invested with authority within the Irish nation-state. In this scene Harry goes to visit his father's grave with his mother and his rather reluctant brother. At the end of the scene the camera lingers on a close-up of his father's photograph on the gravestone and then cuts in quick succession to images of a Celtic cross, a Garda station sign with its Celtic cross insignia, a school building with a crucifix above the door and a church steeple in the background, and a priest walking down a school corridor slapping a wooden rod against his hand. The camera then brings us inside a classroom where children are reciting by rote, and where we see Harry being hit on the head by a priest for making an error. This sequence of images creates a clear visual link between the figure of the father and the institutions of the police and the church. It also suggests that the authority of these institutions is legitimated through an appeal to an essentialised Irish past, as embodied in the image of the Celtic cross. However, the fact that Harry's father is absent and that he is therefore unable to fill the roll of father to Harry renders these images ambiguous and is symptomatic of the wider questioning of power and paternity in Irish culture.

In discussing the preoccupation with father figures within the texts of the Irish literary revival, Kiberd writes that this fixation is symptomatic of a society that is unsure of itself. In a colonised society such as preindependence Ireland, he writes, 'rebellions are conducted not so much against authority figures as against their palpable absence. These gestures rehearse not the erosion of power so much as the search for a true authority, and in them will lurk the danger of re-oedipalisation'.[134] The association in this sequence of the authority figures of church and state with the un-vital figure of the father (existing only as an image) suggests a continued anxiety about authority and its legitimacy in postcolonial Ireland, despite the appeal to an historical nation represented by the Celtic cross. Furthermore, the effects of this uncertainty can be witnessed in the random violence of the priest, who through his wielding of the wooden rod and his physical abuse of Harry displays what Kiberd refers to as 'a nervous patriarchal psychology' resulting from the 'endless crises of self-legitimation' that afflicted the leaders of the new Irish state.[135] This crisis of legitimacy can be seen to persist in contemporary cultural production, as subsequent generations reject the autocratic legacy of nationalist Ireland by effacing the father from the text once more, seeing in him a figure compromised by his renunciation of power in the face of a now devalued Catholic ideology.

Whilst post-independence Ireland saw a re-Oedipalisation of Irish society, with the priest once again assuming the role of the authoritarian super-ego, this continued the emasculation of Irish males experienced under colonisation, who were once again dominated in the public and private spheres by an all-encompassing regulatory Catholicism. If the power structures which emerged in the Irish state could be characterised as 'nervously patriarchal' and autocratic, then the abdication of the father from a position of authority allowed these structures to penetrate every aspect of political and domestic life. Thus, without his father's presence to protect him from the vagaries of public life, to construct a barrier between the private and the public until he is ready to assume his role in the latter, the son is prematurely exposed to the power relations that constitute the public sphere. In *The Boy from Mercury* we witness this in the physical abuse that Harry suffers at the hands of the priests, against which he has no father to take a stand. The lack which Harry experiences is only highlighted by the comically inept attempts of his uncle (Tom Courtenay) to talk to him about life, man to man, over an afternoon drink in a pub; the incongruity of a small boy's presence in this setting further adds to the sense of the adult world being thrust upon Harry before he is ready. When Harry visits his friend Sean's (Sean O'Flanagain) house for an afternoon, his family is portrayed as a model of middle-class contentment, and the absence within Harry's own life becomes starkly evident. Sean's mother cares for the boys, while his father arrives home from work and engages with them good-naturedly before retiring to his chair to read a book. However, the fact that this entire sequence is bathed in a yellow glow and tinged with soft focus suggests that it can only ever be a fantasy, a suggestion reinforced by the titles in which the two characters are listed as 'Sean's Perfect Father' and 'Sean's Perfect Mother'. Nevertheless, Harry attempts to fill this absence through his fantasy that he has been sent from Mercury to study the planet Earth and its inhabitants. He communicates messages back 'home' by flashing a torch out his bedroom window, believing the lights from passing airplanes to be his reply. By appealing to a source that is literally outside of this world, Harry gives a meaning to his life that has not been provided by the discourses of nationalism or religion, and which he must create himself without the guidance of his absent father.

In Spain, too, the father is tainted by the emasculation which he suffered under Francoism and is frequently an absent or ineffective figure within Spanish cinema. Helen Graham argues that in Franco's Spain 'the patriarchal family was seen as representing the corporate order of the state in microcosm'.[136] However, this model of society in which the family was vertically integrated into a corporate model of state power transferred the authority of the father to the supreme authority of Franco. Franco's dictatorial power, strategically aligned with institutionalised Catholicism, infantilised the Spanish male by denying him an effective presence in the public sphere. Once again, this breaks down

7. The blue Jaguar central to Adam's multiple histories

the boundary between public and private as the family is incorporated into a ubiquitous corporate state against which the father is powerless to take a stand. Furthermore, the absence of fathers is an historical fact, as over half a million families were without a male breadwinner in post-civil war Spain. The lingering effects of this can be read in the incomplete families of contemporary Spanish cinema and the representations of an older male generation which carry the burden of an historical complicity with Francoism and a problematic relationship with patriarchal power stretching back to the trauma of the civil war.

The manner in which social forces act directly upon the son in the father's absence is made explicit in *Carne trémula* (*Live Flesh*, Pedro Almodóvar, 1997), in which Victor (Liberto Rabal) is literally born into the public sphere. His mother is a prostitute who gives birth to him on a bus on the way to the hospital. With the identity of his father unknown, the state exploits his birth for propaganda and claims Victor as its own, with the Mayor of Madrid proclaiming him an honorary citizen and the director of the bus company presenting him with a lifetime bus-pass. However, the scene of his birth is the last time we see Victor in the company of his mother. From this moment Victor's fate is intertwined directly with that of the city in which he lives, and its forces act upon his life in emphatic ways. In the first section of the film we see him as a child of the streets endlessly circling Madrid, framed by the camera against its night skyline, firstly on a pizza delivery bike and then by bus. When he does finally halt his wanderings, it is not to go home but to visit the house of Elena (Francesca Neri), a drug addict with whom he had a brief sexual encounter previously. However, this is not a space of refuge and his attempts to stay and chat with Elena set off a chain of events which ultimately lead to his imprisonment. Through sheer misfortune he becomes the victim in a love triangle involving two policemen and one of their wives. He is framed by Sancho (José Sancho), a violent drunk of a cop who shoots and seriously injures his partner David (Javier Bardem) in an act of vengeance but manages to pin the blame on Victor. Here we see the forces of authority intervening directly and detrimentally in Victor's life. The only crime which he is guilty of is naïvety, for believing that his sexual encounter with Elena was meaningful. Like Harry in *The Boy from Mercury*, in the absence of a protective family environment the adult world has been thrust upon him too soon, and for Victor the consequences are several years in jail. After his release, again like Harry, he must create meaning in the world for himself. In Victor's case this meaning comes through his desire to take revenge on David, now paraplegic, by seducing Elena, who has since become his wife. Yet it is revealing that Victor's anger is in fact directed towards the wrong man, suggesting that revenge will prove to be as unsustainable a means of giving meaning to the world as Harry's fantasy of spacemen. Indeed his actions, although governed by this desire for retribution, serve to socialise Victor, turning him into the kind of man which Elena can, and does, fall in love with, until finally he is ready to be the father that he never had to their soon-to-be-born son.

Thus, both *The Boy from Mercury* and *Carne trémula* are narratives of maturation, in which the son, lacking a father to facilitate his path to adulthood, must create his own Oedipal figure against which to define himself. For Harry it is the spacemen who he turns to for guidance and meaning in his life; for Victor it is David, in relation to whom he constructs his own identity and whose position he must ultimately assume. What lingers from these films is the image of a generation cut adrift from its past, for whom the world is precarious and immediate. Having rejected the father and the ideologies of the past, the new generation must forge its own relationships with society. However, the difficulty of achieving this is symbolised by the absent father in these films. For what the father provides is stability and structure in the interaction between the private and the public spheres. He provides a position which the son can accede to and an ideology which structures his relationship to society. Without this, as we have seen, the path to adulthood can be traumatic, as the son, having rejected the meanings bequeathed by history, must forge his own comprehensible narrative, wrought from an ever complex and uncertain world.

About Adam is a playful, post-modern take on this necessity to create meaning in a world without historical certainties. In it the central character Adam (Stuart Townsend) ingratiates himself into a Dublin family of three sisters, a brother and their mother. Whilst the family's absent patriarch is not even alluded to in the film, having assumed, it would seem, the status of a given within Irish cinema, it is Adam's construction of his own past which is interesting. Adam himself is nothing more than a cipher for the desires of the various family members; he allows them to construct his identity according to what they wish to find. What makes this possible is his apparent independence from his own past, which he constantly reshapes to conform to the particular identity which he wishes to assume. This is evident in the various stories he tells about the fate of his parents and the blue Jaguar which he owns. To Lucy (Kate Hudson), his future wife, and her mother he says that his parents died when he was young and that he used his inheritance to buy this car, which his father had always loved, so as to remember them by. This provokes a loving response from both, confirming their image of Adam as a sweet and slightly innocent young man. To Laura (Frances O'Connor), the family's hopeless romantic, he tells how his father bought him this car and then the next day disappeared; the victim of a 'great passion'. To the brother David (Alan Maher) he tells how he bought the car to attract women, on the advice of his dad, whom he 'never liked much', thus confirming his status with David as an attractive male role model. Adam uses the freedom that comes from a severance with the past to create his own multiple father figures, each of which facilitates a particular identity formation in the present. This at once acknowledges the importance of the father in the process of forming identity and disavows the possibility of any essential identity in a society where the certainties of the previous generation have been rejected. It is significant within the film that at no stage is the audience witness to the 'real' Adam beyond his multiple constructions. Neither is Adam ever forced to confront his own multiplicity by an intrusion from the past. We are never allowed access to any 'authentic' past against which his stories can be measured. This is Baudrillard's post-modern history, 'empty of referents',[137] which gives witness to a society seeking to distance itself from its own past. However, the danger of rejecting history as a basis for identity is that it involves a concomitant loss of depth in which identity becomes nothing more than a play of empty signifiers.

8. The father as absence/presence, embodied in the transgendered figure of Lola

In fact, in the majority of Irish and Spanish cinema, the absence of the father is registered as a source of trauma rather than freedom. The past resonates within *Secretos del corazón* (*Secrets of the Heart*, Montxo Armendáriz, 1997) through the absent father figures who haunt the film. Set in the early 1960s, it tells the story of Javi (Andoni Erburu), a young boy who alternates his time between the rural house of his mother, uncle and grandfather and the town where he attends school. Early in the film Javi brings his friend to a supposedly haunted house where one can hear the voices of buried murder victims, who shout because 'they took secrets no one knew to the grave and now they have to tell them'. Here the past is a place of secrets and violence which reverberate in the present. Javi's family home is tethered to the past through the figure of his grandfather (Joan Vallés), who refuses to leave his armchair, and his dead father, whose presence lingers in the still bloodstained chair in which he committed suicide. Javi attempts to uncover the secret of his father's death through a meticulous investigation of the present, combing the room in which he died for clues. This is a world in which present and past are symbiotically linked, in which each provides meaning in the other. The several father figures in the film are all strongly connected to the past. The first we encounter is the father of Carlos (Íñigo Garcés), a friend of Javi's elder brother Juan, who plays the saxophone in an adjoining room while the children and Carlos' mother dance in the kitchen. Although we never see him, his presence hangs heavily over the film and it is strongly suggested that Carlos' mother kills herself due to his physical and mental abuse. Notably, the only visual representation which we do see of him is his army jacket hanging over a chair, thereby connecting this violent patriarch to the autocracy of the Francoist state while at the same time continuing the tradition of non-representation of male violence that was characteristic of Francoist cinema. The displacement and fetishisation of male violence into the masochistic aesthetic which dominated Francoist culture is here replicated by the replacement of the abusive father with fetishised markers of his identity. However, in the suicide of Carlos' mother the film reminds us that although it may be effaced from representations, the reality of abusive patriarchy has been a constant within Spanish society and has had real and tragic effects within it.

The image of the army jacket also evokes the unspoken presence at the heart of this film; the Spanish Civil War. If Carlos' father can be seen to represent the victors of that war, then both the father and grandfather of Juan are representative of that large body of defeated men whose own experiences of the war were denied expression in Franco's Spain. In this context, Juan's grandfather's decision to withdraw from public life and remain cocooned in the domestic sphere becomes comprehensible. Furthermore, the logical extension of this withdrawal is presented as suicide by the grandfather, who cannot explain to Juan why he wants to go on living, but only that he knows he does. His father, on the other hand, could not carry on living in such a context. 'Some of us want to live, others no. That's all', is the most that his grandfather can offer Juan in his search for meaning in his father's death. The film's refusal to confer any greater meaning than this on his father's suicide evokes a pervasive sense of meaninglessness which is the legacy of a war between countrymen and which it falls to the next generation to overcome and relegate to the past.

The father as a traumatic absence/presence is dealt with explicitly in Almodóvar's *Todo sobre mi madre* (*All About my Mother*, 1999), in which Manuela (Cecilia Roth) returns to Barcelona following the death of her son Esteban (Eloy Azorín). She has fled both the city and Esteban's father, the transsexual Lola (Toni Cantó), seventeen years before and now she retraces her journey in search of him. In Barcelona she acquires an alternative family, comprising of the prostitute Agrado (Antonia San Juan) and Rosa (Penélope Cruz), an angelic nun. Lurking at the heart of this family is the figure of Lola, who disappeared previously with much of Agrado's money and belongings and left behind Rosa, impregnated and infected with HIV. Significantly, when Manuela finally meets Lola at Rosa's funeral she declares 'you aren't a human being Lola, you're an epidemic'. The father here is the source of family trauma, an epidemic whose legacy must be overcome by successive generations. As a post-operative transsexual, Lola represents both the absence and presence of the father in the one body, seemingly embodying the worst excesses of *machista* behaviour while lacking its bodily markers.

For Esteban, his father was an absence that prevented him acceding fully to the symbolic/social world. This is suggested in the early section of the film, which depicts Esteban and his mother in an almost pre-Oedipal closeness. On the eve of his birthday they spend an evening together, eating and watching television. Later, as she sits on his bed, he asks her to read to him like when he was a child, his eyes staring at her with a seductive intensity. Without his father's presence the bond between them is unmediated; at the theatre Esteban doesn't watch the stage but its impact on his mother, and later on when she agrees to tell him about his father he kisses her and holds her in a lingering embrace. Esteban makes the impact of his father's absence explicit in his diary entry, in which he writes, referring to a torn photograph which his mother showed him, 'half of it was missing. I didn't want to tell her but my life is missing that same half'. Yet, for Esteban, the opportunity to reconcile his father into his life is gone and he dies before Manuela can tell his story. It is only with the passing of time that the father can be rehabilitated, a possibility which Almodóvar admits in *Todo sobre mi madre*. After the birth of Rosa's son, also called Esteban, Manuela brings him to Lola, along with her son's diary in which he tells of his desire to meet his father. Thus the father is readmitted into the family's life, albeit briefly, as Lola is dying of AIDS. Yet significantly, the baby Esteban neutralises the HIV virus in record time and is free, in Almodóvar's narrative of progress, to live his life unburdened by the legacy of the past.

The ideology of the father as an historic inheritance that must be rejected and overcome by the son is dramatised in the Irish film *Korea*. In this configuration of the Irish Oedipal drama, the son must contend with the overwhelming presence of a flawed father figure rather than an absent and idealised one. The film tells the story of John Doyle (Donal Donnelly) and his son Eamonn (Andrew Scott), who make a living fishing for eels on a lake in the midlands but whose fishing licence is shortly to be revoked as the lake has been redesignated for tourism. From the opening scenes the film invokes the Irish Civil War as a constant presence both in the drama which unfolds and the social context in which the Doyles live, one in which the divides which the war occasioned have not been forgotten, at least by those, such as John, who were on the losing side. His imagination is dominated by the war and he feels betrayed by a state that has failed to fulfil the promises of the nationalist rhetoric which inspired those who fought for it. When the postman delivers him the revocation of his licence John remarks, 'there was a time when all I wanted to see was a harp on an envelope

instead of a crown'. This disillusionment finds a target in the figure of
Ben Moran (Vass Anderson), who fought on the opposite side in the
civil war and who, along with 'those buckos up in Dublin', represents
to John the betrayal of nationalist Ireland by the forces of commerce
and modernity.

The suffocating domestic presence of the father in *Korea* is occasioned by the death of John's wife and by his disempowerment in the
public sphere, so that his control over his son is the only authority he still
maintains. As Eamonn remarks in voiceover over the opening shot of the
men on the lake; 'me and my father, it was always me and my father'.
The extent of John's control over Eamonn is such that a central dilemma
in the film is whether he will send him to America, the consequences of
which would be his enlistment into the Korean War and possible death.
However, this prospect is not viewed entirely negatively by the villagers
due to the soldiers' pension that would accrue to John in this circumstance. In this way Eamonn becomes objectified in a warped system of
monetary exchange. However, the son is unwilling to remain trapped in
his father's world of historical rhetoric, he is aware of the need to escape. He declares in voiceover that he has remained there too long, that
his father's past 'goes with me in my dreams'. It is through his love affair with Una Moran (Fiona Molony), the daughter of his father's civil
war enemy, that Eamonn asserts the possibility of a future that leaves behind the divisiveness of the past. In the film's denouement he finally
confronts his father by challenging him to fulfil the consequences of his
own rhetoric. Having refused his order that he emigrate to America, Eamonn defies his father to shoot him with his old civil war gun, thereby
fulfilling the violent logic of the past which John continually evokes.
Yet, the physical presence of the gun shatters the romanticism of John's
civil war rhetoric and confronts him with its consequences in the present. Without the bulwark of a nationalist historical discourse, John's
power over his son is lost and he can only sit and weep. The film ends
with John being led from his boat by Una before walking away into the
distance. The camera returns to Eamonn and Una, who stand side by
side, symbols of the next generation who will reject the language of the
father and the historical order which it invokes.

The figure of John Doyle, the autocratic father, would seem to question the accuracy of the dominant maternal figure so ubiquitous within
the Irish cultural imagination. It suggests that the Irish male's disempowerment in the public sphere under colonisation increased his need to
exert his authority within the domestic space. However, the fragility of
patriarchal power depicted in *Korea* supports Kiberd's assertion that 'the

evidence of Irish texts and case histories would confirm the suspicion that the autocratic father is often the weakest male of all, concealing that weakness under the protective coverage of the prevailing system'.[138] When the historical nationalist discourse which John Doyle invokes to wield power over his son is punctured, he is revealed as lacking any real power in the public or private sphere. Within *Korea*, the patriarchal values of Irish nationalism are revealed as anachronistic and inadequate for the realities of a modernising nation-state, and their rejection by a new generation reveals the precarious power of the Irish male, who has failed to assume his role as an active agent in the public sphere.

Without the political and symbolic structures that could grant the father authority, the only recourse for the Irish and Spanish male is an expression of power through violence or the hypermasculinity associated with Spain's *machismo* culture. Timothy Mitchell explicitly connects *machismo* to impotency in the socio-political sphere, which is counterbalanced by an emphasis on erotic potency and 'a curious overvaluing of the genitals'.[139] This is the theme of *Huevos de oro* (*Golden Balls*, Bigas Luna, 1993), which even in its title conveys the central character Benito's (Javier Bardem) obsession with his own sexual prowess and his linking of erotic with social and economic power. Benito is depicted as a typically macho Spanish male to the point of parody; his wife at one stage remarking that 'I can't believe I love someone who likes Julio Iglesia.' Throughout the film the erotic and the economic are intermingled, and Benito's sexual prowess is indeed matched by his increasing financial success. In one scene he gives a woman a Rolex watch during oral sex, at the same time an expression of his sexual and economic power over her. However sexual power is ultimately revealed as both transitory and illusory, a poor substitute for social capital. The two women who he holds sway over ultimately reject him, preferring each other's company and caresses to his aggressive sexuality. His economic situation deteriorates when the buildings which he is constructing are found to be substandard. Finally he ends up impotent and broke, living in the promised land of America with the domineering Ana (Raquel Bianca), whose infidelity and declaration that 'I need a man' is the final blow to his shattered masculinity.

The interweaving of male sexual and social power is reflected in Kiberd's slightly altered perspective on the domineering mother of Irish cultural texts. He suggests that 'women sought from their sons an emotional fulfilment denied them by their men, which suggests that the husbands had often failed as lovers as well as fathers'.[140] This image of the male as ineffective to the point of irrelevance is seen in *Agnes Browne*

(Anjelica Huston, 1999), which opens in the immediate aftermath of Agnes' husband's death. As McLoone points out, there is an over-whelming absence of grief amongst Agnes (Anjelica Huston) and her children in the wake of her husband's demise, which contrasts starkly with her anguish following the death of her friend later in the film.[141]When husbands are referred to in the film it is generally in dis-paraging tones, particularly when it comes to sex; in relation to which Agnes asks 'what's to enjoy …? The smell of chips and Guinness?' Equally, in *Rat* (Steve Barron, 2000), a film in which a Dublin father mysteriously transforms into a rat, the central joke of the film is how little the family actually miss him.

However, the effects of Irish male disempowerment are also shown to be tragic in consequence. 'Distortions of sexuality' are cited by Geral-dine Moane as one of the psychological legacies of colonisation.[142] It is easy to read this as a displacement of the male's frustration in the public sphere into the arena of sexuality, as the male's feelings of inadequacy are displaced on to the female, frequently with violent effect. In *Guiltrip* (Gerry Stembridge, 1995) the sexual impotence of Liam (Andrew Con-nolly), an army officer, is matched by the empty manoeuvres carried out by an impotent Irish army, and ultimately finds its expression in an out-break of violence against a sexually confident young woman. Liam bangs her head repeatedly against a cannon, its gun standing proudly erect, but unused, until she is dead. Yet even this show of male force does not serve to assert his authority and is shown in contrast to his waning power in the domestic sphere, as his wife finally rebels against his tyrannical rule. Similarly, in *Country* (Kevin Liddy, 2000), a young girl, Sarah (Marcella Plunkett), is raped by her uncle when she ignores his and her parents dis-approval of the boyfriend with whom she plans to escape small-town life for England. Here we see a disempowered and increasingly irrelevant patriarchy take its violent revenge on those who reject it.

FRAMEWORKS OF MEANING

What is lost in a social and cultural context where patriarchy is devalued and traditional institutions no longer retain the power to structure the symbolic order is any authoritative voice which has the ability to confer meaning upon social reality. This opens a space for competing perspectives and value systems to make their claims on reality, permitting excluded voices to offer new interpretations of the world. However, this loss of certainty can also be experienced as trauma, particularly for those whose patriarchal privileges are most at risk from this new cultural relativism.

In *Abre los ojos* (*Open your Eyes*, Alejandro Amenábar, 1997), we find ourselves in a world where all meaning is indeterminate. From the first scene, the reliability of the visual is questioned as César (Eduardo Noriega), the main character, wakes up and drives out into a street devoid of human life. Firstly we see shots of the empty streets from his own point of view, but as he leaves his car and runs down the middle of the road, the camera lifts up to a God's-eye-view of the abandoned metropolis. Yet this objective eye proves to be misleading, as what we are seeing is revealed as nothing more that César's dream, which we hear him explaining in voiceover to a therapist. Throughout the film successive interpretive layers are peeled away, as initially we believe that we are witnessing César's memories in flashback as he relates them to his therapist. However, these memories prove unreliable, as there is a slippage in identities between the idealised girl of César's past and the figure of the monstrous female, embodied in Nuria (Najwa Nimri), his rejected lover. Yet ultimately, even the position César remembers is revealed as illusory, and we discover that he is in fact dead and existing only in a virtual world of memories. As Chris Perriam argues, in the film 'anarchy is let loose upon the patriarchally constructed worlds of the law, psychiatric therapy, the professional classes … and family'.[143] The revelation that the world is created in César's own head destroys these concepts as means of structuring reality. César experiences this realisation as horror, as it implies the dissolution of his own ego in a world that is meaningless. Furthermore, this loss of self is precipitated by the sexual confusion which Nuria's repeated appearances cause him and the slippage in identities between Nuria and Sofia (Penélope Cruz), the idealised girl of his dreams. For the Spanish male, according to Perriam, 'losing your sense of self, your sense of reality and continuity is palpably connected with losing your virility'.[144] It is the fragility of this virility and the patriarchal identity it supports that the film traumatically reveals, until, for César, the only means of escaping this realisation is to throw himself from the roof of a building to his death.

In Paddy Breathnach's *Ailsa* (1994) there is a similar uncertain relationship between reality and the structures which give it meaning. In the film Miles (Brendan Coyle), a middle-aged man living in a Dublin flat, develops an obsession with Campbell (Juliette Gruber), his new neighbour. As the story unfolds, its events are given an interpretation by a voiceover from Miles. He seeks to create an image of Campbell which he can control by maintaining a distance from the physically present Campbell in his building. He watches her from afar, usually from above. He reads and replies to her letters. And yet, on the one occasion when she is in his flat he is distant and unresponsive to her.

Throughout the film he is associated with problems of representation and the relation of the symbolic to the real. His job is to draw family trees to create 'maps of their past', to represent the lives of those who he suggests 'hadn't really been born until I had written it'. His girlfriend Sara (Andrea Irvine) tells him how she thinks of him during the day until she feels that he's not real, 'that I've made you up somehow'. He turns to external guides to interpret his reality in the form of a palm reading from his neighbour and counselling, yet both ultimately fail to capture any 'truth'. Finally, it is revealed that the voiceover which explains the images before us is in fact a form of suicide note left on an answer-phone by Miles for Ailsa, Campbell's daughter. Thus it is only from the impossible space of death that he can achieve sufficient distance from reality to interpret it and give it meaning. As in the worlds of *Ailsa* and *Abre los ojos*, in the indeterminate social order of modern Ireland and Spain all meaning is immanent to the social context in which it is conferred and any symbolic space that can bestow authority is closed off, is impossible, and is equated with the inaccessible space of death.

In conclusion, we have seen how the problematic relationship to patriarchal power within Irish and Spanish culture can be traced to the legacies of colonisation and civil war respectively. Furthermore, the decline in the Catholic nationalist ideology that dominated cultural discourses within both countries for a large part of the twentieth century has exposed the lack of an alternative authenticating discourse which can legitimise the operations of power as they are represented within popular culture. This chapter has traced the effects of this in contemporary crime films and an inability or unwillingness to depict the police as representatives of a legitimate state power. Yet it is not merely state power that has been called into question within Irish and Spanish culture, and the chapter has gone on to interrogate the continued failure of Irish and Spanish fathers to assume the patriarchal role and to explore the effects of this failure on the generation of sons who succeed them. Finally, it has argued that the demise of the dominant interpretative frameworks within Irish and Spanish culture, namely Catholicism and nationalism, has left those cultures devoid of any symbolic system which can confer meaning and value. This lack is represented as a cultural freedom to create meaning anew in many Irish and Spanish films. However, it can also have a destabilising effect as the cultural frameworks that guaranteed certain subject positions and identities are dismantled in the process of modernisation. The next chapter will explore the effects of this process on the range of identities available to women within contemporary Irish and Spanish cinema.

Femininity, Sexuality and Space

WOMEN AND NATION

Cultural representations of women in Ireland and Spain have been intrinsically bound to the imagining of the nation. This has had frequently negative consequences for women in those countries and for the manner in which they have been both represented within and given access to public discourse. Within the arena of sexuality and reproduction, women's bodies have been disciplined by the state to correspond to a feminine ideal that is held to embody the nation, and the dominant discourses surrounding the female body have been centred on morality and purity rather than on equality and individual rights. This creates a context where statements can be made such as that by Father Dennis Faul in a Pro-Life campaign pamphlet in 1994 in which he states that 'the separation of sexual intercourse from reproduction in Ireland represents *the death of the nation*'.[145] In the context of the abortion referendum debates of the time, this clearly maps the nation on to women's bodies and conflates discourses of sexuality and nation. Thus female subjectivity and the individual, sexualised female body become subsumed within a debate on national identity. This nationalist discourse seeks to erase difference and desire from its own idealised version of femininity, upon which is placed the burden of representing not so much the women of Ireland, but the nation itself.

In her book on Irish cinema, Ruth Barton argues that 'the embodiment of Ireland as young and feminine and an object of pure love, or alternatively as an old woman sheltering her sons in times of adversity, has a long representational history.'[146] Lacking from both these figures is sexual desire, and indeed female subjectivity. In the first instance Ireland is figured as a female object of purity, a victim of seduction or rape at the hands of the invading coloniser. However, for this metaphor to function within the terms of Irish nationalism female desire must by definition be effaced, for to admit its presence would be to figure the colonial relationship in terms other than those of domination and abuse.

It is this symbolic appropriation of the female body which explains the absolute taboo on relationships between Irish women and the British armed forces, evidenced in the ritual humiliation of Rosy Ryan (Sarah Miles) at the end of *Ryan's Daughter* after her relationship with an English officer is discovered. It is significant that her punishment is to be publically shorn of her hair, thereby denying her femininity and restoring the integrity of Ireland's symbolic identity as the unwilling female victim of an aggressive colonising force.

Alongside the figure of the purified love object, the nationalist elevation of the female to the role of symbolic embodiment of the nation was realised in the person of the Irish mother. Within a nationalist Catholic discourse which frequently equated her with the figure of the Virgin Mary,[147] the Irish mother has been reified as a desexualised being, defined solely in terms of her maternal role as the figure of domestic authority. The dominance of this image can be traced to specific social and economic developments within Ireland, as well as to the cultural economy of nationalism. As argued previously, post-famine Ireland saw a change in succession practices that necessitated the strict regulation of sexuality in order to prevent marriages which were economically unsustainable. According to Joe Lee, post-famine economic and social changes 'drastically weakened the position of women in Irish society'.[148] The reasons which he gives for this are threefold: the collapse of domestic industry; the shift from tillage to livestock farming, which reduced the need for female labour on the farm; and the decimation of the labouring classes by the famine. Within the poorer classes, he claims, women enjoyed greater equality and there was greater opportunity for marriage than in the post-famine middle classes, for whom marriage was a strictly economic arrangement. Within post-famine Irish society, for the vast majority of women the choice was marriage or emigration, as evidenced by the consistently higher rates of female emigration than male up until the 1960s.[149] Women who remained in Ireland were defined primarily by their role as child-bearers. As Rosemary Cullen Owens argues, 'once married, the female became a reproducer rather than a producer',[150] as evidenced by the practice known as the 'Country Divorce', whereby a man could send a barren wife back to her parents.[151]

The Catholic Church assumed a newly central role within this new social and economic order through the 'devotional revolution', which occurred in the aftermath of the famine. With this came what Dympna McLoughlin refers to as 'the triumph of respectability'; the new moral code wherein a respectable woman was one who remained in the domestic sphere and whose sexuality was totally contained within marriage.[152] Women were assumed to have no sexual desire and were thus entrusted with the necessary role of regulating unorthodox expressions of sexuality. Furthermore, the trend for Irish men to marry late to younger women, after having inherited the family farm, meant that many farms fell into the hands of widows, who often resisted the marriage of their inheriting son.[153] Therefore Irish mothers continued to exercise control over their sons' sexuality, as well as that of their potential sexual partners, well into adulthood. Within ecclesiastical discourse women were constructed as responsible for the morality of the country, as seen, for example, in the exhortation by bishops that Irish mothers should police their daughters' dress.[154] Although this moral code was expressed in terms of Catholic ideology, 'sexual prudery in nineteenth-century Ireland had little to do with the church and all to do with the economics of the emerging middle class'.[155] As Lee states, 'sex posed a far more subversive threat than the landlord to the security and status of the family'.[156]

Thus, for a variety of social, economic and cultural reasons Irish women became reimagined within the dominant discourses of nineteenth-century Ireland as non-sexual figures whose role was primarily in the domestic sphere. This confinement of Irish women to the domestic arena is perhaps reflected in the census figures, which show a decline of women in employment in Ireland from 846,000 in 1861 to 550,000 in 1901, down to 430,000 in 1911.[157] Within this time period, sexuality in Irish society became dominated by the emerging prudishness of the tenant farmer classes. That this was a result of specific social and economic circumstances rather than the expression of any innate Irish characteristic is evidenced by the prior existence of an Irish folk culture in which sex was 'a vital and pleasurable act in both an affirmation and a continuation of life'.[158] This included traditions such as the playing of sexually explicit games at wakes and the administering of love potions and remedies for the sexually 'lethargic'. However, historical variations in attitudes to sexuality were not acknowledged within the dominant nationalist Catholic discourse, which instead promoted a generalised equation of Irishness with sexual purity.

A similar connection between socio-cultural change and available models of femininity can be traced in turn-of-the-century Spain. In the late nineteenth and early twentieth centuries Spanish national identity was shaken by the political and cultural turmoil occasioned by the loss of its colonies in Central America and the Caribbean. This loss caused a strain on the ties between Spain's various regions, which had up till then united out of colonial interests. The effect of this, along with the more general impact of modernisation, created a plurality of identities in more developed parts of Spain.[159] Correspondingly, the promotion of a unified national identity became the preserve of conservative forces such as the church and the army. The national images that emerged from this conservative discourse included that of the 'uniquely beautiful and devout' Spanish woman and the valiant Spanish male with his highly developed sense of honour and 'manliness'.[160]

Once again, it is the image of a devout, desexualised woman that is summoned to represent the national collectivity, and it is her morality which is considered to uphold the morality of the nation. As Pilar Primo de Rivera, the daughter of Spain's ruling dictator through the 1920s, stated, 'we believe that it is the women of Spain, as a block, who safeguard the traditions of our nation'.[161] This image of Spanish femininity must be considered in relation to the Spanish concept of 'honour', according to which 'it was the woman's responsibility to safeguard morality and the family's honour depended on her virtue'.[162] According to the Spanish code of moral values, honour was an objective asset that could be lost through one's own or one's relatives' actions. Thus, a daughter who became pregnant before marriage was frequently expelled from the house so that the family could save itself from dishonour.[163] The strict regulation of female sexuality was therefore necessary, leading to discourses on women within Spain tending to be constructed around a reductive virgin–whore dichotomy. Ironically, women who were ejected from the family home frequently found themselves unable to find work and were therefore forced to enter into prostitution. As John Hooper declares, 'in this way, [Spanish] society has divided women into whores and Madonnas not just in theory but in practice'.[164]

Helen Graham describes the conservative attitude to women in Spain in the context of an interwar, European-wide response to the anxieties of modernism whereby reimposing traditional gender roles for women became a substitute for the loss of control caused by social change and 'a whole pathology of modernity was written on women's bodies via repressive state legislation'.[165] However, within Spain this outlook became enshrined within the Francoist, Catholic ideology of post-civil war Spain. Within this ideology the patriarchal family was seen as representing the state in microcosm. As an institution, the family was unthreatening to autocratic Francoism 'because it connected vertically with the state rather than horizontally within society'.[166] Thus a focus on the family as emblematic of the Spanish nation forestalled the development of a class-based solidarity which might threaten the harsh post-war regime.

Within the patriarchal institution of the family, it was in fact the mother who was frequently depicted as the figure of domestic authority in Spanish literary and cinematic representations. As Marsha Kinder argues, in the recurrent Oedipal narrative of Spanish cinema, 'mothers frequently stand in for the missing father as the embodiment of patriarchal law' and, mimicking the situation within Irish culture, 'thereby [become] an obstacle to the erotic desire of the daughter'.[167] As in the Irish context, the emergence of the dominant mother figure can be traced to both social and cultural causes. The first is a Catholic discourse that, as in Ireland, idealised a purified femininity which found its ultimate expression in the desexualised figure of the Virgin Mary. Furthermore, depictions of the mother as head of the family also reflected a social reality in a post-war Spain in which 'it has been estimated that at least half a million families were without a male breadwinner'.[168] Therefore, as in Irish culture, the Spanish woman became the embodiment of a specific, conservative imagining of the nation; in the process becoming both subject to and the symbol of a repressive sexual discourse which denied to women their reality as sexually desiring beings.

Although ostensibly situating women in a position of power and agency, these narratives constrained the development of any genuine female subjectivity. As Luke Gibbons points out, within the nationalist elevation of the female to the realm of the symbolic 'the materiality of women's bodies is emptied out to carry what are essentially masculine ideas'.[169] This is emphasised by the absolute denial of female sexuality within these discourses, but can also be illustrated by a variety of historical examples which illustrate the degree to which femininity was relegated within Irish and Spanish culture to a subcategory of nationality. First is the degree to which non-conformative models of femininity were written out of Irish history, such as the female agitators involved in the tithe wars, election time riots, food riots and anti-slavery societies of the 1830s.[170] Furthermore, those historic figures such as Queen Maeve, who embodied a femininity which was both powerful and sexual, were sanitised within official nationalist histories. Similarly, Helen Graham discusses the tradition of 'spontaneous female mobilization' across Spain in instances such as the food riots and rent strikes of 1898 and 1909 which does not conform to the modes of behaviour available to women within official nationalist discourse.[171]

A further effect that can be traced to the reductive models of femininity available within nationalist discourse was the historical failure of feminism to develop as a political position within Ireland and Spain.

Although an active suffragette movement developed in Ireland from the early part of the twentieth century, its relationship to nationalism was a cause of much debate within its own ranks as well as within the nationalist movement. Agnes O'Farrelly, leader of the nationalist women's organisation Cumman na mBan, argued against putting suffrage over Home Rule, declaring 'there is one price we must not pay [for suffrage], and that is the price of nationality'.[172] The suffrage paper the *Irish Citizen* voiced concern in 1917 that 'so few republican women post-1916 held or articulated feminist ideals'.[173] This is illustrated by the reluctance of the few female deputies in the Oireachtas in the 1920s and 1930s to support women's issues, even as the equality of Irish women was eroded by a series of bills excluding women from public life.[174] Even for the liberal Republican regime in 1930s Spain, women were primarily considered as 'the ideological and physical reproducers of the nation'.[175] Although Republicans supported education for women, its value was that it enabled them to pass on republican values to their offspring, once again reducing femininity to its maternal constituents and employing it in the service of the nation. However, the difficulty of attempting to challenge these models of femininity from a feminist perspective is illustrated by Elizabeth Butler-Cullingford's experience of being labelled a 'British imperialist bitch' for criticising, in a 1991 article, the Irish nationalist use of women as icons of land and nation.[176] Her feminist critique of nationalism is all too easily reinterpreted within nationalism's Manichean imagination as pro-British sentiment. It would seem, to misquote Eamon De Valera, that in an historical context where nationalism claimed pre-eminence as an interpretative discourse, feminism would have to wait.

REPRESENTATIONAL SHIFTS AND THE NEW SOCIAL ORDER

As outlined above, the dominant image of womanhood within Irish and Spanish culture for the majority of the twentieth century was an idealised, desexualised motherhood. Although the strong maternal figure did have roots in the social and economic realities of Irish and Spanish life, its prominence as a cultural icon is due to the Catholic nationalist ideologies which posited this purified image of femininity as the embodiment of nation. It has been further argued that the nationalist appropriation of the female as symbol has limited the expression of female subjectivities and has denied the reality of women as sexually desiring beings. Thus, it is unsurprising that the rejection of Catholic nationalist orthodoxies within recent Irish and Spanish society has seen a concomitant reimaging of the female within contemporary film. Frequently, this has involved either a rejection or a sexualisation of the mother figure, who, no longer a reified symbol of church and nation, has been reinscribed as a fully embodied woman.

In Francoist Spain the figure of the strong patriarchal mother was often exploited by an oppositional cinema, which, forced by censorship to express its antagonism through allegory, saw in her 'the perversity at the heart of the arch-conservative Francoist notion of the family',[177] and by extension the nation itself. Furthermore, given the negative associations which clustered around the maternal figure, it is only logical that post-Franco films would seek to expel that figure of repression from the text. This reaction is seen in films such as *Furtivos* (*Poachers*, José Luis Borau, 1975), released just after Franco's death, which 'collapses unconscious and real or socially authentic versions of motherhood in a nightmarish projection of the "phallic mother"'.[178] In it Martina (Lola Gaos), the possessive mother of Angel (Ovidi Montllor), grows ever more desperate in her attempts to hang on to her son in the face of competition for his affections from a young woman, Milagros (Alicia Sánchez), until ultimately Angel is driven to matricide. As Maria José Gámez Fuentes points out, this matricide acquires great significance in the context of the transition from Francoism, as the film is 'trying to eliminate the repressive force that kept Spain immobilized for almost forty years'.[179]

However, the film, whilst physically expelling the figure of the repressive mother in an attempt to reject the legacy of the Francoist past, also reveals the continuing legacy of that past for ongoing representations of women in Spanish cinema. Having been denied any role other than the maternal by Francoist ideology, the threat to that role from a younger, sexual woman provokes a response from Martina that becomes increasingly more hysterical and ferocious, until she eventually murders Milagros. Her desperation reveals the impossibility for her of any alternative form of female subjectivity outside the maternal. The threat from Milagros is a threat to her very existence as a woman. As Peter William Evans argues, Martina in *Furtivos* is 'twice a victim'. She is a victim of the phallocentric order which disempowers her even as it asserts her as an emblem of that order; and she is a victim of the violence visited by the next generation on the mother as a symbol of the repressive regime which they reject.[180]

As the power structures that situated the mother figure as an embodiment of patriarchal law were rejected, the precariousness of the woman's position within patriarchy became evident. The symbolic power which was acceded to the mother figure was revealed as illusory, designed merely to support and legitimise a patriarchal order which, in fact, denied women an existence in the public sphere. In this context, Martina's control over her son's behaviour becomes her only means of negotiating what Evans describes as her 'problematic relation to the symbolic realm'.[181] Thus, the oppositional and post-Franco cinema, by invoking the figure of the paternal matriarch only to reject it as a symbol of a repressive Francoist past, nevertheless retained Francoism's reductive model of femininity. In these films

> the matriarch was ... marked as a perverse distortion – of both traditional notions of the feminine and of the patriarchal order itself. Consequently, although this image was highly effective in political terms, it also attached further negative connotations to the image of the strong, powerful woman.[182]

These films were more interested in utilising the figure of the female as a symbolic riposte to Francoism than expanding the range of female subjectivities represented on film. Once again, it seemed that feminism would have to wait.

This symbolic shift, whereby social and cultural change is written on to women's bodies, is also evident in much Irish cinema since 1992. Again, this shift is frequently expressed through the figure of the Irish mother. An example of this can be seen in *Last of the High Kings* (David Keating, 1996), a coming-of-age drama set in a wealthy suburb of Dublin in the late 1970s. It depicts Frankie's (Jared Leto) struggle to negotiate a path between the childhood world of his family and the adult world which awaits him with uncertain promises of sexual fulfilment. His family life in the film is portrayed as a parodic version of the Irish Oedipal setting. His father (Gabriel Byrne) is a typically ineffectual figure, an actor who spends most of his time away from home, while his mother (Catherine O'Hara) is an over-the-top version of the domineering Catholic mother. Throughout the film she rails against Protestants, the British and sex; the constant preoccupations of any 'good' Catholic mother. Her attempts to police her son's burgeoning sexuality at times slip into the hysterical, such as when he returns home after having lost his virginity to a local Protestant girl. She accosts him in the stairway, ranting to him 'when I think of the all the noble Irishmen who gave their lives for Ireland, and my son takes up with a devious little Prodie bitch'. Her white nightgown and flaming red hair luminescent in the dark of the hallway, she appears as the archetypal Irish mother, asserting her control over her son's sexuality. Her conflation of national heroism and sexual purity parodically encapsulates the sexual rhetoric of Irish Catholic nationalism. However, there is a sexual cadence to her despairing accusations, as she tells Frankie to return to his 'prodie slut', flinging his records out his bedroom window after him like a jealous lover. Although a sexually attractive woman, as evidenced by the local politician's attempts to seduce her, her sexual fulfilment is prevented in the film by the absence of her husband. The suggestion of sexual jealousy towards Frankie's lover, therefore, evokes Declan Kiberd's comment on the 'over-intense' relations between mother and son in many Irish texts.[183] Thus, as in *Furtivos*, her sexual jealousy is provoked by a younger, sexually attractive woman, who threatens not only her maternal authority but her very identity as a woman.

The film clearly reflects the ideological prejudices of 1990s Ireland and, as Martin McLoone points out, 'evinces a kind of middle-class smugness' in the manner of its depictions.[184] It leaves us in little doubt that Frankie's mother is a relic of the past, an historical figure who is of little relevance to contemporary Celtic-Tiger Ireland. Although it offers us an upbeat resolution in which Frankie's father returns and frees Frankie to form a relationship with his mother's blessing, the dominant image of the film is Catherine O'Hara's over-the-top depiction of Irish matriarchy and the continued symbolic link between female and nation. In the extreme, yet comical, version of traditional Irish motherhood that the film offers us, 'the Irish mother is being parodied out of existence and by extension so too is the Ireland that she has come to represent'.[185]

In its response to the Catholic nationalist exhortation of nation and motherhood, *Last of the High Kings* can be seen to commit the parodic equivalent of the symbolic matricide in films such as *Furtivos*. A similar dynamic can be seen in a cycle of films within Ireland in the last ten to fifteen years which Ruth Barton describes as a 'backlash that elided the figure of the Irish mother with that of Norman Bates' parent in Psycho'.[186] She includes as examples films such as *A Mother's Love's a Blessing* (Charlie McCarthy, 1994), *Driftwood* (Ronan O'Leary, 1996), *The Fifth Province* (Frank Stapleton, 1997) and *Home for Christmas* (Charlie McCarthy, 2002). In *The Fifth Province*, Timmy (Brian F. O'Byrne) is driven to a psychiatrist by his domineering mother, with whom he still lives, despite apparently being in his thirties. The psychiatrist suggests that his mother may be terrible because he imagines her that way and refers to a mystical being known as a 'talpa', which is brought to life by the imagination. There is, however, a hitch, as once a 'talpa' is imagined into existence he says, 'the bloody thing can take on a life of its own'. Its hard not to read this as a reference to the ubiquitous Irish mother imagined into life by romantic nationalists which proceeded to dominate the Irish cultural imagination for the best part of a century. Once again, though, the film invokes the figure of the phallic mother only to confirm her demise, and the last we see of Timmy's mother is her floating to the bottom of a lake, embalmed in a shower curtain, as Timmy dances into the sunset with the young, sexy European woman who has taken her place.

Alongside the violent rejection of the domineering mother evident in the texts discussed there are also examples from the Irish and Spanish films of the last few decades wherein motherhood is reimagined in a positive or benign light, suggesting a re-evaluation rather than a rejection of the past. In many of the films of Pedro Almodóvar, and most explicitly in *Todo sobre mi madre*, maternal love is experienced as empowering rather than suffocating. Similarly, in *My Left Foot* it is Christy Brown's mother (Brenda Fricker) who insists on her son's humanity and it is her dedication which enables him to develop into an artist and a writer, despite his physical disability. However, although the mother is reinscribed in these films as a positive figure, her subjectivity continues to be defined through her relationship with her offspring, frequently within a narrative of self-sacrifice. For example, in *Home for Christmas* a somewhat dysfunctional family is haunted by the empty place set at the table each Christmas for the father, who has been missing for years. However, a glimpse of a dead body at the bottom of a garden drain prompts a chilling revelation from the mother, Mona (Dearbhla Molloy). The body is that of her husband, who she found hanging in the garage on Christmas Day many years previous and who she undertook to bury in the garden without telling the children, thereby saving them the knowledge of their father's suicide. In carrying out this act she suppressed her own inevitable feelings of pain and loss as a wife in order to protect her children and forced herself to carry on as if she was unaware of her husband's death. Mona's calm, detached demeanour as she reveals the gruesome truth suggest that the traumatic effects of this self-denial may include the inability to feel and experience as an emotional, desiring woman. The irony is that until this moment she had been portrayed within the film as a cold figure, the typically repressive Irish mother whose relationship with her offspring is one of mutual antagonism and emotional distance. Thus the revelation of her self-sacrifice is, by extension, a revelation of the sacrifice that Irish mothers have been repeatedly called on to make in Ireland's patriarchal culture; that is the distillation of their beings into the narrow world of motherhood and the suppression of those aspects of their subjectivity which exceed this narrow remit.

THE SEXUALISED MOTHER

The association of the mother figure with a particular ideological regime in Irish and Spanish culture has problematised the representations of motherhood which have been produced as that ideology has lost its cultural power. Maternal authority, and by extension the inherited tradition of which it is a symbol, has been challenged by a generation who have instead embraced a youthful modernity, frequently signified by a sexual openness and confidence. Indeed, to the extent that a kind of ubiquitous hyper-sexuality has become the signifier *par excellence* of modernity in both societies, the figure of the desexualised mother is by definition excluded from the new cultural order. In the recent cinema of Ireland and Spain, we see a breakdown in the hierarchical structures of the traditional family and increasingly women are defined through their sexuality as opposed to their relationship with offspring. Whilst this broadens the range of female subjectivities available in these films and escapes the previously narrow equation of femininity with motherhood, the increased sexualisation of culture is often depicted as traumatic for a generation of older women. Unable to easily assume the maternal role within this new cultural context, these women are often shown to be uncertain of their identity in a society which celebrates youthful sexuality.

The difficulty of reconstituting the maternal role within the sexualised sphere of modernity is a central theme within *Solas* (*Alone*, Benito Zambrano, 1999). This film centres on María (Ana Fernández), a woman from rural Andalucia who is living and working in Madrid, and her mother (María Galíana), who is staying with her in order to look after her abusive husband while he is bed-ridden in a nearby hospital. Frequently belittled by her husband, scorned by her daughter and alienated by her urban surroundings, the mother (named in the credits only as *madre* [mother]) is initially defined entirely through her maternal role. We are first introduced to her as she shuffles down a hospital corridor in a white coat, stopping at an observation window. The camera cuts to inside the room, her husband's tube-covered body filling the foreground while in the background, framed by the window, she gazes down at his prostrate form, watching over him as a dutiful wife. Her daughter then takes her from the hospital and she is thrust into the unfamiliar modernity of Madrid. The camera lingers on her as she disembarks from a bus

near María's flat, her shifting gaze provoking a point-of-view shot of a
man rolling a joint beneath a tin shelter. A medium shot depicts her uncertainly surveying her surroundings while in the background men loll
by the side of the road and passing traffic disrupts the image. The effect is to signify her discomfort in these unknown surroundings, an effect which is heightened when María leads her to her local bar, which
she refuses to enter as 'there are a lot of men'. The mother's uneasiness
in this milieu is captured visually when she returns that night to make
a phone call. She pauses at the threshold of the door, the light spilling
out from the bar to illuminate her face, while the frame is filled with
men gesturing and shouting at a television screen. Their image remains
out of focus, heightening the sense of the bar as a foreign space which
she eventually turns away from. Her attempts to engage with María,
meanwhile, are rejected by her daughter, who is unwilling to accept
her maternal gestures. Inside María's flat it is the daughter who in-
structs her mother, while in the hospital her husband replies to her concern only with abuse.

Thus from the film's start the mother's identity is threatened by the
shift to urban modernity within which, unlike her daughter, she is uncertain of her role. Her daughter has already rejected her rural past and
embraced the lonely individualism which the city seems to offer. Unlike
her mother, María is represented to a large part through her sexuality
as a woman, and sex is revealed as the only binding force in her relationship with Juan (Juan Fernández), her sometime sexual partner. This
is made explicit by Juan when she tells him she is pregnant and suggests
they might form a family. His reply that 'if you want a dick you can
use mine, but that's all we have' precludes any possibility of a deeper
bond between them. Indeed, the film sets up an opposition between
María and the maternal, encapsulated in Juan's comment that the mis-
take in having a child would be 'a mother like you'. It is this opposition
which leads Candyce Leonard to read the film as a conservative appeal
to traditional family values. She claims that María's character 'reflects
the tension between the active presence of female sexuality in society
and the restoration of the family by restricting female sexuality to reproduction'.[187] The film resolves this tension, she says, by restoring the
family unit through María, who returns to the rural space to form an
alternative family with her newborn child and elderly neighbour (Carlos Álvarez-Novoa), who becomes a surrogate father and grandfather.

However, the film does offer a more complex reading through the
trajectory of the mother. As the story progresses she develops a subjectivity outside her roles as wife and mother through the relationship

9.Tentative exploration of sexual desire in *Solas*

which she develops with her daughter's aforementioned elderly neighbour. Their relationship is initially depicted as a replication of her marital and maternal roles, as she cooks him lunch and even showers him after he soils himself. Nevertheless, although never becoming explicitly sexual, there is an undercurrent of desire within their growing friendship. Their relationship is depicted as almost childlike in its development, both of them unpractised in the expression of their desires as sexual beings. Furthermore, as this relationship grows, her relationship with her daughter begins to improve and we see her tending to María's sore hands with aloe vera and knitting her a cardigan. Thus the film suggests that the maternal and the sexual can coexist in the one figure, even if for the mother this discovery has come too late in life.

In a poignant scene, as María leads her mother from her apartment for the final time, she requests that her daughter wait a moment while she calls on the neighbour to say goodbye. On hearing her knock, he pauses to compose himself before answering the door, his careful fixing of his hair and suit betraying the desire for companionship which is evident beneath their polite exchanges. As they stand in the doorway, the camera frames them in an uncomfortable three-shot, with María hovering in the background. The demeanours of the mother and neighbour suggest that they feel embarrassed to reveal themselves in her presence, like a teenage couple in front of a parent. This role reversal is complete when María tells her mother she will wait for her in the bar; seemingly blessing her mother's desire to express herself outside of her maternal role. The neighbour then launches into what appears to be a prepared speech, declaring that in the lonely hours before him, she 'will always be a pleasant memory'. His practised words can only reinforce the sense that their relationship has come too late, that the world of sexual relations must be left to the young. As he takes her by the arm and leads her down the stairway, his growing distress at the ending of their relationship is matched by her practicality as she prepares herself to return to the world that she previously knew. He cannot telephone her, she says, as she does not have a phone, nor write to her as she cannot read, and when he suggests that he may call on her she orders him to stop, declaring 'we're acting like kids'.

Thus the film's representation of femininity and motherhood is more complex than Leonard allows. Although the mother ultimately accepts the role she has been allotted in life, and is depicted as a benevolent representative of tradition, nevertheless the film permits a more radical reading by admitting the sexuality of an older, maternal figure into the text. It reveals the difficulty for an older woman, whose identity has been constructed through the kind of conservative family values that Leonard decries, of maintaining that identity within the sexualised culture of modernity in which, lacking the sexual ease of youth, she risks rejection and ridicule. The unease and insecurity which this can engender is encapsulated in María's mother's fear that in experiencing sexual desire she is acting like a child. Similarly, the resolution of the film, in which the mother's tentatively sexual relationship with the neighbour is replaced by María's filial relationship to him, reveals the range of potential relations available within modernity. Within this new family configuration, María's mother is a possible rival to María for the neighbour's affections, a potential which is disavowed within the film by the mother's return to her unhappy marriage and her eventual death.

The confusion of the maternal and the sexual within these films often has traumatic consequences, most particularly for the mother figure, who attempts to regain the maternal role through her sexuality. In *Carne trémula*, Clara (Ángelina Molina) is a middle-aged woman in an abusive, childless marriage with Sancho, an alcoholic, corrupt cop. When the film's main protagonist Victor gets out of jail, having been set up by Sancho for the shooting of his police partner, Clara begins a sexual relationship with him. However it is a relationship depicted as maternal, with Clara promising to teach Victor to be a great lover. He becomes the child that her failed marriage has denied her and at one stage she gazes at a photo of him whispering *'mi niño'* ('my boy'). However the only means left to her to express her maternal instinct is through her sexuality; she assumes the mantle of the *puta madre* (literally whore-mother) which in Spanish refers to something of exceptional value or esteem. This conflation in one body of the two polar characteristics of womanhood within Spanish culture may be the ultimate fantasy of Spanish *machismo*. However its cost for the woman who embodies it is great, as it is a role which proves unsustainable. Clara performs the role of mother for Victor by teaching him how to express his sexuality; socialising him so that he can enact his male role proficiently in society. Yet the trajectory of this process is inevitably one which sees Victor separate from her as he becomes more sexually (socially) proficient; for this is the role of the mother, to lose her son to another (sexual) woman. However, unlike the non-sexual maternal relationship, Clara's bond with Victor cannot withstand the intrusion of another woman. As the relationship progresses we see the power balance within it begin to shift, with Clara expressing her love for him, and his rejection of that love. Ultimately he leaves Clara for Elena, a woman of his own age who he truly desires. For Clara, the logical conclusion to the self-sacrificing role of *puta madre* is death, as she sacrifices her own life in order to protect Victor from the vengeful wrath of Sancho.

It is significant that in *Carne trémula*, the younger Elena is unproblematically depicted as both maternal and sexual. The point is not that these positions are mutually exclusive, but that the association of the mother with the forces of tradition within Irish and Spanish culture has problematised the depiction of older women. Within the sexualised culture of modernity the maternal identity as constituted within Catholic nationalist culture is no longer easily available, and indeed there has been an ongoing concern to reject this model of maternal femininity as an expression of distance from the Catholic nationalist past. The difficulty of Clara's position is not that she is a sexual woman, but that she uses her sexuality to inhabit a maternal role in a manner that can only be precarious. For Elena, on the other hand, the maternal and the sexual are merely two coexisting aspects of her person; one does not preclude or even necessarily relate to the expression of the other. When she and Victor finally make love, it occurs in the children's refuge which she runs, the sexual and the maternal temporarily coexisting in this one space. The camera celebrates their sexual union; lingering on their bodies in a series of artistically composed images; capturing their pleasure in the soft lighting, the romantic music, and their own physical expressions. It is never suggested that Elena's expression of her sexuality in such a setting is in any way wrong or diminishes her maternal suitabil-

10. Victor and Elena's sexuality is celebrated by Almodóvar's camera

ity. In fact, this sexual act sets in motion the climactic action of the film, which will see all other models of masculinity and femininity expelled from the text in order to propose Victor and Elena as paradigms of a reimagined Spanish family. It is a family model which acknowledges their sexuality even as it celebrates the power of parental love through their dedication to the children at the refuge as well as their soon-to-be-born child.

In order to construct this celebratory reimagined family-as-nation those older, unacceptable models of femininity must be rejected. This perhaps explains the astonishing level of both literal and displaced matricide in the films listed above. In *The Fifth Province* and *A Mother's Love's a Blessing* sons are driven to kill their overbearing mothers, whilst in *Carne trémula* and *Solas* the maternal figure dies by the end of the narrative, freeing the next generation to escape the burden of a repressive past. Nevertheless, representations of older, sexualised females which escape the restrictive binary equating sexuality with youth do exist within recent Irish and Spanish cinema. But despite offering the image of an older generation capable of expressing sexuality, these films do not necessarily represent such expressions in a positive light. A key scene in this respect occurs within the 2003 Irish black-comedy *Intermission* (John Crowley), in which the romantically unsuccessful Oscar (David Wilmot) drags his friend John (Cillian Murphy) to a nightclub that caters for older clientele. When John remarks that you would need to be 'desperate' to go there, Oscar replies 'but I am John, you know I am'. Thus from the start, the form of sexuality embodied by these older women is established as deficient, suitable only for 'the desperate'. This view is reinforced when we enter the club and the camera picks out various elderly couples moving awkwardly on the dance floor. Although they all seem to be enjoying themselves, it is clear that we are expected to share the feelings of John and Oscar, whose somewhat horrified faces the camera quickly cuts back to. Nevertheless they continue on and John soon finds himself being seduced by an older woman who frankly expresses her sexual desire to him, declaring that since she's been on hormones she's 'been feeling very erotic'. Although she takes his initial brush-off with equanimity, when she later sees him dancing with a younger woman she attacks him with venom. Slurring her words in anger and drunkenness she leers over him, declaring that she's been 'coming here long enough not to be lied to'. As John quickly makes his exit, she is left standing in the middle of the dance floor shouting after him, her abandoned figure suggesting the difficulties of age in an era obsessed with youthful sexuality.

In many ways this scene encapsulates in microcosm the ideological shift that has occurred in Irish cinema since the start of the 1990s. The film is primarily occupied with the romantic entanglements and criminal activities of young Dubliners and therefore this elderly display of sexuality is a jarring intrusion into the world it presents. This is the generation whose ideologies have been rejected by modern Ireland, their

11. Capturing the shift in generational power in recent Irish cinema

place in the social and cultural fabric disturbed by the rush to urban modernity. The middle-aged Irish woman, once a figure of maternal authority and a symbol of unchanging values, now turns to the younger generation for recognition of her femininity, as the sexual supplants the familial as the primary form of human relation. Yet it is hard not to also read this scene as a return of modern Ireland's repressed, as an acknowledgement of those whose subjectivities and desires have been effaced from this revised Irish cultural identity. As John stands at the bar, the camera roams around the room, lingering on the face of a middle-aged man, sitting alone in tears. Cutting back to John, the barman hands him his drink and berates him, 'you dirty bastard, fancy a bit of mature? I know why you're here', before turning away from him disgustedly. This combination of images and the barman's rebuke constructs the older generation in the room as vulnerable and in danger of being preyed upon by youth. As such, it reverses the power structures of traditional Irish society, with its deference to age and oppressive parental figures, and captures the precarious position of those for whom modernity does not offer possibilities, but the loss of their cultural frame of reference.

MOTHERS AND DAUGHTERS

It has already been described how changes in cultural values have caused a shift in the representation of a generation of women, previously coded exclusively as maternal, who are now shown struggling to assert their subjectivity through a newly acknowledged sexuality. However, it is not merely the mother who is affected by this new-found sexuality. Within this changing sexual economy the mother becomes an obstacle to the daughter's sexual fulfilment; not through the regulation of her sexuality, but through her status as sexual competition. Although not as frequent as the type of film discussed previously, there are several recent Irish and Spanish films in which an older generation of women are seen to embrace the new sexual possibilities available to them in contemporary society. However, this is frequently seen to have negative consequences for younger women; a generation of either literal or figurative daughters who struggle to negotiate their sexual identity in relation to a mother figure whose own sexuality can no longer be disregarded. In short, the prominence of sexuality in human relationships often puts an unbearable strain on inter-generational relationships, and these films resolve this through a variety of strategies, from acknowledgement to disavowal to death.

The Sun, the Moon and the Stars is a family melodrama in which two daughters are shown struggling to come to terms with their parents' separation over the course of a summer holiday with their mother Molly (Gina Moxley). The eldest girl, Shelley (Elaine Cassidy), has particular difficulty accepting her mother as an individual with sexual and emotional needs. Molly, meanwhile, tries to balance her role as a mother with attempts to restart her life after her husband. Thus we see her on one of the first nights of their holiday in a bar with the girls, clearly being attentive to them, yet wearing a sexy silk dress which catches the attention of a local worker Pat (Jason Donovan). It is the development of Molly and Pat's relationship that Shelley finds disturb-ing. Shelley cannot accept that Molly can be both mother and lover, as evidenced by her retort when told to obey her mother that 'you don't exactly act like my mother'. By engaging in sexual behaviour, Molly loses her aura of authority in the eyes of Shelley. It causes Shelley to challenge her mother's power to regulate her behaviour by suggesting that her own behaviour is not beyond reproach. Thus when Shelley is asked by her mother why there is a boy in her bed she responds by ask-ing what Pat was doing in Molly's bed. By positing their behaviour as equivalent, Shelley implies that sex is inimical to maternal authority, that to engage in sexual activity implies a fall from maternal grace so that the mother now inhabits unmistakeably the same sphere as the daughter. Yet rather than experiencing this diminished authority as free-dom, Molly's exploration of her identity beyond the maternal role causes Shelley her own identity crisis, which she attempts to contain by constructing her own interpretative narrative. In order to make sense of her mother's changing behaviour, Shelley is forced to turn to a su-pernatural explanation, namely that Molly has been possessed by a witch. The fantastical lengths to which Shelley goes to account for her mother's actions illustrate how the sexualisation of the mother may be experienced as trauma by a younger generation attempting to negoti-ate their own paths through the confusing terrain of sexuality.

In *About Adam* the eponymous character seduces all three sisters of a well-to-do Dublin family and eventually becomes engaged to be married to the youngest, Lucy. Throughout the film their mother Peggy (Rosaleen Linehan) is depicted as having a loving relationship with her daughters as well as being welcoming towards Adam, and encourages her daughters to express their sexualities. However there is a brief but pointed scene in the film which suggests that Peggy's relationship with Adam may be more than just one of maternal approval. The action cuts from Adam and Lucy lying arm-in-arm in bed, having finally consummated their relationship, to Adam and Peggy stumbling arm-in-arm down the side of a mountain

12. Peggy's suggestive glance

while Lucy waits in the car. As they make their way down Peggy turns to Adam and declares 'it was so invigorating'. Back in the car, Peggy adoringly tells the story of how Adam acquired his blue Jaguar, relating it to the death of his parents when he was young. Throughout this Lucy is somewhat excluded, leaning forward from the back seat to hear the story. The camera switches from Peggy to Adam as she speaks, keeping Lucy at the edge of the frame. Having finished her tale and declared that Adam is wonderful, Peggy begins to suck on her ice-cream in a suggestive manner. As Lucy hugs Adam, the camera switches back to a close-up of Peggy, showing us her eyes moving briefly, but very definitely, down to his crotch as she smiles mischievously. Here Peggy's sexuality is very clearly introduced into the film and she is shown to be no more impervious to Adam's sexual charms than the rest of the family. Regardless of whether this attraction was consummated on the mountain top, which is certainly a possible interpretation of the sequence, it is clear that Peggy's sexuality cannot be dismissed and as such she represents further sexual competition for her daughter. The film's light-hearted means of resolving this threat to Lucy's happiness is to imagine a Utopian world of unchecked sexual desire devoid of judgement or reproach. In the final scene Adam is embraced by Lucy and her entire family as the camera whirls joyously about them. It seems to suggest that, if *Carne trémula* imagines a family model which can admit both sexual and filial relations, this is a family in which the sole binding force is sex. Despite the film's upbeat ending, it is difficult to imagine this as a sustainable solution to the renegotiation of gender and sexual relations demanded by modern life.

Sexual competition between the mother and the daughter is a key feature of *Jamón Jamón*, in which Carmen (Anna Galiena) and her daughter, Silvia (Penélope Cruz) have sexual relations with Silvia's fiancée José (Jordi Mollá). Indeed, the film plays as an exaggerated satire of the sexual dynamics that have been outlined in this chapter. Although Carmen's relationship with her daughter Silvia is depicted as a positive one, characterised by maternal love, the eruption of sexuality into every relationship within the text can here only be resolved by death and the reconstitution of relationships along purely sexual lines. The relationship of Conchita (Stefania Sandrelli), José's mother, to her son is like that of a jealous, possessive lover. When he informs her that he is planning to marry Sylvia she thrusts him against a wall, her body pressed against his in a posture of sexual dominance as she demands, 'Don't you love me?' However, when Conchita begins sexual relations with another young man, Juan (Javier Bardem), she loses interest in her son and becomes more concerned about Juan's relationship with Sylvia. Thus by the end of the film both Carmen and Conchita are aligned, not with their biological offspring, but with the objects of their sexual desire; surrogate sexualised sons. Following a fight in which Juan kills José, the camera slowly pulls away from the grieving women, depicting the characters arranged in tableau against the desert landscape. Carmen cradles José, recalling the image of the Pieta, while Conchita kneels on the ground holding Juan beside them. In the background José's father (Juan Diego) stands with his arms around Sylvia, the realignment of relations along sexual grounds complete. Thus in the film the mother–daughter and mother–son relationships are shown to be unsustainable in a cultural climate which is defined by unconstrained expressions of sexuality.

FEMALE IDENTITY AND SPACE

One effect of this breakdown of traditional family relations within Irish and Spanish cinema has been the reconstitution of spatial divisions as the divide between public and private space has begun to dissolve. The integrity of the private, domestic sphere has been central to much of the cultural rhetoric that has equated the health of the family with that of the nation. This is captured in article 41 of the Irish constitution, in which 'the state recognises the family as the natural, primary and fundamental unit group of society'. Article 41 goes on to recognise the support that

'woman' gives to the state by her life within the home. Thus, the
Catholic nationalist use of motherhood as a symbol for nation is based
on the concept of domestic space as distinct and inviolable. Inglis traces
this to the beginning of the nineteenth century, when a general differentiation of space began to occur in Irish society.[188] As work practices
changed there was an ensuing shift in the understanding of space, with
an increased separation between the arenas of work and domesticity.
These new spatial arrangements permitted novel forms of subjectivity
and modes of behaviour to emerge, including those associated with domestic family life. Kiberd links the model of motherhood which came
to be dominant in Irish culture with this differentiation between the
work and domestic spheres of life.[189] Within this emerging set of spatial divisions, the female was increasingly equated with the domestic, an
association that continued through twentieth-century Irish culture and
society.

This correlation between private space and femininity is not, of
course, limited to Irish and Spanish cultures. It is a recurrent motif
across cultures whereby public space is defined as masculine and private
feminine in a set of terms that prove consistently disempowering for
women. Carole Pateman captures the imbalance inherent in this division of space in her description of it as that between

> the universal sphere of freedom, equality, individualism, reason,
> contract and impartial law – the realm of men or 'individuals';
> and the private world of particularity, natural subjection, ties of
> blood, emotion, love and sexual passion – the world of women, in
> which men also rule.[190]

This is a binary in which there are clear implications of dominance and
subjugation, with private space constructed as a necessary subsidiary of
public space rather than as an alternate or equivalent space. As Janet
Wolff argues, 'the public could only be constituted as a particular set of
institutions and practices on the basis of the removal of other areas of
social life to the invisible arena of the private'.[191] Thus the divide also
has clear implications for issues of visibility, with certain behaviour and
types of people concealed within the private arena while other, ap-
proved behaviour is permitted public visibility. One effect of this has
been to confine behaviour designated as feminine to the private sphere
and to severely restrict the ways in which women have historically accessed public space.

In Irish and Spanish culture this divide has been further complicated
by the manner in which domestic space has been imbricated within the

public discourse of nation. In his study of the *Irish Homestead*, the weekly publication of the Irish Agricultural Organisation Society at the turn of the twentieth century, James MacPherson traces an 'increasing perception of the home as the cornerstone of the Irish nation, with Irish women being assigned the role not only of homemakers but also of nation builders'.[192] Thus, although not perceiving women as public actors in an actively political sense, the journal did allow them a public position through their domestic role. This connection between the public and the private is suggested by the 1914 inaugural address by the leader Agnes O'Farrelly to Cumann na mBan, the revolutionary nationalist organisation of women. Referring to the arming of members, she declares, 'each rifle we put in their hands will represent to us a bolt fastened behind the door of some Irish home to keep out the hostile stranger'.[193] The call to political action is phrased in terms of protecting the domestic space in a rhetorical move which accurately reflects the ideology of Catholic nationalism.

However, as Pateman reminds us, the private sphere is 'the world of women, in which men also rule'. Although the domestic space may often be controlled by females, ultimately it is subject to the laws and restrictions of a patriarchal society. This was made explicit under Francoism by the *patria potestad*, a law which granted the husband legal control of his children, of the wealth accrued within a marriage, and even his wife through the concept of the *permiso marital*, which prohibited a wife from embarking on any activity outside the home without her husband's permission. Thus under Franco's repressive regime the banishment of women from the public sphere was enshrined in law, as was the absolute subjugation of the private to the public, pervaded as the domestic was by the dictates of an authoritarian regime. This is not to suggest that the domestic could not also be a site of resistance, for as Helen Graham reminds us, in post-civil war Spain the domestic space was often experienced as a haven from the sexual and physical abuse frequently suffered on the streets at the hands of the police and fascist party.[194] Nevertheless, the spatial hierarchy remains in which the (feminine) domestic space is defined and controlled by the discourses and dictates of the patriarchal public sphere.

The division of private and public space was further complicated in Spain by the effective exclusion of the entire population, both male and female, from the public sphere. Discussing Francoist cinema of the 1940s, Jo Labanyi outlines how a spate of war films glorifying fascist soldiers were replaced from 1942 by films which focused on the home and family 'in a depoliticizing strategy that encouraged men as well as

13. Manuela's comfort within the sexualised environment of the city space

women to identify with the private sphere'.[195] The motive for this is clear, given the exclusion of citizens from any meaningful participation in the political sphere under a dictatorship. Similarly, in Ireland the gendered nature of the public–private dichotomy was historically problematised by the exclusion of Irish males from the public sphere under colonisation in a process that is frequently described in terms of their feminisation. It is this exclusion from the public sphere which generated such a focus on the domestic as a site of purity and the source of resistance to the colonial power.

However, as has been established, the achievement of independence in Ireland did not lead to the breakdown of gendered spatial binaries. The concern to regulate women's access to public space is illustrated by the Irish clergy's reaction to the new amusements that developed in the twentieth century, particularly the cinema. These were viewed as undesirable as they were seen to contain emancipatory potential through their construction of a specifically female public space.[196] Thus the public–private divide has been shown to be one which consistently serves to regulate and prohibit female behaviour in the interest of maintaining a set of rigid gender divisions, which are clearly imbricated within the power structures of patriarchal society. Furthermore, this divide has been both strengthened and complicated in Irish and Spanish culture by a Catholic nationalist rhetoric that has confined the feminine to the domestic sphere while at the same time incorporating that sphere into public discourse as a symbol of nation. This chapter will now examine the effect on representations of public and private space as that rhetoric has lost its cultural power.

THE SEXUALISATION OF SPACE

Caricias (*Caresses*, Ventura Pons, 1998) combines eleven interlocking narratives into a dense mosaic in which a series of characters seek to establish emotional connections within an alienating city environment. Within the film, family relationships are shown to be disintegrating under the pressures of modern life. A husband and wife physically abuse each other, a daughter rejects her mother's attempts to love her, a mother robs her son and labels him a sadist for abandoning her. The domestic space is depicted as one of isolation and despair. However, the caresses of the film's title are not absent, they are merely displaced from the private sphere of family life to the chance encounters of public space. The film is divided into eleven distinct chapters, with each chapter being linked to the previous by one of the characters. Through this structure the film allows a series of interpersonal connections to evolve and circulate within the city space. What ties these people together, in the absence of strong family bonds, is sexuality. A variety of spaces within the city, both public and private, become sites of sexual encounter within the film. The rejected mother finds solace in a lesbian kiss as she dances in an old-folks' home. A father and son compare penis size in the bath, as sexuality becomes the binding force around which even this parental role is enacted. In the next sequence, the father ends an affair with a woman in the public setting of a train station. Surrounded by fellow commuters, he loudly declares that her 'cunt smelt terrible'. The same woman's father is seen picking up a rent boy before bringing him back to a rented apartment, complaining that 'there's no privacy'. In these encounters, we see the categories of public and private space dissolve in the presence of a ubiquitous sexuality, which is depicted as the only plausible means of relating to others within contemporary Spanish life.

Many recent films have depicted the everyday space of Irish and Spanish life in a manner that has served to undermine the gendered division of space so central to those previously dominant discourses. This has frequently involved a shift from the rural to the urban as the representative space of national life, the full implications of which will be explored in the next chapter. However, the defining theme which could

be said to run through these depictions is a rejection of gendered pub-
lic/private space for a conceptualisation of all space as sexualised space.
The consequences of this include a breakdown in spatial and
social hierarchies, the admittance of previously restricted behaviour to
the public sphere and the reimagination of family life.

When Manuela first returns to Barcelona in *Todo sobre mi madre*
she takes a taxi to a piece of waste ground on the outskirts of the city
in search of Lola, the father of her dead son. This is a liminal city space
that has been reappropriated as a site of sexual encounter. As Manuela's
taxi approaches on a dirt road the taxi driver momentarily pauses, ask-
ing Manuela, 'Shall I keep going?' Given the type of space they are
about to enter, it is tempting to suspect that Manuela's gender is the
cause of his hesitation. The camera then cuts to a long-shot of their car
passing underneath a motorway, the cars and trucks passing by overhead clearly belonging to a different spatial order to that which
Manuela is entering. We then see an overhead shot of the waste ground,
circled by cars and prostitutes advertising their wares, before cutting
to Manuela's point-of-view from inside the car. We are shown a series
of women leering towards the window and beckoning to Manuela with
their half-naked bodies. The camera circles past, offering us a disorient-
ing sequence of sexual images. Although the purpose of Manuela's visit
is not sexual gratification, this scene can nevertheless be considered significant in relation to the sexualisation of space. What is striking is
Manuela's absolute comfort in these surroundings; she is nonplussed by
the display of female sexuality for her benefit, and does not hesitate to
get out of the taxi in order to aid a prostitute being attacked. Furthermore, it is noteworthy in itself that we are presented with these images
through the eyes of a woman, as another binary which has structured
the spatial order historically has been that between looking and dis-
playing, with the power to do the former resting exclusively with the
male.

The division of public and private space has never simply involved
the confinement of sexuality to the private sphere, but has rather constructed the public sphere as a space of sexual freedom for men while
denying female sexual desire. 'For women, the public spaces thus con-
strued were where one risked losing one's virtue, dirtying oneself; going
out in public and the idea of disgrace were closely allied. For the man
[on the other hand] going out in public meant losing oneself in the
crowd away from … demands of respectability.'[197] Central to this divide
is the power to look and to be looked at. Pollock describes the twin
ideological formations of bourgeois society as 'the splitting of private

and public with its ... freedom for men in the public space, and the pre-eminence of a detached observing gaze, whose possession and power is never questioned as its basis in the hierarchy of the sexes is never acknowledged'.[198] This detached gaze is embodied in Walter Benjamin's figure of the *flâneur*, the male city stroller who observes city life with a look 'which is both covetous and erotic'.[199] As Pollock's statements suggest, the power to look is implicated within hierarchical gender relations, implying an objectifying gaze which is rarely turned back upon the male.

Unlike the male *flâneur*, the female is defined in public spaces by her 'to be looked at-ness'; her identity constructed through the eyes of the (male) observer. The very act of appearing in public contained a potential for loss of identity and social standing. Quoting Pollock again, 'it has been argued that to maintain one's respectability, closely identified with femininity, meant *not* exposing oneself in public'.[200] Returning to *Todo sobre mi madre*, whilst public space has always been able to accommodate prostitutes, it is the depiction of Manuela as the bearer of the look which makes this image of prostitution potentially subversive. She is seen to comfortably inhabit a sexualised space while searching for the father of her son, himself a transsexual prostitute; a situation which combines the familial and the sexual, the domestic and the public, in a manner that cannot be contained within established spatial arrangements.

Wilson argues that when women have been present in cities within literature it has been 'as temptress, as whore, as fallen woman ... but also as virtuous womanhood in danger, as heroic womanhood who triumphs over temptation and tribulation'.[201] Missing from this range of female identities is the desiring woman who enters the city in order to seek out temptation. *Goldfish Memory* is one of several recent Irish films, such as *Snakes and Ladders*, *About Adam* and *Intermission*, which have inserted female desire into the public spaces of the city. The film depicts the lives and loves of attractive young people in a modern, cosmopolitan Dublin. It manages to represent an array of sexual identities and romantic permutations within its narrative. Characters switch sexual partners and sexual orientation with dizzying regularity in a narrative of self-discovery, which they experience for the most part as positive. Thus the film fits squarely into a Utopian discourse that reimagines Dublin as a space of sexual and personal liberation. Its narrative structure allows desire to be represented within the text from a number of subject positions. Heterosexual, gay male and lesbian desire are granted an equivalency, both through the on-screen time devoted to each and in their manner of representation. In

an early scene Clara (Fiona O'Shaughnessy), who has just ended a relationship with her lecturer Tom (Sean Campion), responds to a drink invitation from a lesbian woman Angie (Flora Montgomery). She enters
'Miss Julie's Ladies Club', the location easily recognisable to a local audience as a well-known city-centre bar, to be met by the stares of several women obviously coded as lesbian. The sequence is filmed in a
shot–reverse-shot style; close-ups of the women being followed by repeated full-length shots of Clara's body which, although not exactly
matching the women's point-of-view, clearly construct Clara as an object of desire for these female 'bearers of the look'. What is unique
about this in an Irish cultural context is that the desire so represented
is lesbian; a previously disavowed desire is now inhabiting the heart of
the city. Although Clara seems to experience this initially as discom-
forting, she quickly relaxes and engages in a process of mutual seduction with Angie. The action then cuts to her apartment, where the soft
light, soothing Brazilian jazz, and tasteful close-ups reproduce all the
conventions of a Hollywood sex scene. The filmic language employed
in this sequence establishes lesbian desire as unremarkable, and by extension challenges the exclusion of formerly unapproved desires and
identities from visible, public space.

As in *Caricias*, the city here is predominantly depicted as a sexualised space. The locations the film inhabits are by and large those
which facilitate sexual encounters, such as bars and clubs. However,
sexuality is also portrayed as the dominant motivation for interpersonal
exchange, even in those spaces not normally associated with such interactions. Thus Tom, a lecturer verging on middle age, uses his lecture
hall primarily as a means of meeting younger women. Angie, whilst
supposedly interviewing Clara for a television programme, quickly
shifts her tone from professional to seductive. Traditional family
arrangements are conspicuous by their absence from the film. In the
one instance in which the traditional Irish family is represented, the
purpose of the sequence is to negatively contrast it with the new model
of human relations which the film proposes. As Larry (Stuart Graham)
and Rosie (Lise Hearns) drive through the countryside to meet her
mother, his future mother-in-law, Rosie learns to her horror that he is
not a Catholic and insists that he convert, declaring that if he doesn't
'it'll break mammy's heart'. When they arrive to Rosie's family home
in the country, her mother remains off-screen but fulfils her role as the
oppressive Irish matriarch by answering the door with a curt 'you're
late'. It is significant that this is one of only two occasions in which
characters travel outside the city, clearly suggesting that this family

model belongs to the past and has no place in the urban spaces of modernity. An alternative family is proposed through the film's romantic resolution, in which a lesbian and a gay male couple share the parenting of a child conceived during a brief heterosexual liaison between a member of each couple. Although this could be conceived as a reconstitution of the hetero-normative family, away from the free expression of sexuality earlier proposed by the text, the film remains an important intervention in the representation of sexual and spatial relations within Irish culture. It ends with four gay parents doting over their newborn child in the public space of a city bar, an image which offers a fundamental reimagining of family, sexual identity and the division between private and public space in modern Irish life.

SEX AND NATION

The relationship between sexual freedom and modernity which films such as *Goldfish Memory* propose has been a recurring feature within Irish and Spanish cinema. This must be seen as a cultural response to the symbolism of Catholic nationalism, in which a desexualised maternal figure and the traditional nuclear family became paradigmatic of the nation. By rejecting these traditional gender roles, these films are by extension rejecting the ideology which sustained them and are asserting their own modernity. This can be seen in the wave of soft-core pornography which emerged from Spain in the years following Franco's death. As Daniel Kowalsky points out, the escapades of the female protagonists in these films 'were pointedly political; her presence on the screen heralded the arrival of a new generation that was savvy, continental and rebellious, a Spanish youth that questioned the mores of their elders'.[202] According to Marsha Kinder, this cultural response to the demise of Francoist ideology has 'succeeded in establishing a mobile sexuality as the new cultural stereotype for a hyper-liberated Socialist Spain'.[203] Or as Ricardo Roque-Baldovinos describes it, in liberated Spain, 'the law of the father ... is dissolved in a feast of lust'.[204]

A feature of many Irish and Spanish romantic comedies, the genre in which this mobile sexuality tends to be expressed, is their unwillingness to impose any limitations on individual behaviour. Again, if we read the embrace of sexual freedom as a rejection of the personal strictures perceived to have been a feature of traditional national culture, then it becomes clear why this may be so. This can be clearly seen in *About Adam*, in which Adam's sexual relations with his fiancée's sisters are devoid of any negative consequences. A similar unwillingness to impose limits on the possibilities for sexual self-expression can be seen in *El otro lado de la cama* (*The Other Side of the Bed*, Emilio Martínez Lázaro, 2002). This depicts the frantic inter-coupling of two sets of cohabiting twenty-somethings, Javier (Ernesto Alterio) and Sonia (Paz Vega), and Pedro (Guillermo Toledo) and Paula (Natalia Verbeke). The irreverent attitude to romantic and sexual relations in the film is signposted by the film's tag-line 'If love is only a game … why not cheat?' We are first introduced to the latter couple as they are breaking up, Paula informing Pedro that she is in love with another man. We soon discover that other man to be Javier, Pedro's best friend. Javier, for his part, divides his time between consoling Pedro, prevaricating over his relationship with Sonia and sneaking off for illicit afternoon sex with Paula. The scene is set for a sexual farce. However what is remarkable about the film is the lack of consequences experienced by the characters, regardless of their behaviour. Tension is created over whether Pedro will discover that his friend is Paula's lover, but is then completely dissipated as Pedro begins a relationship with Sonia behind Javier's back. There is no credible reason offered for this narrative development; it merely seems that all relations are so infused with sexuality that the development of multiple sexual relations is inevitable. Following a protracted sequence of close shaves, the narrative resolution brings the original couples back together. However, in the final sequence we see them at a party where one by one they slip off for a sexual liaison with their old lovers. The celebratory tone of the film's finale leaves us in no doubt that their relationships are secure, and suggests that their sexual dalliances are no longer even secretive. The image the film offers is of a modern, youthful Spain in which carefree expressions of sexuality connote a society at ease with itself and unburdened by the sexual repressions of the past.

The irony of these representations is that they repeat the earlier metaphor equating sexuality with nation, although now the Catholic nationalist elevation of sexual purity to the status of national characteristic has been replaced with a celebration of sexual freedom as the paradigm of modern society. Yet the difficulty with this metaphor is that it effaces the limitations on sexual identity, which persist into modernity. Lance Pettitt addresses this difficulty in his discussion of *The Last Bus Home*, a film depicting the rise and fall of a punk rock band in late 1970s Dublin. The drummer in the band, Petie (John Cronin), is gay and hopes that the band will take him away from the repressive atmosphere of Dublin to London, where his sexual desires can find expression. When these hopes are dashed Petie apparently kills himself rather than continue to deny his sexual identity. The problem, as Pettitt outlines it, is that the film suggests that an answer to Petic's experiences of homophobia can be found in the modern space of London, thereby disguising the fact that even there homophobia still exists.[205] In *Goldfish Memory* the characters no longer need to leave Ireland to find modernity, yet the danger remains that the representation of the modern as a space of sexual freedom may be equally Utopian. In the Spanish context, according to Paul Julian Smith, homosexuality has been offered as 'the essence of modern, secular society in opposition to the old Spain of family and religion'.[206] This is particularly evident in the films of Pedro Almodóvar, which frequently position homosexual and transsexual characters at the centre of the narrative. The danger, as Smith argues, is that by depicting modern Spain as a space in which homosexual identity can be freely expressed he 'places the spectator in a position of indifference or disinterest with regards to homosexuality within the film, without necessarily challenging her or his attitudes towards the subject outside the cinema'.[207]

This final caveat reminds us that the appropriation of sexual identities as a symbol of nation will always be problematic. Within Irish and Spanish culture, the elevation of women to purified symbol of nation denied the reality of women as sexually desiring individuals. As the Catholic nationalist ideologies that gave cultural power to this symbolism declined, the shift in cultural values was often given symbolic expression within cinema by a rejection of the maternal figure, who represented the oppressive values of the past. This has had both a liberating effect on the range of identities available to women within Irish and Spanish film and a destabilising effect on the family-based identities that previously constituted female subjectivity. The potentially negative effects for those women whose identities were sustained by the cultural discourses of Catholic nationalism is captured in the troubled depictions of maternal relations in many of the films analysed. The dismantling of these cultural discourses and the gender relations that they supported have also been expressed spatially within recent Irish and Spanish cinema, through a breakdown in the gendered division of space which characterised traditional culture. This has led to a new relationship between sexual identity, space and nation within contemporary Irish and Spanish films, wherein the sexualised spaces of modernity have become a new metaphor for the modern Irish and Spanish nations. Central to this spatial reimagining is the shift to the city as the representative space of Irish and Spanish national life, as will be explored in greater detail in the next chapter.

The City Space

A key transformation in the experience of space which occurred in the shift to modernity, according to David Clarke, was that within the new urban formation, social and physical spaces were no longer equivalent. In contrast to the rural experience, space within the city environment is fragmented and rigidly delineated according to its function within capitalist work/leisure practices. It is an experience of space that is embodied in the figure of the stranger, who is concurrently physically proximate while being socially distant. Clarke describes the modern city as 'concomitantly, the world as experienced by the stranger, and the experience of a world populated by strangers – a world in which a universal strangehood was coming to predominate'.[208] The encounter with the city as one defined by strangeness is an idea with a long literary lineage. Raymond Williams describes Wordsworth's central concern in his depiction of London life as 'a failure of identity in the crowd of others which worked back to a loss of identity in the self, and then, in these ways, a loss of society itself'.[209] In Virginia Woolf, he argues, 'the discontinuity, the atomism of the city were aesthetically experienced, as a problem of perception which raised problems of identity'.[210]

These associated problems of identity and perception are central to the experience of the city within modernity. Issues of identity within modernity must be understood as spatial in their origin and their articulation, as related to the ways in which people attempt to belong within the city space. Unlike urban space, pre-industrial space could be taken for granted; 'place and the social sphere out of which a person might be confronted with behavioural expectations coincided'.[211] Yet within the city, this knowable space becomes shattered, and attempts to construct a coherent identity are forced to occur across a series of fragments, of disparate and disconnected physical and social spaces. As David Pinder states, 'it is the very condition of the city to be plural with a multiplicity of stories, an inexhaustibility of narratives, peopled with strangers and difference'.[212] Equally, our perception of space is necessarily altered within the city environment. In his discussion of the 1978 film *Visions of a City*, Scott MacDonald describes how within the film 'the reflective surfaces so common to modern urban construction shatter our sense of continuous space'.[213] Within the city the gaze is frequently disrupted, or reflected back on itself, as in those reflective surfaces of buildings which create a spectator 'positioned as both subject and object simultaneously'.[214]

It is this process of 'making strange' through a fragmentation of space which gives the city charge as a cultural force, one which destabilises the fixed and allows new connections and structures to develop; potentially challenging the existing cultural order. However, it is important to remember that any spatial order is inherently political. As Edward Soja argues, 'spatial fragmentation as well as the appearance of spatial coherence and homogeneity are social products and are often an integral part of the instrumentality of political power'.[215] The particular spatiality which is inherent to the city must be understood within the wider network of power and spatial relations that is international capitalism. To quote Soja again:

> The geography and history of capitalism intersect in a complex social process which creates a constantly evolving historical sequence of spatialities, a spatio-temporal structuration of social life which gives form to and situates not only the grand movements of societal developments but also the recursive practices of everyday life.[216]

Therefore, whilst the city does offer the possibility of escape from reified power structures, it is not in itself a space of liberation. It is a set of spatial relations which imposes its own limits on behaviour. These spatial relations have both occurred throughout history and are also emblematic of a particular historical moment, that of modernity. MacDonald reminds us that 'the city has always been with us';[217] but yet its significance within the set of economic and political relations which characterise global capitalism is a distinct one. Increasingly cities 'relate primarily to other cities in the network rather than to the particular national or regional space in which they are physically located'.[218] Any attempt to theorise the city space and its implications for national and other forms of identity must acknowledge the political nature of space in general, and the role of capitalism in the 'spatio-temporal structuration' of city life in particular.

Many cultural commentators have drawn connections between the city and the cinema as organisers of experience. The development of both was inseparable from the nineteenth-century process of industrialisation and both have come to be the signifiers *par excellence* of modernity. It is no surprise, therefore, that urban life and the 'city experience' have been constant cinematic preoccupations since the first street actualities were exhibited at the end of the nineteenth century. Within German cinema, expressionism and the city symphony films of the 1920s attempted to portray the desires, possibilities and fears evoked by the urban experience. Through the use of montage, movement and expressionistic imagery they sought to represent the fundamental changes which the city implied in our experiences of time and space. MacDonald discusses the impact of European city symphonies on the New York City films of the 1930s, tracing this lineage through to contemporary cinema such as Spike Lee's *Do the Right Thing* (1989).[219] American cinema was, of course, central to the dominant representations of the city which developed through the twentieth century. From the shadowy streets of film noir to Woody Allen's New York homages, the city has existed throughout cinema's history as a visual and social space that facilitates and demands distinctive modes of representation and ways of being.

For Walter Ruttman, director of the archetypical city film *Berlin, Symphony of a City* (1927), 'the essence of a city [was] its rhythmic spatial organisation and time structure'.[220] The city's relationship to time is a complex one, for it is at the same time a form of human settlement which has occurred throughout history; a collision of the old and new, the past and present; and also a space which strives towards the Hegelian 'end of history', wherein time is 'solidified and fixed within the rationality immanent to space'.[221] Time becomes a function of the structures which organise it such as the law, the localised and transnational spaces of economic exchange, and the spatial organisation of the city. At this 'end of history', history itself is 'transformed from action to memory, from production to contemplation'.[222] And yet history is still productive within the city; there is still a tension between modernity's rationality and the forces of tradition. The city continues to have a different resonance in relation to the postcolonial metropolis than to the western centre of power. It is this tension within the city and the manner in which it unfolds within Irish and Spanish culture that this chapter will examine. The city's position as both space of liberation from traditional institutions and site of new forms of rationality and control is particularly marked by those nations' encounter with modernity.

THE MONUMENTAL CITY

Near the beginning of *Irma La Douce* (Billy Wilder, 1963) there is an extended sequence introducing us to the characters and setting of the story. The camera tilts up from a street-cleaner sweeping the streets of Montmartre to an elevated shot over the skyline of Paris. As it does so a voiceover informs us, 'the place is Paris, the time is 5 o'clock in the morning'. There follows a montage of shots, presenting us with some of the city's most well-known sights, unaccustomedly bereft of people due to the early hour of the morning. In quick succession we see the Arc de Triomphe, the Place de la Bastille, the Eiffel Tower, and a view over one of the Seine's more opulent bridges. But the voiceover warns us that if we want excitement at this hour we must 'forget the high rent district. You must come to our neighbourhood'. With this the camera cuts to an aerial shot of the food market at Les Halles, teeming with life and activity, before transporting us around the corner to the red light district, the setting of the story that follows. What is interesting about this sequence is firstly the economy with which the director can signify Paris, through a series of images which register instantly with the viewer and carry a weight of cultural meaning. Also interesting however, is the manner in which the film urges us to leave this well-known Paris, 'the high rent district', behind, and offers instead to show us the exciting underside of Paris, the unknown neighbourhoods teeming with life, away from the official monuments and the city they represent.

As Irish and Spanish cinema of the nineties increasingly turned towards urban stories for material, the necessity arose to represent the city experience in a way that was meaningful within the respective cultures. Thus the challenge was to show city life in a way that was distinct from the rural but also recognisable as an expression of the national life. However, the relative absence of the city from the cinematic heritage of the country meant there was no repository of imagery that could be utilised in order to connect a particular cinematic representation of the city back to the national culture. This is in contrast to cities such as Paris and London, which are saturated with meanings and myths to the extent that Jill Forbes can comment on an ideal 'original' Paris, 'which we carry in our mind's eye'.[223] It would not seem possible to make such a statement for Dublin or Madrid. There is no sequence of images which could represent those cities and carry an equivalent resonance as those at the beginning of *Irma la Douce* could for Paris. The frequency with which Liberty Hall, a building bereft of aesthetic quality or cultural significance, occurs in establishing shots of Dublin only illustrates the poverty of images available to filmmakers as they seek to establish the cinematic identity of the city.

The Eiffel Tower, Arc de Triumph, Place de la Bastille; these are images which carry meaning within a variety of discourses, from the historical narrative of the French Revolution to the touristic promotion of Paris as the City of Romance. Furthermore, through sheer weight of repetition they have come, as argued above, to act as a visual shorthand for the city, in the process occluding other parts of Paris from representation. Hayward refers to the 'imagined body-Paris', 'an over-exposed, too-visibilised cinematic city', which she contrasts with a 'repressed, invisibilized' city which is not shown and is refused cultural currency.[224] Thus our knowledge of Paris as cinematic audiences is limited to monuments, to specific areas and to the circulation of people within those areas. This 'cinematic city' is so burdened with semantic and ideological weight from its constant recurrence through cinematic history that it serves to close down meanings and limits the ability of contemporary representations to make the city 'strange'. Thus the city as a place of cultural change and fragmentation becomes replaced by an 'official', 'monumental' city which is situated firmly within an historicised national culture.

This is not to say that dominant representations of Paris and London cannot be challenged, but rather that any attempt to represent the experience of these cities as fragmentary must do so in the context of a lengthy cultural heritage which has sought to fix their meanings within political, national, economic and touristic discourses. In *Irma la Douce* we are offered a journey into the hidden side of Paris; into, the film seems to suggest, the 'real' Paris. Yet this journey from the official to the 'real' is not one which is easily reversed. After the camera cuts from the bridge over the Seine to the low-rent district, it is there that we stay. The world of the film, seedy and unlawful though it may be, is firmly separated from the sites of power within the city. The dominant meanings of the city are not challenged, but instead the characters in the story, and the film itself, accept and embrace their marginal status. Or to take an example from an entirely dissimilar film, the protagonists of *La Haine* (Mattieu Kassovitz, 1995), despite their brief intrusion into the space of the centre, have their exclusion and marginality confirmed by the narrative and ultimately the centre remains undisturbed.

Lefebvre describes monumental space as 'the metaphorical and quasi-metaphysical underpinning of a society ... [within this space] the authority of the sacred and the sacred aspect of authority are transferred back and forth, mutually reinforcing one another in the process'.[225] The monument, therefore, provides meaning and legitimacy to the social relations which constitute society and to the power structures these relations express. As Lefebvre argues, it confers an air of the sacred upon authority, one which stretches back into history and promises continuity into the future. 'Monumental space offer[s] each member of a society an image of that membership, an image of his or her social visage.'[226] The monumental acts as a force of social cohesion, yet in its attempts to codify space it inevitably exists in a state of tension with the heterogeneous reality of the city. Furthermore, Paul Julian Smith reminds us that 'the reverse of the monument is the unspeakable violence of colonial racism, a violence at once expressed and concealed by the abstraction of space imposed by the imperial metropolis on all its subjects, both near and far'.[227] The power of the centre is built upon a history of and a potential for violence. It is this violence which the grandeur of the monument sanctifies and consecrates.

Colm Lincoln writes on a book of Dublin photographs that 'one finds a world denuded of the symbolic places, the monumental buildings, by which we normally identify a city. Instead we see people moving from one place to another; the reality of their Dublin captured in a series of photographs taken on buses'.[228] Without a set of recognisable landmarks to symbolise the city, it must be signified in some other way; through the circulation of people within its confines and the network of power relations they embody and enact. This lack of monumentality has been a defining feature of the city's relationship to national culture within Ireland, as without monumental spaces the city struggles to offer the members of the national society an image of that membership. It suggests a failure to connect the city space with the historical narrative of the nation and a more general crisis in the connections between past and present. As Hayward argues, 'the crisis of the monumental is the loss of meaning and therefore memory'.[229] And yet at the same time, this lack also suggests the city's greatest potential, for a weakened monumentality facilitates a heterogeneous city space, one whose meaning is still contestable and open. Smith connects a weakened monumentality to 'the restoration of sociality to the city' and a space 'which tends towards tension, movement and festivity'.[230] This ambiguity is one of the lingering effects of Ireland and Spain's encounters with modernity, one which can be read in the city films of their respective national cinemas.

One of the first attempts to address the city in Irish film was the 1987 thriller, *The Courier*. The film opens on the chimney stack of a power station, colloquially known as the 'pigeon house' and one of the most visible landmarks on Dublin's skyline. It then cuts to a shot of Dublin port, then to Liberty Hall, previously Dublin's sole high-rise building. This is followed by shots of car-filled streets, a toll bridge over

the river Liffey and an office space, before we cut to a rubbish truck in
Ballymun, Dublin's monument to misjudged urban planning. Rockett argues that attempts to adopt US genres in Irish cinema have been 'unable
to overcome the visual handicap of the modest scale of Irish cityscape'.[231]
This opening sequence from *The Courier* attempts to create an urban setting within which this drugs thriller can be played out. Yet the signifiers
of urbanity it presents us with are nothing more than a collection of utilities. Transport, power, the solitary high-rise betraying Dublin's underdeveloped business sector; these are necessary features of urban life,
yet more than anything they symbolise an absence. What is lacking is
the space that holds these images together, which gives these utilities
purpose. In these images, as in representations of Dublin on screen generally, there is no centre, and without a centre 'there is no urban at
all'.[232] As Soja states, 'the nodality of the centre defines and gives sub-
stance to the specificity of the urban'.[233] Without the central sites
around which meaning can cluster, Dublin remains a non-entity in Irish
cultural life. In Lincoln's words, 'Dublin is everything and nothing,
having failed to generate a tangible imagery which is in any real sense
distinctive.'[234]

At the most basic level, this absence of monumental spaces can be
equated with a lack of recognisable landmarks in Dublin-set films. Even
the General Post Office, a building with the strongest of connections
with Irish nationalism, appears relatively few times in Irish cinema. It
may well be that the mark of the coloniser is just too visible in Dublin's
most impressive architecture, a fact that is borne out by the wilful destruction of much of Dublin's Georgian architecture up until the 1990s.
Indeed in a speech to the Dail in 1970, Kevin Boland 'effectively described the Georgian city as the expendable left-over of an arrogant
and alien ruling class'.[235] A reliance on the imagery of Georgian Dublin
to signify the city, therefore, threatens to confirm the city's status as
outsider within the national culture, too tainted by its previous status
as the centre of colonial power.

This is not to argue that a discursive Dublin does not exist. Clearly
there are a number of discourses surrounding the city; from the writings
of James Joyce and Sean O'Casey to those touristic discourses of the past
ten years that have remarked the city as one of Europe's premier party
destinations. A collation of the discourses that have surrounded Dublin
historically, such as that provided by the anthology of writings in *Dublin:
A Traveller's Companion* (1988), reveal the range of ways in which the city
has been perceived and discussed; from its status on the social calendar
of the English aristocracy to the perennial scourges of poverty and

disease in its slums. However, the thread that runs through all these discourses is the fact of Dublin's one-time status as a colonial city. It is this which has rendered it an ambiguous space within nationalist rhetoric, as its identity is too closely associated with both the coloniser who formerly occupied it and with an international modernity irreconcilable with the imagined rural Irish nation. This ambiguity is captured in Terry Eagleton's description of *Ulysses* as a work which 'celebrates and undermines the Irish national formation at a stroke, deploying the full battery of modernist technique to re-create it while suggesting with its every breath just how easily it could have done the same for Bradford or the Bronx'.[236]

It is this troubled relationship with Irish nationalism that has governed, in particular, Dublin's relationship with power. Dublin's marginalisation within Irish culture in the aftermath of independence conferred upon it the position of outsider, despite its position as the centre of state power. The irony of this is, of course, that the romanticised rural nation which could not accommodate the urban reality was the product of a resolutely urban sensibility. Nevertheless, its dominance within the national imagination meant that those both within and without the urban centre could deny the reality of the power relations that constituted the state; with those within claiming marginalisation from the nation, and those without asserting their peripheral status within the state. The result is a situation where, in Fintan O'-Toole's words, 'we end up with two sets of people who have immense power yet manage, through their complementary myths of persecution and marginalisation, to avoid responsibility for the state of the place'.[237] Thus, through the range of discourses that circulate around Dublin, there is continued ambivalence about its position of power within the Irish nation-state and its ability to regulate the national space. This is further emphasised in filmic representations of the city by virtue of their novelty within the national cinema. Its occlusion from the on-screen Irish identity for the large part of the twentieth century is symptomatic of its more general effacement from the national culture. Therefore, although cinematic Dublin does not exist in a representational vacuum, it does lack a representational tradition that situates the city at the heart of the national life.

The city's existence within Spanish culture has been complex and multiform. Within the *Sainete*, for instance, part of the popular Spanish theatre tradition, sketches portrayed romantic dalliances within everyday urban life. Deborah Parsons, discussing poster advertisements for Madrid's *fiestas*, suggests that pre-Franco these posters 'consistently acclaim[ed] the position of Madrid as a city of social and aesthetic modernity',[238] and 'evoke[d] an atmosphere of urban sexuality within an unprohibited zone'.[239] Modernist writers such as Ramón Gómez de la Serna and Ramón María del Valle-Inclán celebrated the everyday life of Madrid in the first decades of the twentieth century, much as Joyce did for Dublin. However, what these expressions of city life shared with Joyce's was the manner in which they were suppressed by the nationalistic, conservative rhetoric of the Franco administration. Parsons' comparison of pre-Franco *fiesta* posters with those of the 1940s reveals that the previous modernist representations of Madrid were replaced by images which evoked traditionalist notions of Spanish identity. Subversive aspects of the *Sainete* were sanitised under Franco; such as the figure of *lo castizo*, similar to the London Cockney and associated with street culture and ingenuity, which was resemanticised as an unchanging Castilian peasant.[240] This new relationship with the city was given intellectual expression by the group of writers known as the '1898 generation', who displayed an anti-urban sensibility that was in keeping with the rural rhetoric of the Francoist years.

Therefore representations of the city in contemporary Irish and Spanish cinema must be read in the context of political and cultural nationalisms that historically rejected the validity of the city as an expression of the nation. This has lead to a deficit in cultural meanings connecting the city and the nation, and to the necessity of and opportunity to creating the city anew. It is this possibility and this deficit which spawned Madrid's *movida* of the early 1980s, in which artists, musicians and filmmakers, the most famous of them being a young Pedro Almodóvar, sought through their artistic expressions and their personal lives to create a city of sexual and personal liberation, one in which the strictures of Francoism were an historical irrelevance. It is this possibility and this deficit which has seen Dublin's cinematic representations encapsulate both a progressive space of personal liberation and a non-place incapable of asserting its own identity against the universalising march of global capitalism.

THE ABSENT CENTRE

About Adam and *Goldfish Memory* could be considered emblematic of one new direction within recent Irish cinema, what McLoone has labelled 'hip-hedonism'.[241] These are films that celebrate Ireland's modernity and the liberal, consumer culture it has engendered. Resolutely urban in disposition, they portray the romantic entanglements of predominately

14. *Goldfish Memory's* re-imagined cityscape

young, affluent, attractive Dubliners. However, in this embrace of
modernity, Dublin tends to fade into 'any-city-whatever', to rephrase
Gilles Deleuze. In *About Adam* any sort of establishing shots are es-
chewed and the only explicit visual reference to Dublin is when two of
the characters go walking in the Dublin Mountains and we are offered
a view of the city spread out below them. 'Isn't Dublin huge', one character remarks, and yet for the remainder of the film the size and complexity which is suggested by this view of the city in its totality is
disavowed. Dublin is reduced to a few affluent streets, the characters'
impressive dwellings and a series of cafés and bars, all of which are
adamantly universal in appearance. The characters do not interact with
the specificity of the local environment in any meaningful way. They are
not shaped by the city, but rather inhabit the globalised world of consumer capitalism.

Whilst *Goldfish Memory* does seem specifically concerned to
reimagine Dublin as a space of personal freedom, the shots of the city,
which act as punctuation for the film's cyclical storylines, are significant. The camera seems reluctant to stray too far from the river Liffey,
as if this were the only reliable anchor for the city's identity. We see repeated images of the river, of the bridges over the river, of the Customs
House and the ubiquitous Liberty Hall, both positioned on the river.
We see the city's revitalised dockland area, now a paean to the promises of international capital; even the bar which serves as one of the primary settings within the film is itself situated on the Liffey Basin. Once

again this suggests a city that lacks density and complexity, where to stray too far from the river is to enter a semantic vacuum. The relationship of these representational spaces to the lived spaces of the city, where the film's action takes place, is never articulated. What is more, the images of Dublin we see have been digitally enhanced in the post-production process, their colours exaggerated, further distancing these on-screen markers of identity from the lived city.

A large number of films set in Dublin would be more aptly described as suburban rather than urban. The opening shot of *The General* shows a Dublin skyline, black against the night sky, seemingly establishing itself in the genre of the urban gangster film. And yet what we see silhouetted is not the downtown city streets, but a row of suburban houses. Similarly, other Dublin films of the past fifteen years such as *Pete's Meteor* (Joe O'Byrne, 1998), *Rat*, *The Snapper* (Stephen Frears, 1993) and *The Boy from Mercury* are all situated in nondescript, frequently economically disadvantaged suburbs on the outskirts of the city. Within these films, the urban centre does not hold any sway over its peripheral spaces. They seem disconnected from the urban and rural spaces that have dominated the Irish cultural imagination. The fragmentary nature of this cinematic city is made explicit in the credit sequence of *Intermission*, which consists of a series of roughly drawn fragments of maps, with streets and places of interest apparently sketched in hastily. There is no sense of the connections between these places, something which is continued into the narrative, in which the spatial relations within the story are frequently unclear.

Far more than the lack of recognisable landmarks, it is the absence of clearly defined spatial relations that suggests a failure to develop a monumental city. In his discussion of cinematic representations of Rome, David Bass outlines several categories of urban film these representations can be divided into. The first category he discusses is what he labels the outsider's view of the city. These films feature a touristic gaze with an 'out-of-sequence litany of landmarks'[242] and manipulate scale as 'the protagonists experience the city as relatively small ... [with] frequent chance meetings'.[243] Rather than being bound by spatial relationships, the films 'reconfigure [their] decontextualized contents at will'.[244] These films depend upon the audience's familiarity with the famous landmarks of Rome in order to construct an image of the city, albeit an unrealistic one. Examples of such films include *Roman Holiday* (William Wyler, 1953) and *Gidget Goes to Rome* (Paul Wendkos, 1963), which transport the viewer around the city's sights while playing out their tales of comedy and romance.

Bass contrasts this with the insider's view of the city, which 'sees the city as a strict itinerary of repulsions'. The freedom of movement associated with the previous category is rejected and instead the characters' actions are 'guided and squeezed by [the city's] intransigent topography and the character of its areas'.[245] The touristic view of the city is replaced by a realist attention to the social and geographical conditions that shape the lives of its protagonists, as seen in *Bicycle Thieves* (Vittorio De Sica, 1948) amongst other neo-realist classics. This view of the city as a set of spatial relations is elaborated in a further category outlined by Bass; those films which explore the periphery and '[seek] to uncover the poetry of the outskirts'.[246] These feature protagonists for whom the centre holds no attraction, who inhabit the space of 'not-Rome'. Thus, the monumental city of Rome is represented either through reference to its specific landmarks, around which meanings cluster, or by depicting the strict set of spatial relations which exist around this monumental centre. Characters may struggle against their spatial confinements or exist happily in the periphery, but, regardless, it is the centre which fixes their position.

In Irish and Spanish cinema, however, this strong centre, and the fixed spatial relations it engenders, are noticeably absent. Even in those films that are concerned with representing the ways in which their characters inhabit the city, and would therefore seem to fit within Bass' second category of films, there is nevertheless a certain disregard for the realities of spatial relations within the city. For example, *Last Days in Dublin* (Lance Daly, 2001) depicts the frustrated attempts of Monster (Grattan Smith) to escape from the city and start a new life abroad. As such it is explicitly concerned with the intransigency of geography and the limits it imposes on economic and personal freedom. Yet there is a curious lack of consistency in the representation of Dublin space, with central and peripheral spaces apparently existing in absolute proximity. This is clearly illustrated in a scene where Monster is chased by a gang of thugs through the streets of Dublin. At first we see him running through Smithfield and on to Dame Street, both central Dublin locations, he then briefly takes refuge in a junk yard, before returning to another city centre street and escaping from his pursuers. At first this may seem merely another example of the inevitable spatial liberties taken when transforming the physical space of the city into the imaginative space of the cinematic city, one which is all the more striking to the Irish viewer due to the relative novelty of experiencing Dublin cinematically. However, it is the incongruity of the junk yard in this series of images which is striking. This is a space that belongs to the periphery, much like the abandoned train yard where Monster sleeps, yet there is no sense of the distance between centre and periphery. The centre exists as just another space alongside many others, one which can be moved into and out of without difficulty. Despite its attempts to illustrate the limitations imposed by the city space, the film reveals Dublin as remarkably fluid. Without a cultural sense of a strong urban centre, the city loses the power to impose restrictions upon its inhabitants.

This lack of a clear distinction between centre and periphery is also visible in *Adam and Paul* (Leonard Abrahamson, 2004), a black comedy depicting a day in the life of two Dublin junkies as they try to score a heroin fix. The film opens with the two eponymous characters waking up in a field in some unknown part of Dublin. As they stand and survey their surroundings the camera frames them from behind, against the Dublin skyline, the 'pigeon house' power station visible in the distance, in the only shot of the film that allows the viewer a clear spatial orientation. As they look out over the city Adam (Mark O'Halloran) asks 'Where the fuck are we?', suggesting that they have left their familiar surroundings behind. This is reinforced in the next shot, which silhouettes the characters in the distance against a grey sky, the foreground filled with the desolate field across which they walk, the setting apparently rural. There is then a cut to a grass-covered hill from behind which the characters emerge, only to be confronted by a grey, decrepit apartment block, which prompts Paul (Tom Murphy) to declare that 'I haven't been out here in years.' This opening sequence seems to position the characters outside the city and suggests that the journey back to the city centre will, at the very least, require effort on their part. However, following a brief stint on a bus, cut short by Paul's bout of nausea, the camera shows the two characters wandering up the grass centre of a motorway, cars streaming past them in either direction. It then immediately cuts to a shot of O'Connell Bridge, in the heart of the city, and then to Adam and Paul standing by the Daniel O'Connell monument nearby. Thus, in a single cut, the characters have journeyed on foot from wherever they were stranded outside the city to the city centre. After initially setting up a distinction between being inside and being outside the city, the ease of this transition between the two serves to eradicate this very distinction.

This spatial ambiguity persists through the film as the two characters, despite existing on the absolute social margins of the city, appear to move about the city space without any impediments to their mobility. As in *Last Days in Dublin*, the juxtaposition of incongruous geographical spaces can be specifically related to the failure to develop a strong sense of urban place and the consequent limitations this imposes on behaviour within specific spaces. Although private spaces are shown to be highly controlled, with the characters frequently excluded from them, the public spaces of the city are depicted as interchangeable and fluid. For example, a series of images in the film show Adam and Paul successively standing down a deserted side-street waiting for a car to break into; emerging from a dilapidated building in the undeveloped docklands; sitting in a café; walking down another back-street; and finally walking through the Irish Financial Services Centre, with its modern office blocks and clean, spacious streets. Here they pause to get some food and rest, sitting on a bench with a Bulgarian immigrant, before moving on once again to beg on a busy central street. In this sequence we see them move through a variety of spaces within central Dublin, from the deserted back-streets in which we might expect to find a couple of heroin addicts, to the centre of international finance in the city. Yet there is no apparent distinction between these very different spaces. The particular urban spaces they inhabit in no way impact upon their behaviour and there is no attempt to prohibit their movements between them. There is no sense that the set of power relations which constitutes the city is capable of regulating their access to the heterogeneous city space.

A similar relationship between the centre and periphery is evident in *Barrio* (*Neighbourhood*, Fernando León de Aranoa, 1998), which depicts the attempts of three teenage boys living on the outskirts of Madrid to deal with their family problems and fill their days over the course of a summer holiday. Although it is not infused with the same anger or indictment of injustice, certain comparisons can be usefully made with the previously mentioned French film *La Haine*. Both concern youthful protagonists who exist on the fringes of urban society, both geographically and socially. The protagonists within both are forced to search for spaces they can temporarily inhabit, in the face of an inhospitable urban environment. In *La Haine* it is the rooftop of an apartment block, in *Barrio* a makeshift parody of a sitting-room constructed by the boys underneath a motorway. However, the relationship of both sets of protagonists to the centre is particularly revealing. In *La Haine* there is a clear distinction between the peripheral estates of Paris in which the three main characters live and the centre into which they journey. The characters, young men of varying ethnic backgrounds, remark on the differences between the two spaces, such as the price of a chocolate milk or the fact that here a policeman addresses them as 'sir' when asked for directions. Crucially, it is a space which

seeks to occlude them, and when they visit an apartment block in an up-
scale part of town, their arrival is swiftly followed by that of the police.
Despite there being no evidence of wrongdoing, they are arrested and
taken into custody, where they are physically abused and tormented,
one officer telling them they are on their own here, 'not on your estate
with your thieving friends'. The distinction between centre and periphery is clearly established here, and the space in which the young men
belong is left in little doubt. When they are finally released from custody it is so late that they miss their last train, which leaves them
stranded in the centre for the night. In stark contrast, the journey to the
centre in *Barrio* is not a traumatic one. At one stage the boys go to visit
Rai's (Críspulo Cabezas) older brother in his job as a security guard.
After a brief shot on a train, we see the boys walking down a street,
with office tower blocks in the background clearly signifying their entry
into the financial centre of the city. After their visit, the camera immediately cuts back to one of the boys returning to his bedroom. The unremarkable nature of this sequence reveals the ease with which the boys
can move between centre and periphery. Unlike Paris, Madrid does not
possess a centre with the cultural and historical power to fix its periph-
eries in their place.

The fluidity of the centre and its openness to reappropriation is explicit in the title and narrative of *Kilometre Zero* (*Kilómetro Cero*,
Yolanda García Serrano and Juan Luis Iborra, 2000), which is the point
in Madrid from which all distances are measured nationally. Therefore,
it is quite literally the centre of both the city and the country. The narrative of the film concerns the sexual relations of a diverse group of people who descend upon this spot on a hot summer's day. It includes a
middle-aged woman who sleeps with a male prostitute only to discover
that he may be her son, an uptight young (straight) man who is mastur-
bated by his male guardian angel in a bar toilet, and two gay men who
spend the afternoon having passionate sex. Thus a range of identities
and behaviour, which might more usually be consigned to the margins,
here inhabit the centre. Furthermore, there is no sense within the film
that their position at the centre is in any way problematic, their right to
be there is assumed by both the film and the characters themselves.
Without a fixed set of cultural meanings which have been historically associated with the urban centre, it can be imagined and reimagined according to the political agenda of the filmmaker. The city's semantic
openness has allowed it to act as a space in which the nation can be
reimagined and previously suppressed gender and sexual identities can
be normalised at the very centre of this newly imagined national space.

Jeff Hoplans describes 'place' as 'a centre of felt value ... a centre of meaning constructed by experience'.[247] For de Certeau, 'a place is ... an instantaneous configuration of positions. It implies an indication of stability'.[248] Thus, the city in Irish and Spanish cinema can be understood in terms of its failure to turn city space into place. This can be explained by the lack of instances in which the city was 'experienced' within the cultural output of these countries historically and thus its failure to accrue meanings over time. However, de Certeau's description of place as an indication of stability begins to suggest why even over the last twenty to thirty years, despite recurring frequently in Irish and Spanish films, the city has failed to develop a distinctive sense of place. For stability implies a source, a centre of power that can guarantee perpetuation. Yet the city in Ireland and Spain has been repeatedly implicated in the rejection of the power structures of conservative nationalism. The city has been posited by filmmakers from Almodóvar to Gerry Stembridge as a space of liberation from the past.

Ewa Mazierska and Laura Rascaroli distinguish between three different areas in European cities: 'the "historical centre", which works as a constant reminder of the past and as a gravitational pole for the whole city, and is therefore exemplified by the figure of continuity; an external area exemplified by the figure of the fragment; and an even more external and peripheral area, characterized by the dispersion of countless fragments'.[249] The examples outlined above suggest that the historical centre which exists in a relationship of continuity with the national past is absent from the Irish and Spanish city and that it is this absence which structures all other spatial relations within the urban space. In 'The image of the city', Kevin Lynch outlines four factors which structure the spatial environment: paths along which the observer ordinarily or potentially moves, edges separating distinctive spaces, districts, and nodes or foci which become symbols of certain sections of the city.[250] The ease of movement of characters around the city suggests that the paths which may be taken are arbitrary rather than determined by geographical, political or economic relations. Equally, the effortless transition between distinct spaces reduces the ability of edges or districts to construct a spatial sense of the city. Furthermore the relationship between the affluent districts of *Goldfish Memory* and the marginalised districts of *Adam and Paul* is unclear and, in fact, the two frequently overlap, assigning a different meaning to the same space. Similarly, the ability of certain foci, such as the buildings of the financial centre or the bridges of the river Liffey, to become symbols of certain sections of the city is undermined by the competing meanings that attach themselves to them. Thus, either space can be associated with and occupied by a pair of heroin addicts as easily as an affluent member of cosmopolitan Dublin. Without an established set of power relations, the city space is permanently contestable and open to new and unforeseen alignments.

THE CITY AS A DESTABILISING FORCE

Rockett describes the choice of 'the country' as the site of authentic Irish culture as 'an attempt to enter a romantic Arcadia with man in dialogue with nature, rather than with man'.[251] This produces an essentialised notion of culture predicated on notions of permanence which are inherently bound to the unchanging landscape against which this culture is set. The shift to the city, therefore, with its increased emphasis on man's dialogue with man, inevitably acknowledges that culture is always provisional and negotiable. To accept the existence of dialogue is to accept the possibility of the 'other'; it is to accept that identity is negotiated rather than essential. Thus the very existence of the city within the cultural sphere has served to destabilise nationalist ideologies and other essentialist structuring discourses. And yet, in the same breath, the city's identity has been destabilised, for, without recourse to these discourses to give it meaning, it is subject to the competing claims of all those who seek to describe the city.

The result of this destabilising effect in Irish and Spanish cinema has been a tendency towards representing the city as either a threatening site of crime and disarray, or a site of hedonism and liberation from societal and sexual strictures. As the shift to the city occurs within modernity, existing social structures are undermined, along with the power bases, such as the Catholic Church, which sustain them. Thus, the competing representations of the city as threatening or hedonistic can be seen as polar responses to this shift.

Within post-Franco cinema, the city was initially portrayed overwhelmingly as a site of freedom, as 'the place of liberation from the tyrannical sexual and social codes of patriarchy'.[252] This representation of the city can be seen in the early films of Almodóvar as well as other films of the transition and beyond, such as *Opera prima* (1980) by Fernando Trueba, which explored the possibilities for sexual encounters in the newly liberated (urban) Spain. This representation of the city as hedonistic persists in the continuous wave of romantic comedies showing endless sexual permutations amongst attractive young people in a modern urban milieu, such as *El otro lado de la cama*. The trend towards representing the urban as a site of sexual freedom began in Ireland relatively recently, with films such as *About Adam* and *Goldfish Memory*. However, if to certain sections of society the city offers the possibility of liberation, it is inevitable that the city will also be conceived of as a place of danger and even anarchy. The dissolution of power structures will predictably be viewed with anguish by those who lose the authority conferred by those structures. Thus, as the traditional social order itself decays, it is likely that it is the city, as the exemplary feature of modernity, which will be posited as the site of disorder and decay. This can be seen in the inferno-like Madrid of *El dia de la bestia* (*The Day of the Beast*, Alex de la Iglesia, 1995), filled with fire, smoke and lost souls wandering the streets; the depressing drug-ridden inner city of *Crush Proof* (Paul Tickell, 1996); or the personal despair engendered by the drab working-class areas of Madrid in *Barrio*.

This is not to suggest that certain films should be positioned within a progressive discourse that claims the city as a site of liberation, and others within a traditional cultural discourse that positions the city as a place of decay. Rather, these are the cultural parameters from within which representations of the city emerge. Both discourses can be traced back to the failure to develop a cinematic representation of the strong, urban centre that can regulate space. An illustrative example occurs in *Crush Proof*, a film which explores the horse-riding sub-culture within the more economically deprived areas of Dublin. Typically these horses are owned by young males and are frequently left to graze in wasteland adjacent to the housing estates in which they live. In a key scene, the police seek to impose their authority on the group of young people who are the film's protagonists and who have inadvertently killed an ex-member of their group. In a series of hand-held long-shots, suggestive of a surveillance camera, we see a group of horses grazing in long grass, as a voiceover on the police radio declares 'we punish them. They've got to see we mean business'. The sequence that follows is an ever-escalating depiction of chaos as the police attempt to regulate the space which the protagonists and their horses occupy. Constant pans and slipped focus add to the impression of disarray, as first we see wardens attempting to corral the horses into vans. However the wardens themselves are swarmed, first by protesting children and then by a group of men who emerge, carrying flaming torches, from behind the grassy hill. The camera remains almost exclusively in close-up as the chaos increases. A car burns. Hooded men arrive on horseback. We see a child running, clutching a police hat. In the midst of the mayhem sits a police van, the symbol of order and authority. From the supposed refuge of

15. The regulated space of rural Ireland in *This is my Father*

this van, the police detective (Michael McElhatton) who is leading the investigation into the activities of Neal (Darren Healy), the leader of the group, telephones Neal to taunt him. However the scopic regime which supposedly characterises this power relationship, the police surveillance of the criminal, is in this instance reversed. For, although Neal is hidden from the detective by the bedlam which surrounds him, it is the very visibility of the Garda van which makes it a target. As the phone call progresses it is Neal who taunts the detective with this fact. The camera switches back to the action, which reaches a crescendo as the van is attacked and smashed to pieces, while a police officer is wrestled to the ground by a bunch of youths. The efforts of the police to impose order on this peripheral space has been prevented through the use of disorder on the part of those who are confined to these spaces. The power of the centre is insufficient to regulate the urban space which surrounds it or the behaviour of its inhabitants.

This contrasts sharply with the depiction of rural space in films such as *Korea*, *The Ballroom of Romance* or *This is My Father* (Paul Quinn, 1998). These films portray a world where space is rigidly ordered by the institutions of church, state and family so as to regulate behaviour according to the expectations of Catholic morality. Within the spaces of rural society, hierarchical power relations are highly visible and behavioural norms are clearly established, particularly with regard to sexual relations. This can be seen in *This is My Father* when, after a fight breaks out at the local dance, the priest (Eamonn Morrissey) denounces the behaviour from the pulpit the following morning. 'Fists and blood were flying', he declares, 'and all this over who would have the next dance with a certain young girl.' He goes on to condemn 'the band that played the fast music to stir up the passions of these young people', and bans further dances from being held in the parish. In these few lines we can see the absolute control which the church wields over sexual behaviour in rural Ireland, or certainly within its cinematic representations. It maintains this both through the control which it exerts over those public spaces where interaction between the sexes takes place, and through the scopic regime which it institutionalises, one characterised by constant communal surveillance of behaviour and the threat of public exposure for those who flout social norms. As the priest pronounces that the fight took place over the attentions of a particular girl, the camera cuts to a close-up of Fiona (Moya Farrelly), the 'certain young girl' in question, suggesting through its visualisation of the 'culprit' the power of the pulpit to make social transgressions publicly visible. Indeed, rural society, as portrayed within Irish film, constitutes a space of absolute visibility where the public regulation of space is internalised and repeated within the domestic space, usually through the figure of the mother. It leads the mother of Fiona to report her daughter's sexual tryst to the public figures of priest and police, an act which leads to Fiona's exile and her lover's suicide. Space is regulated to such an extent that deviant behaviour, whether occurring publicly or privately, is almost certain to be discovered and its perpetrators either publicly reprimanded or, in the case of extreme transgressions, expelled from the community's space.

The distance between the representation and regulation of space in these two films is obvious and illustrates the relation between changes in the spatial order and potential models of behaviour. Thus, the city space, with its weakened central control, can be represented as a space of disorder and danger. However, this weakened control is also celebrated in many films as an opportunity to break down inherited meanings and imagine new and unexpected alliances within the urban space. The city, as both a space of disorder and possibility, is captured in *El dia de la bestia*, an apocalyptic thriller set in Madrid in which a priest and a heavy metal fan must combine to prevent the Antichrist being born on Christmas Day. Madrid is depicted in the film as an inferno of fire and smoke where all sense of order seems lost. The streets are filled with thieves, beggars and violent policemen, who attack civilians at will. Yet, the city is also shown as a space of freedom, where Padre Ángel (Álex Angulo) is not constrained by the usual limitations on priestly behaviour. He forms an unlikely alliance with José María (Santiago Segura), a greasy, long-haired heavy metal fan who lives at home with his foul-mouthed mother and who engages in violence and theft in his fight against the forces of fascism, which are behind the plot to unleash the Antichrist upon the world. The freedom of the city space is shown here to be a source of disorder, but also to facilitate the emergence of new and unpredictable forms of identity.

Obviously, the notion of the city as a site of personal freedom and also of personal danger is not unique to Irish and Spanish cinema. However, I would argue that the city is so charged with meaning due to the recent cultural shifts in these countries that it continues to be striking by the very fact of its inclusion in films. The city, in Irish and Spanish cinema, is not merely a place where things happen, it is a place which is constantly trying to lay claim to a role beyond that of the 'other' within national culture. It exists always in relation to that which it is not: the imagined rural nation that has dominated cinematic representations. City films cannot only tell the stories that occur within them, they must also tell the story of the city itself. The image of the nation as highly regulated, rural space was dominant until comparatively recently; it was only in the 1970s that it began to be genuinely challenged as the default cinematic landscape within both countries. Indeed in Ireland's case it is only in the 1990s that an urban cinematic cityscape could be said to have emerged. Therefore, the relative novelty of the city in Irish and Spanish cinema means that the distinctive reality of urban experience and urban space continues to interact with received models of national culture and historical cinematic representations of the nation-space. It is still a short distance in space and time from the cosmopolitan culture of Dublin or Madrid to either nation's rural past, and it is this contiguity which lends the city continued cultural resonance within the national cinemas of Ireland and Spain.

THE ABSENT HOME

The moving about that the city multiplies and concentrates makes the city itself an immense social experience of lacking a space. [253]

16. The parody of domestic space in *Adam and Paul*

De Certeau's equation of movement with lack is an apt description of urban space as experienced by the characters in much of Irish and Spanish cinema. To take one recent example from each, *Adam and Paul* from Ireland and *Barrio* from Spain, for the main protagonists of each film de Certeau's assertion that 'to walk is to lack a place'[254] certainly captures their relationship to their urban environment. What is lacking for these characters, what cannot be assured within the urban space is, to borrow bell hooks' term, a 'homeplace'. Hooks describes homeplaces as spaces which 'act as sources of self-dignity and agency, sites of solidarity in which and from which, resistance can be organized and conceptualized'.[255] Therefore, whilst it is possible for the characters in these films to resist the forces that structure their environment and their lives, theirs is always a resistance which is spontaneous and contingent. They have no space of refuge from which they can survey these forces and plan a concerted act of resistance or escape. Theirs is the logic of the 'tactic', in de Certeau's terms, a practice that insinuates itself 'into the other's place, fragmentarily, without taking it over in its entirety, without being able to keep it at a distance'.[256] The lack of a homeplace ensures that they must act in the space of the other, in 'a terrain imposed on it and organized by the laws of a foreign power'.[257] The characters in the films discussed are forced to act from moment to moment, scoring occasional victories over the forces of power but without a base where they can 'stockpile [their] winnings'.[258] Although a tactic may be successful, what it wins it cannot keep.

Adam and Paul opens in a parody of the domestic scene, the camera lingering on the characters asleep on a mattress in the middle of a desolate field. As the setting suggests, far from acting as a space of refuge, the field is another stop on an endless series of displacements for these characters. For, if it is true that, as argued above, these socially marginalised characters are permitted a remarkable degree of mobility between city spaces, it is also true that the city denies to them a homeplace in which they can rest. They operate permanently in the space of the other, a fact emphasised by their bewilderment on awakening as to where they are or how they got there. The remainder of the film can be read as an attempt by the two protagonists to overcome their lack of place and find a space of refuge within the inhospitable city. The first space which offers them respite on their journey is a city centre park, in which they encounter the friends and relations of their own recently deceased friend, Matthew. Despite an element of hostility towards Adam and Paul, they are offered a can of beer and a marijuana joint to smoke. Throughout the scene the sound of the wind blowing through the leaves is audible on the soundtrack, a constant undercurrent beneath the dialogue, seeming to isolate this space from the city which surrounds it. This sense of a space removed from the endless experience of lack which constitutes the protagonists' lives is furthered when one girl reminisces about their past; that of Adam, Paul and the late Matthew. Speaking to Matthew's sister she asks, 'Do you remember them three Orla, years ago?', a time when Adam and Paul 'practically lived' in Matthew's house. For a moment there is a sense of connection with others and with the past, but the group soon move on, leaving them sitting alone beneath a tree, draining the last dregs from the beer can.

Thus, the characters continue to move about the city, searching for the opportunities which it may offer them, unable to construct a coherent and systematic attempt to achieve their goal of attaining heroin, but instead stumbling from place to place in a vague search for 'what's his face'. They experience the city as a 'strict itinerary of repulsions' as they are kicked out of a café, moved on from the outside table of a bar, constantly driven onwards, walking back and forth across the city. Their lack of a homeplace is emphasised in a degrading fashion when Paul is forced to 'have a shite' down a back alley and clean himself with torn-up newspaper. Shortly after this is a scene which reveals their journey as actually a yearning for escape from the streets and for the solidarity and human warmth of home. On visiting the flat of an ex-addict friend of theirs, Janine (Louise Lewis), they discover that the place is empty

17. The city space transformed by heroin

except for her baby. Although their first instinct is to rob the flat, they soon become distracted by the baby's cries. The baby's room is bathed in a soft light, diffused by the curtains, as Paul gently picks the baby up and holds her, whispering in her ear. When Janine arrives home she sees the two of them sitting on the bed crouched over the baby and whispering to her. There follows a short sequence which is clearly a fantasy, although it is not revealed whose fantasy it is. The soundtrack goes still as Adam, Paul, Janine and the baby hold each other close, the camera lingering on their faces in close-up. They caress each other, and smile, and rub their faces together savouring the warmth of human contact. For a moment we see the people they could have been, the life that was taken from them by heroin. Then the camera cuts back to reality, to the home which is not theirs, and their necessity to move ever onwards, searching.

After this, it is only heroin that offers them any respite, which instead of taking them from the streets, transforms the streets so that they may inhabit them. Having finally acquired the drugs when they, quite literally, fall to them from the sky, they proceed to shoot up by a dirty wall in the shadow of a block of flats. Immediately the scene is transformed. Music rises on the soundtrack, obliterating all other sound. The lights of the flats now sparkle like a Christmas tree. The world has become saturated with colour as they wander through the shoppers on a city street. They lie down on a bridge over the river Liffey, the camera focusing on details; the crushed cigarette box, the half-eaten apple, their eyes and faces, the luminescent supports of the bridge. It is the city recreated through the eyes of a heroin addict. It is the streets made into a home. Adam and Paul have momentarily inhabited the other's space, remaking it fragment by fragment. And yet, it can only be temporary, they will always come down to find themselves within the same space, lacking a place once more. The only escape for them, as the film bears witness, can be in death.

As this analysis reveals, their relationship with the city space is ambiguous. It grants them a certain mobility and is semantically open enough to allow them to reimagine it for us, the viewer. Through a camera which offers us their heroin-induced point of view, our received images of the city are destabilised. Yet, ultimately, they can only ever exist as an other within the city space. The homeplace which could be taken for granted in the rural space, oppressive as it may have been, is now subject to breakdown under the economic and social pressures inherent in the shift to the city. Although the disruption of power relations this shift engendered does allow characters such as Adam and Paul the mobility they possess, it also cuts them adrift without the networks of support provided by family and community. In the breakdown of existing social structures, there is not only the potential for freedom but also the possibility of becoming lost.

In *Barrio* it is explicitly the failure of an elder generation that denies the homeplace to the younger; specifically, the inability of the father to protect his sons in the face of the economic and social forces which structure the city. We are first introduced to Javi (Timy Benito), Manu (Eloi Yebra) and Rai in the environment in which they seem most at home: the street. Indeed, the street is presented as the locus of city life within the opening sequence, which features a series of fast-paced cuts suggesting the vitality and heterogeneity of street life. We see boys playing football, men arguing, the graffiti on walls, the homeless and aged who sit on street corners, dogs, cars, women hanging out laundry, even a group of men playing instruments with a dancing goat. All these images suggest that the street is a public space that is occupied in a variety of different ways; from the conventional, as captured in shots of cars commuting, to the potentially oppositional, such as is suggested by the graffiti-covered walls. Furthermore, the street is in a sense privatised by those who occupy it, as illustrated by the makeshift living-room which the boys construct out of discarded furniture in the shadow of a motorway. More accurately, as explored in the previous chapter, it should be understood as the boundary between public and private space becoming fluid in the congested urban environment; a fact suggested by a long-lensed shot of a woman in her nightdress hanging clothes out the window of her flat; an image that belongs to private, domestic life but is thrust into the public sphere as she leans out her window, miniaturised against the façade of the tower block which surrounds her.

It is in these streets that the boys spend most of their time during the long summer holidays, fighting boredom while dreaming of exotic locations and sexual encounters. Movement is a constant for the boys, and the film is punctuated by shots of them on the subway, the tunnel whirring past the window while a song repeats on the soundtrack, the words declaring, 'I walk in concentric circles. I'm not the owner of my dreams. Every step is a repeated longing. I repeat, every step.' The boys move in circles because they have no place to stop; their dreams are provided by the ephemera of everyday life, which they encounter in the streets, from the holidays advertised in the travel agency window to the sex ads they find in scraps of magazines. What they long for, the desire that these dreams cloak, is a space of escape from the relentlessness of the street. They seek it in a record shop, where they stop to listen to music but are ejected by the security guard. They enter a bar to sell flowers that they have stolen from graves, but soon become embroiled in an argument and have to move on again. Most importantly, this space of refuge is denied them in their homes. Manu's mother is dead and his father (Francisco Algora), it seems, is lost in mourning; sitting quietly in the darkened house, unable to offer Manu the comfort that he may need. Javi's father (Enrique Villén) is an embodiment of the violent Spanish autocrat, who hits his mother and verbally abuses the maternal grandfather who lives with them. The only time we see Rai at home, his father (Pepo Oliva) accuses him of stealing money from his pocket. The boys have no space that can act as a 'source of self-dignity and agency', no 'site of solidarity' from which they can plot their own position in the world. The home, like the street, is for them another space in which they must struggle to find an identity.

Whilst this may seem the case for any teenage boys seeking to negotiate the journey to adulthood, what is significant for Javi, Manu and Rai is the failure of their family homes to provide them with the protective space from which they can make this journey. Javi's father, Ricardo, is eventually barred from their house by his mother, and is forced to live in his van in the square by their building. Shortly after this happens, he and Javi sit drinking coffee in the back of his van while passersby look in. Within this improvised living space the barrier between public and private is dissolved and the father can no longer protect his son from the myriad forces which constitute the city. Significantly, the next time we see the family sit down to dinner, Javi takes his father's seat at the table so as he can 'see the television better'. Although he is clearly not ready to assume the role of the patriarch, the only other male within the family space is his grandfather (Claude Pascadel), who is unable or unwilling to speak, even when being abused by his son-in-law. It is as if, through his rejection of language, he has abdicated his position within the symbolic world of patriarchal power. His silence suggests the silence of all those defeated Republicans of his generation, who were denied a public existence in Francoist Spain. He is a feminised figure with whom Javi is closely associated through the bedroom that they share. Indeed, it is an excess of femininity which characterises the household, as illustrated by Javi's discomfort as his sister walks around in her underwear, and it is from this that he escapes to the streets. Yet, unlike in the traditional configuration of the public and private spheres, wherein it is autonomy in the private sphere that grants the male access to the public, Javi is powerless in both, and is therefore prey to the multitude of forces which impact upon his daily life.

Manu's family home provides even less refuge than Javi's; steeped in the grief of his father, it is filled with darkness and silence. In contrast to Ricardo, Manu's father has cut himself off from public space and stays confined within the domestic, desperate but unable to communicate with Manu. Yet the breakdown in the relationship between public and private is no less effecting and leaves Manu suffocated in the latter and without guidance in the former. The only glimmer of hope in his life is the promise of escape that is embodied in his successful brother, who Manu never sees but who apparently leaves presents and messages for him with his father. However this fantasy is shattered when he discovers that his brother is in fact a drug addict, living under a bridge and surviving on food which his father brings him. It is this failure to protect his son which is perhaps the true source of the father's grief, and it is a failure which he is in danger of repeating with Manu. His inadequacy as a father is only reinforced when Manu, having secretly learnt the truth, gives him his earnings from his summer job and tells him that his brother gave it to him to pass on, in the process infantilising him by acquiescing in his fantasy. This domestic world is isolated from the streets in which Manu lives, and the fantasy which he and his father inhabit cannot protect him from the streets' reality.

It is Rai, however, who suffers the tragic consequences of the boys' vulnerability on the streets of Madrid. Earlier in the film, he illustrates his precarious position through a literal example of de Certeau's tactics in operation. Having previously discussed his fantasy with the other boys of an exotic sun holiday, Rai discovers a competition for such a prize on a yoghurt carton. His mother is unwilling to purchase the requisite number of yoghurts but Rai tactically utilises 'the possibilities offered by circumstances'[259] and steals the tops from a carton of yoghurts while he and Javi are shopping in the local supermarket. Surprisingly his entry is successful and he wins a jet ski, which is delivered to his house, much to the amusement of the other boys, living as they do in Madrid. However, as argued above, what the tactic wins it cannot keep, and Rai is unable to protect his belongings in the fragile environment in which he lives. Unwanted in their flat by his mother, he ends up chaining the jet ski to a lamppost from where, eventually, it is stolen. Without an autonomous private space from which they can operate, Rai and the other boys are unable to accumulate capital in the public space of the city. Yet, for Rai, the consequences of his overexposure to the city are ultimately fatal. His life on the street slowly drifts into crime, as he seeks the money that can offer him some escape from those streets. Having already had an encounter with the police, when he is arrested for running drugs only to be released back on to the streets, he is shot at the end of the film by Javi's neighbour, a fascistic cop. Thus in its final twist, the film undermines the forces of authority, which supposedly offer protection to the boys within the public space of the city. It is endemic of a general failure of legitimacy for the forces of authority in Spanish culture, tainted as they are by their associations with the past. Yet, this is a failure that, the film suggests, has consequences for Spain's future generations. They are denied the protection of the institutions of family and state which can allow them to negotiate their own ascent into the public sphere. As *Barrio* ends, Javi and Manu are back on the same train, travelling in circles, and the only response Javi can offer to Rai's death is to kick repeatedly at the carriage door in futile rage.

This narrative of displacement is also evident in *Crush Proof*, as the story narrates the aftermath of the central character Neil's release from prison. His first act, following his release, is to call on the house of Aisling (Fiona Glascott), his ex-girlfriend and the mother of his child. However, it is here that he is first excluded from the possibility of a homeplace, and we witness the range of forces which will deny that possibility to him. Aisling refuses entry to Neil, who can only clutch his baby's hand through the barely opened door. His only demand is to be allowed to be a father, but yet, when Aisling's refusal leads him to angrily bang on the door, she calls the police, who quickly arrive with sirens blazing. Although only out of prison a matter of hours, he is already a fugitive from the law, and it is clear that his search for a home will be thwarted. The instant arrival of the police reinforces the notion that, due to his own self-destructive nature and a social system which has no sympathy with his plight, Neil is condemned to exist as an other to the forces of authority; to those who deem the legitimacy and legality of actions in the city. So begins Neil's flight from the law, which will take him through the streets and wastelands of Dublin before finally ending up outside the city in the mountains and in death. His friends become his family on this journey. However, theirs is a family with no home apart from the streets and fields in which they ride their horses, and the bars in which they seek comfort. When Neil does return to his family home, significantly, he enters through his sister's bedroom window rather than through the front door. He can only enter the house like a burglar because, despite his sister's love for him, he does not belong there. When his mother discovers him in the kitchen she declares that she has no son, and he is forced to move on again. At one stage he also seeks refuge in a church, yet his own quiet reflection is interrupted by a priest who admonishes him for smoking and asks him if he would like to talk, to which Neil's answer is to 'ask me bollox'. Thus, the traditional institutions of family and church cannot provide Neil with any respite from his battle for survival on the city streets.

However, Neil's relationship to authority is in fact ambiguous, and, as his journey unfolds it becomes clear that what he seeks is not freedom, but the legitimate authority of a father figure. As he wanders the city, he seeks out his own father in a pub, where he finds him drunkenly propping up the bar. Yet this father is so inadequate that he cannot even remember his son's name. This failure to grant Neil even the recognition of the name that links them drives him into a vicious assault on his father, who is incapable of defending himself. Although outwardly self-assured, Neil is increasingly burdened by his friends' need for leadership and his own lack of place in the world which surrounds him. Although it is the law which drives him to ceaseless movement, the other potential father figure for Neil is in fact the detective who is leading the search for him. He is clearly a flawed father figure, as is evident by the vindictive nature of his desire to capture Neil and by the petty taunting he engages in during their frequent telephone calls. Nonetheless, he is the only figure whose authority can grant Neil the recognition of his own identity, as becomes clear when his attempt to arrest Neil turns into a gun battle. This ends with Neil standing over the detective, holding a gun, and demanding that the detective say his name. 'Say my fucking name' he implores, seemingly about to shoot. When the detective manages to utter 'Neil', he puts down the gun and declares that 'you may have just saved your own skin'. Neil finally gets the recognition he desires, but by this time the possibility of a homeplace in the city has been forever put beyond his reach by the deaths of those closest to him. All that is left for him is to drape his dead friend over his horse and ride out into the mountains, beyond the city's reach, where the inevitability of his own death awaits.

If *Barrio* and *Crush Proof* focus on the consequences for the son of the father's failure, *Los lunes al sol* (*Mondays in the Sun*, Fernando León de Aranoa, 2002) examines the economic and spatial disenfranchisement of those men who are unable to provide for their family and for whom, therefore, the homeplace has become not so much a refuge but a reminder of their own inadequacy. It follows a group of men in the port city of Vigo, a more peripheral urban space than the capital Madrid, who are unable to find work since being made redundant from the now closed shipyards. Unlike the previously mentioned films, the characters in *Los lunes al sol* do have a 'site of solidarity'; the bar in which they spend their days talking and drinking. However, as the film progresses we realise that this space is an imperfect substitute for the real homeplace which each man is lacking. Santa (Javier Bardem), the charismatic leader of the group, lives in a boarding-house in which he is not permitted female visitors. Lino's (José Ángel Egido) position as patriarch in his home is undermined by his increasing desperation to find work. In an effort to appear younger at interviews he borrows his son's clothes and seeks his advice on using computers. Jose's (Luis Tosar) masculinity is even further threatened by the fact that it is his wife who is the breadwinner, a fact that is made clear when they meet with their bank manager to ask for a loan and he is excluded from the conversation. The link between his economic uselessness and his virility is implied by the suggestion of an affair between his wife and a work colleague, and her subsequent decision to leave him.

For Amador (Celso Bugallo), the eldest of the group, the consequences of his economic exclusion and the consequential deterioration of his home life are particularly tragic. When Santa, against his friend's wishes, enters Amador's flat he discovers that his wife has left him and is not, as Amador had claimed, visiting a sick relative. In her absence the flat has become a dingy hovel, in which old newspapers and rotting food compete for space. It is clear why Amador is so unwilling to return home from the bar, and why he has begun drinking so much. However, being the imperfect homeplace which it is, the bar must close each night, and Amador, like the others, is forced to return to this domestic emptiness until finally he kills himself.

With its story of disempowered males, *Los lunes al sol* asks us to consider all the victims of a modernised economic and social system. Significantly, the shipyard has been closed in order to build apartments on its lucrative site, while the manufacturing of the ships has been shifted to Korea. It is the logic of global capitalism which Santa captures in his pithy declaration that 'they'll build luxury apartments and the fucking Koreans will come and live in them and laugh in our fucking face'. Whilst *Barrio* and *Crush Proof* lay the blame for their protagonist's vulnerability partly at the door of absent or ineffective fathers, this film reminds us that the father is not just a representative of illegitimate authority, tainted by association with a colonial or dictatorial past, but also a real figure who has suffered disempowerment at the hands of those elusive forces of capitalism that have driven the shift to modernity. Furthermore, it insists that we understand these forces in terms of their spatial effects, which can be read in a very real way in the homes, workplaces and public spaces within which the citizens of the city interact.

PROBLEMS AND POSSIBILITIES IN THE (POST-)MODERN CITY

An analysis of the spatial operations that operate within the Irish and Spanish cinematic city as begun in this chapter allows us to move away from the liberating–threatening dichotomy which has informed much of the debate surrounding the city. Rather, we can understand the city in terms of the power relations that operate within it and the ways in which the specificity of the cityscape serves to both challenge and conceal the operations of power. The intention is not to replace one set of binaries with another by assigning worth to films according to the extent to which they challenge existing power structures. Instead, it is to acknowledge both the liberating potential of the city within a conservative national culture and the reality of economic and social forces that impose limitations on behaviour and opportunity within the urban space. Within Irish and Spanish culture, the city has been strongly associated with escape from an oppressive past, and the relative exclusion of the city from traditional constructions of national identity has given cultural producers the freedom to imagine a city space which fits their own political agenda. The city's semantic openness has allowed it to act as a space in which the nation can be reimagined, and where previously suppressed gender and sexual identities can be normalised within the national space. It has resulted in an aestheticisation of the city that is consistent with the practices of post-modernism. However, the danger of constructing the city in such a way is that the forces which structure the lived city are rendered opaque, dissolved in an aesthetic of playfulness. Thus, the challenge is to both acknowledge the radical potential of the city and to explore the operations of power in a modernised social formation.

Bell argues that by the time modernism arrived in Ireland as a cultural force in the 1960s, its political force as an international movement was spent, and it had been recuperated by the forces of consumer capitalism.[260] Therefore, Ireland did not experience the kind of oppositional cultural politics which characterised this movement and, instead, 'prematurely entered the post-modern era'. If we fast-forward to the cinema of the 1990s and 2000s, it can be seen that a body of work critiquing modernity and its ills, along the lines of British social realism, has not developed in Ireland. With their youthful casts and attractive settings, films such as *Goldfish Memory* and *About Adam* offer a celebratory discourse around the city; de Certeau's 'hero of modernity';[261] and, by extension, around modernity itself. This celebratory discourse also defined the *movida*'s relationship to the city in 1980s Madrid. This can particularly be seen in the early films of Almódovar such as *Pepi, Luci, Bom* (1980), which revels in the possibilities afforded within the liberated space of the city. In both cases, modernity is offered unproblematically as the means to escape a restrictive past and in the process any degree of social analysis is lost. Even in films such as *Adam and Paul* and *Crush Proof*, which deal with those marginalised in the city, there is little attempt to explore the social and economic causes of their marginalisation. In *Crush Proof* the relationship between the forces of law and the socially excluded is reconfigured as that between a corrupt authority and a mythic Celtic past.

David Harvey warns that 'the rhetoric of postmodernism is dangerous, for it avoids confronting the realities of political economy and the circumstances of global power'.[262] The danger of the post-modern aesthetic is that 'when all that is seen is so fragmented and filled with whimsy and pastiche, the hard edges of the capitalist, racist and patriarchal landscape seem to disappear, melt into air'.[263] It is easy to believe when watching the endless sexual configurations of *Goldfish Memory* that identity politics have been transcended in cosmopolitan Ireland, and that sexual repression has been left in the country's rural past. Yet, this is to ignore the battles which continue to be played out in the political arena over the state's control of women's bodies and the issue of abortion, not to mention the level of homophobic violence which occurs on Dublin city's streets. Although it may seem misguided to

18. The encroachment of capital on *La Ventilla*

accuse a film which is positioned as generic entertainment cinema of failing to address political issues of identity, it is the assumptions that the film feels able to make about the city and the cultural climate in which this occurs that must be interrogated. As Linda Hutcheon argues in relation to feminist discourses, the post-modern deconstruction of identity can only be attempted after denied or alienated subjectivities have been affirmed.[264] It is this stage of identity politics that Irish cinema has lacked in its rush to celebrate the liberation of modernity.

Writing on the redevelopment of dockland spaces, which has been a feature of the post-modern, de-industrialised city, Antonio Sanchez writes that the emphasis on 'aesthetics and playfulness' in these revitalised spaces hides the economic forces at work. The economic logic of these redevelopments sees those capitalist forces that previously abandoned the modern city now restructuring its environments for profit, 'often eradicating long-established communities in the process'.[265] This destruction of urban communities is explicitly referenced in *Carne trémula*, in which the main character, Victor, lives in a slum area of Madrid known as *La Ventilla*. Although run-down, it is depicted as a vibrant communal space in which children play in the street while the older generations sit and talk. However, the manner in which we are introduced to the area is significant. The camera pans from a pair of high-rise buildings, known as the 'gates of Europe', to the ramshackle houses that sit conspicuously in their shadow. The forces of capital are encroaching on this communal space, and Victor informs us that soon *La Ventilla* will cease to exist, as it is to be expropriated by the city in order to build an avenue. It is this process of displacement that is concealed by the digitally enhanced vistas of *Goldfish Memory*. The celebration of urban aesthetics effaces the social reality of urban development.

However, despite this gesture towards social analysis, ultimately *Carne trémula* reinforces a celebratory urban discourse. Although the body of the film explores the operations of power in the city through the prism of marital relations and the corrupt or otherwise enforcement of the law, this strategy is undermined by the prologue and coda of the film, which firmly situate the city as the progressive alternative to Franco's repressive past. In the opening sequence of the film, captioned 'Madrid, January 1970', we witness a young prostitute giving birth to Victor on a city bus in the deserted streets of Madrid. We learn that a state of emergency has been called in order to defend 'peace and progress in Spain'. Contrast this with the film's end, in which Victor and his pregnant wife drive to hospital while he whispers to his soon-to-be-born son. The camera, through the window of the car, shows us a footpath thronging with people, as Victor tells his son how 'it's so different now. Look at the sidewalk, full of people. When I was born there wasn't a soul on the street. People were shut up at home, scared shitless. Fortunately for you, son, in Spain we stopped being scared a long time ago.' Here, the streets filled with shoppers and the cars are a symbol of progress, consumerism has supplanted Francoism, and fear has been consigned to the past. Yet the film itself has borne witness to the fear in which many in Spain continue to live, suffering brutality at the hands of abusive husbands or marginalisation due to the social and economic realities of capitalism. However, in his desire to insert the film into a narrative of emancipation from the past, Almodóvar undermines his own exploration of the lived city in order to embrace the city as symbol.

If power relations are a constant in the city, within *Carne trémula*'s Madrid of 1970 the source of that power is much more clearly visible. The film opens with a radio address by the government denouncing the social unrest in the country and invoking the use of emergency powers. This is a power which is explicit, identifiable and, therefore, susceptible to tactics of resistance such as terrorism or civil disobedience. In the Madrid of the 1990s the operations of power had become more discreet, but no less effective. *La Ventilla* will be destroyed because the logic of capitalism denies it a place in the city; no bomb or demonstration can alter this. The nationalist space of Francoist Spain has become the 'any-space-whatever' of the modern city. Deleuze coined this term in his analysis of cinematic space, and it is described by Mark Shiel as 'a space in which the source of control, the centre of power, is curiously difficult to apprehend'.[266] The rural space within Irish and Spanish cinema is nationally specific, and power within it is rooted in church and family and legitimised through appeal to an historic unified nation. The 'any-space-whatever' of the city is international in its immediate referents. It exists in a network of cities and increasingly takes form according to the requirements of a globalised economy. Thus, the operation of power becomes more and more difficult to circumscribe. There is 'no tangible oppression, no identifiable enemy, no centre of power', only 'two disjointed spheres of human experience ... people live in places, power rules through flows'.[267]

Yet it is this lack of spatial specificity that also gives the city potential as a liberating cultural force, particularly in national contexts such as Ireland and Spain, which have had a relatively late experience of modernisation and urbanisation and have been dominated by a rural, conservative national rhetoric. The difficulty in representing power structures within the city is reinforced in Ireland and Spain by these cultures' problematic relationship with authority and the consequent difficulty in giving it positive representations. This ensures that the city remains a space that is very much up for grabs and its meaning eminently contestable. It allows a cinematic city that is as easily occupied by a pair of heroin addicts as by the middle-class representatives of the Celtic Tiger. It positions the city as a liminal space, between the national and the transnational, in which both can be reimagined. It is a space that allows unexpected and unforeseeable alliances and which, rather than representing a simple rejection of traditional values, reshapes those values through their encounter with the city's heterogeneity.

Writing about those elements of Paris marginalised within French cinema, Hayward claims that 'if, according to the body politic, you are invisible and cannot therefore perform the city so (paradoxically) any performance is possible'.[268] Thus, marginalisation can become empowering through a freedom that comes from an absolute severance from the dominant culture. To take this formulation one step further, if the city itself cannot perform the nation, then it too achieves a freedom from the dominant culture and any performance becomes possible. Furthermore, if power in the city is pervasive yet fleeting, if its effects can be read in the interstices of international flows of capital and increasingly supranational politics, then it also eludes the grasp of 'territorially based institutions'.[269] Therefore, denied identification with the national past by dominant nationalist rhetoric, and denied political and economic autonomy by the realities of global capitalism, the city becomes curiously disempowered as a political entity. To operate in the city is to conform to the logic of the tactic, in de Certeau's terms. For, if the goal of the strategy is to regulate space from an external vantage point and thus establish spatial and power relations with others, the tactic is always immanent to and contingent within the space in which it operates. Without a dominant discourse that assigns the city meaning or autonomous control over its spaces, the authorities which operate within the city can never strategically control the city, but must operate tactically, from moment to moment. This allows the city to be a progressive, destabilising force within Irish and Spanish culture, because any control over it will never be complete.

Thus, in the queered Madrid of Almodóvar's films, or the addict's vision of Dublin that constitutes *Adam and Paul*, marginalised social positions become central to the narrative of the city. Although the characters are prey to the economic and social forces operating within the city, their behaviour can never be regulated to the extent that it is in the rural spaces of Irish or Spanish cinema, or the cinematic Paris of *La Haine*. As de Certeau declares, 'although they remain dependent upon the possibilities offered by circumstances … *tactics* do not obey the law of place for they are not defined or identified by it'.[270] It is in this understanding of the tactic that the city's true potential as a progressive national space is suggested. If behaviour and identity in the city remain contingent upon, yet not reducible to, the specificities of the city space, then this allows us to reimagine the nation and nationality away from the spatial determinism that has characterised so many regressive versions of nationalism. It is this understanding of space as intermediary which protects the city from dissolving into 'any-space-whatever', without attempting to recuperate it into a unifying nationalist discourse. In a city space lacking a strong connection with historical nationalist discourse and subject to the fluctuations of the international political economy, the dominant cultural position is one of marginality. In this context all marginalities in effect become equal, every speaking position becomes a valid one, space becomes contested, and the nation experiences unpredictable encounters with the heterogeneous forces and identities which constitute modernity.

To conclude, we have considered the depictions of urban space in contemporary Irish and Spanish cinema in terms of their semantic openness. The city can be seen as both a space of liberation and also as a space that is particularly subject to the economic and cultural forces which constitute global capitalism. The city's disassociation from the national past in Ireland and Spain has ensured that it is a space in which cultural identity can be reimagined. However, the city's own lack of identity can see it appropriated by the homogenising and depoliticising discourse of inter-national consumer capitalism. It is against this possibility that the nation becomes a potentially radical category, one which allows for the re-assertion of a politicised national identity against an increasingly ho-mogenised global modernity. Bearing this in mind, the final chapter will now turn to the national past and its representation within Irish and Spanish cinema.

The National Past

Discussing the rapid process of cultural change that occurred in 1960s Ireland, Conor McCarthy claims that from this time 'modernisation became a narrative in which the "imagined community" of the Republic understood itself, and envisioned its future'.[271] This embrace of the modernising process as a symbol of national progress has been dominant within both Irish and Spanish culture since that time. However, this progressive narrative depends upon a negative conception of tradition and the national past as that which must be left behind. Given the association of tradition with the oppressive cultural forces which had dominated Irish and Spanish society up until that point, its rejection is not surprising. Nevertheless, this binary view of culture, centring on the opposition between tradition and modernity, has forestalled a critical engagement with either of these terms. Pheng Cheah's assertion of the importance of national politics as 'it is only through the nation that global capitalism can be resisted'[272] suggests that the national past could constitute an important resource in this resistance. With this in mind, this chapter will turn to representations of the past within contemporary Irish and Spanish cinema. It will firstly outline the conventional representational strategy of visualising the past in terms of an urban–rural divide and suggest the limitations of this approach. It will then take three separate case studies, finding in them indications as to how Irish and Spanish cinema might productively engage with the past.

URBAN–RURAL

Discussing the symbolic figure of the bridge, de Certeau claims that it

> gives objectivity (that is, expression and re-presentation) to the alterity which was hidden inside the limits, so that in recrossing the bridge and coming back within the enclosure the traveller henceforth finds there the exteriority that he had first sought by going outside and then fled by returning.[273]

The bridge establishes a limit and an other beyond that limit, yet it also reveals the existence of the other within those limits. His formulation suggests that to leave a space and then return fundamentally alters the experience of that space by revealing that the feared and sought-after other is an inseparable aspect of the known. In this description of the bridge, de Certeau expresses the division of urban and rural space so central to the cultural imagination of Ireland and Spain.

As has already been argued, within the Irish and Spanish nationalist imaginations the rural became equivalent to the nation, in the process eliding the city from the national space. In contrast, as nationalist ideology has lost its dominance in the modernising period of the last thirty years, there has been a corresponding concern to represent previously neglected urban spaces. Nevertheless, the shift towards the urban as the representative site of national life has not dismantled the fundamental urban–rural divide, which has structured both national cultures. The perpetuation of this divide as a structuring opposition within the respective national cinemas has precluded the exploration of the spatial complexities of Irish and Spanish life in their totality. It has perpetuated the nationalist association of the rural with an essentialised past, only now that past has been assigned a negative value. It is this which allows the bridge to continue to function as a descriptive symbol for the relationship between urban and rural space, concealing, as in de Certeau's description, the interpenetration of these supposedly opposing spaces.

O'Toole has argued that the urban–rural divide is no longer a descriptive one in a modern Ireland which is increasingly penetrated by a globalised media and leisure culture.[274] Indeed, given the small size of the country and the ever-increasing suburban sprawl of Dublin, the rigid separation of urban and rural spaces seems even harder to sustain. Yet it is one which persists in much recent cinema within Ireland and Spain, both in the period reconstruction of the rural past and in the representation of the rural in contemporarily set films. We can see this in the violent rural order which must be overcome by youth in *La vida que te espera* (*Your Next Life*, Manuel Gutiérrez Aragón, 2004); in the restorative rural space of *Solas* or *Into the West* (Mike Newell, 1992); and in the recognisably repressive spaces of *This is My Father* and *The Fifth Province*. Despite adopting a range of viewpoints towards the rural space from regressive romanticism to subversive satire, these films all perpetuate the ubiquitous binaries within Irish and Spanish cultural life which equate the rural with the past and the urban with modernity, thereby concealing the full complexity of both history and contemporary life.

19. The rural as a space of death

In one of the final sequences of *Intermission*, a film that has until this point been confined to the suburbs of Dublin, the policeman Gerry (Colm Meaney) is involved in a high-speed car chase with his criminal nemesis Lehiff (Colin Farrell). As they race through the streets, their surroundings shift from suburban to rural, tree-lined lanes. The camera lingers on Gerry's face as he ominously mutters, 'He's going to the country. You're out of your element now pal'; to which his partner Ben (Tomás O'Suilleabháin) replies, 'So are we Gerry.' Suddenly a tractor appears in Lehiff's path and he is forced to swerve to avoid it, causing him to spin out of control and slam into a sheep. As Gerry and Ben struggle from the car an eerie silence descends, offset by the rising tones of Gerry's beloved Celtic music. Gerry and Lehiff face off against the background of a desolate field and distant mountains, a confrontation that ends in injury and death. Here the rural has been reimagined as a space of alienation and disquiet, a space beyond the pale of modern rationality and the known. It is a space in which these characters, clearly marked as modern, are out of their element. The fact that it is a combination of tractor and sheep that has caused the car to crash can be read as an ironic overstatement of the markers of rural life in Irish cultural representations. Yet despite the irony, the sequence does nothing to alter the perception that there is a fundamental difference between urban and rural space. The tone of the scene is significant; the unsettling use of sound and the unease of the characters are prescient of the impending confrontation and mark the rural as a space of death, an association heightened by the sight of Gerry performing a mercy killing on the sheep. The characters have stepped outside the everyday, into the extraordinary and the tragic; a shift which is marked by the spatial shift from urban to rural in a move that is characteristic of one of the major tropes within Irish culture.

PRESENT–PAST

As has been pointed out by Ernest Gellner, amongst others, the concept of nation is a relatively recent one and is linked to the industrial and social changes which occurred in nineteenth-century Europe.[275] Gellner, along with Benedict Anderson, argues for the importance of modern communications systems, such as the printing press, and a national education system in forging a consciousness of 'belonging' to a nation. Central to any process of nation building is the construction of a shared cultural heritage, a national narrative in which the modern nation-state is the inevitable end point of an historical process of becoming. The nation, therefore, posits itself as a unified space which has unfolded historically within a linear narrative of progress, such as the overthrow of colonial domination. Yet, paradoxically, this concept, which emerges within modernity, struggles to account for the experience of modernity itself, which is inevitably far more heterogeneous than the narrow narrative of nation is capable of admitting. Thus, the modern nation seeks to construct a linear sense of time within a unified space, yet the difficulty of accounting for the diversity of modern life within this linear model ensures that ultimately a break must be acknowledged with a prior temporal order, which is then designated as History. This begs the question as to where this history may persist in the modern social formation, the answer to which has been for the large part sought by Irish and Spanish cinema in all the wrong places.

If we consider the most recent stage of modernisation in Ireland and Spain – the rapid process of urbanisation, cultural and social liberalisation, and economic change which has occurred since the 1960s – such are the transformations that have occurred within a short space of time that it acquires the status of an epochal shift. This creates the sense of a prior time period that has now ended and become history. In the case of Ireland and Spain, this prior period tends to be characterised as rural, Catholic and frequently repressive. The question that must be addressed by those cultural products that seek to engage with the national space is how to account for the relationship between these two periods, the contemporary or everyday, and the historical. In the case of national cinemas, this has led to much fraught debate on the apparently conflicting desires to represent contemporary life within the state while still registering in some way the uniqueness of the nation. However, this is based on a false view of history, one which sees it as a discreet set of images and concerns rather than as an ever-evolving process. History is not to be found in a fossilised construction of the past, but is a set of conditions from which we have moved, the traces of which can be read in the interstices of the everyday.

In contrast, the sequence from *Intermission* illustrates the dominant approach within Irish cinema, which posits the historical as something external to the everyday. Gerry's love of traditional Celtic ballads has been a source of humour throughout the film, adding to his characterisation as something of a dinosaur, an anachronistic relic in this Brave New Ireland. It is no coincidence that as they enter the rural space, non-diegetic Celtic music plays on the soundtrack, clearly marking this as a space apart. The presence of death here is appropriate, for this is not a living space; it does not even exist. It stands in here not for a place, but for a time that is now past. As such it can have no easy relationship of continuity with the everyday of the urban present. It is not merely a question of driving from one space to another, but something more fundamental. It is travelling back in time. This is why Gerry believes Lehiff is out of his element; such a compromised creature of modernity has no place in Gerry's romanticised Celtic past. Yet, as Ben's remark illustrates, despite his 'fondness for Celtic mysticism' Gerry too is lost in this space, for the past is a place where nothing can survive.

If the rural is equated with the past within Irish and Spanish culture, then this problematises the representation of contemporary rural life. To acknowledge contemporary rural experience is to deny the possibility of any alternative temporal sphere to the unceasing present in which all experience necessarily occurs. The projection of the past into the rural space constructs a unified, unchanging space, a constant against which the flux of urban modernity can be measured. For this model to function, modernity must be excluded from the rural, an act which clearly strains the representational possibilities of cinema. Evidently, there are films set in contemporary rural Ireland and Spain, which must inevitably admit the impact of modernisation on rural life. Nevertheless, the bridge metaphor persists, which constructs the rural as a space of 'otherness' to that of modern urbanity. This image of rural space endures through a continued focus on certain key features that are associated with this space: on the positive side, regeneration and authenticity, and on the negative, repression and backwardness.

Cuando todo esté en orden (*Everything in Place*, César Martínez

Herrada, 2002) tells the story of a heroin addict, Pablo (Daniel Guzmán), who returns to the village where his father lives in an attempt to rebuild his life. His family house is closed up and shuttered, a space which lingers in the past, haunted by the memory of his dead mother. Indeed, there is an air of decay about the town generally, captured in the long-closed factory Pablo's father takes him to, the camera prowling through the now dilapidated building. As they wander through this space his father speaks proudly of his past, how he was the first of his family not to work in the fields. To this Pablo replies that he was never around for him as a child, distracted as he was by union meetings. The run-down space and Pablo's retort prevent any celebratory perspective on his father's claim for dignity as a worker, suggesting that both he and his ideology are a relic of the past, now irrelevant in the new social order. Yet despite, or because of, its association with the past, the town acts as a redemptive space for Pablo. At one stage we see him climb from a tank, which he has been cleaning in the local oil factory, and hosed down by a fellow-worker. The camera lingers on this scene, suggesting in its imagery Pablo's rebirth and cleansing of his past. As the film progresses he reunites with his estranged son and forges anew his relationship with his father. The film ends as he boards a bus to once again leave his home-town, as there is no work there for him. Nevertheless, he leaves a different man from the one who arrived; although it cannot sustain him, the rural has renewed him, and he returns to urban modernity with the requisite skills for survival.

A similar restorative power is granted to the rural space in *Spaghetti Slow* (Valerio Jalongo, 1997), a film in which a teenage Italian exchange student (Giulio Di Mauro) and the daughter of his host family (Niamh O'Byrne) flee the drabness of Dublin and set off in search of a rave party on the west coast of Ireland. The film climaxes in a field by the sea, where the two teenagers arrive, followed, after a series of mishaps, by their respective fathers. Tomasso (Ivano Marescotti), the father of the Italian boy, is depicted as an uptight businessman whose interaction with the laid-back Irishman, Frank (Brendan Gleeson), is a source of much conflict. However, in an illustration of the mystical qualities of the Irish countryside, the western seaboard changes him. The field to which they arrive has been appropriated by young people and hippies; the atmosphere is one of carnival. Having found his son, Tomasso spends the evening smoking marijuana in a caravan. The next day he gazes out on the beach and the surrounding hills and is moved to telephone his wife in Italy. With a tenderness which seems to shock her, he asks, 'Do you remember the first time that we met?' The surroundings have reawakened the romanticism within him, which had been suppressed by the rigours of modern life. As the film ends he is playing football on the beach, having recaptured the joy within. Once again, the film suggests, although he must return to his everyday life, he will do so a changed man.

The rural as repressive backward space is present in numerous Spanish and Irish films. In *Country*, repressed family history haunts the two sons of a violent father in a small Irish town. Violence is ubiquitous, inflicted on the travellers who are not tolerated as outsiders, and on Sarah, whose rape at the hands of her uncle destroys her dream of escape to the city with her boyfriend. In *The Fifth Province* rural repression is embodied in the overbearing mother of Timmy, whom he must murder to set himself free. In *La vida que te espera*, a son returns to his father's farm and embarks on a relationship with a local girl. However, in order to find happiness they must first struggle to overcome the violent heritage of their parents. *Silencio roto* (*Broken Silence*, Montxo Armendáriz, 2001) depicts the much visualised rural space of Spain's Francoist past, in which fear and silence hang over a village still riven by the destruction of the civil war.

All these examples represent the rural as a space of difference, a difference that stems from its connections with the past and its opposition to modernity. They propagate a particular view of history, which sees it as being 'more present' in certain places than others. However, this is of course a gross simplification, for just as there is a rural present, there is also an urban past. Furthermore, the relationship between past and present, between the historical nation and the transnational encounters of the modern, is far more complicated than the simplistic spatial divisions outlined above would allow. Through an exploration of this relationship, Irish and Spanish cinema can begin to dismantle the binaries which have structured so many films and explore the different ways in which history persists in everyday life.

One way in which history persists within the modern is through the process of remembering, through people in the present who have the capacity to remember. History persists in the physical subjects who perform it and who act as foci around which social, cultural and historical forces converge. However, to talk about history in such a way is to deny the possibility of a singular history, but instead to suggest that there are as many histories as there are subjects in the present. Indeed, the process of remembering itself is the product of a complex arrangement of social forces. As Ryuzo Uchida states, the 'public comprehend their social environment within a framework that is configured through the historical arrangement of cultural resources, such as the modes of thought, the structures of visibility and the modes of perception available at the time'.[276] It is in this sense that history and modernity can be seen to coexist, through what they make visible about the other, what history deems important within the modern and vice versa. If the present, the everyday, is always contingent and incomplete until it becomes past,[277] then this allows us to see that history too is contingent, wholly dependant for its form on the social and cultural formations within the era which looks back.

Rather than residing in a particular space, history is present in the competing discourses that circulate around every space and in the manner in which they interact. An illuminating example of this can be seen in the competition for legitimacy between incompatible discourses which forms the plot of *Mapmaker* (Johnny Gogan, 2001). The story concerns the efforts of a cartographer (Brian F. O'Byrne) to produce a map of an area within Northern Ireland at the request of the local council. Through the use of a camcorder and GPS he seeks to produce a model of the countryside; to abstract space and incorporate it within a rational–scientific discourse – to make it knowable. Yet, the contingency of truth and knowledge is made clear when the existence of a tomb is denied because it wasn't in a previously produced archaeological report, despite the fact that he sees it with his own eyes. On this occasion, historical truth is a more powerful discourse than the evidence of the senses. Furthermore, there are competing historical discourses, all of which make their own claim to interpret the land and which impose meaning on geographical space. Thus space is divided between 'our country' and 'theirs' on religious grounds, and at the heart of the story is the disappearance of a local man many years before, which is linked to his knowledge of the surrounding country. The man, Nolan, showed ancient trails of 'historical value' to archaeologists who were surveying the land. However, these trails' meaning as historically valuable spaces had been superseded through their use by the IRA and their designation as secret knowledge, to be protected from outsiders. Nolan's interpretation of these spaces according to the former discourse ultimately led to his murder as an informer. Thus it is seen that space is not neutral, but is the subject of competing historical discourses, which seek to impose meaning upon it.

To return to de Certeau's metaphor of the bridge, he states that 'in recrossing the bridge and coming back within the enclosure the traveller henceforth finds there the exteriority that he had first sought by going outside and then fled by returning'.[278] To apply this again to the divide between urban and rural, present and past in Irish and Spanish culture, this reminds us that what we leave the urban to find in the rural, that is a sense of continuity with the past, was there with us all along. The past is inevitably present; in memories, in ways of being, in popular discourses which are shaped but never defined by their encounter with modernity. Writing on the ways in which societies remember collectively, Paul Connerton draws an analogy with Freud's directions for exploring the relationship between past and present within analysis. He writes, 'there is a rule of thumb in Freud's technical writings which advises the analyst to direct attention to the past when the analysand insists upon the present, and to look for present material when the analysand dwells upon the past'.[279] If we apply this to the collective sphere of culture, it suggests that the more a society insists on talking about its present, the more it is really discussing its past; and conversely, in the manner in which a society chooses to depict its own past much can be read about the present. This advice should be remembered when we, as cultural commentators, dismiss cinema's attempts to engage with contemporary urban life as products of a homogenised global culture, or search for history in stereotypes of the past. This allows us to reimagine the past as a potentially subversive force which shapes our interaction in a nationally distinct way with the forces of global capitalism, a process begun by each of the three films discussed below.

HISTORICISING THE PAST – SYMBOLISM, ALLEGORY AND THE RURAL SPACE

Recalling the aftermath of Franco's death, Carmen Martín Gaite declares:

> all the years of his reign came tumbling down on top of me. To me they felt like a homogenous block, like a dark brown mountain range such as the ones you see on geophysical maps. The only thing I realised ... was that I am incapable of discerning the passage of time during that period, or of differentiating the war years from the postwar ones. It struck me that Franco had paralyzed time.[280]

This quotation captures the sense of cultural stasis that characterised the Francoist regime and conveys the extent to which the official culture of that period attempted to resist the changes wrought by modernisation. A similar cultural stasis is captured in Inglis' description of 'the long nineteenth century of Irish Catholicism',[281] which saw the Catholic Church retain its cultural dominance in Ireland at least until the 1960s. This sense of stasis is also fundamental to the nationalist view of culture, which is centred on a continuity between the national past and present which cannot admit the changes wrought by time. However, if one of the characteristics of nationalist movements is the attempt to dehistoricise the past, to project an essentialised nation backwards in time, then an insistence on the unfolding of time can be seen as a radical intervention in the imagining of the nation-state. It is an insistence on allegory over symbolism, in Walter Benjamin's terms:

> The symbol ... sought to achieve the transfiguration of nature and the arrest of time under the auspices of eternity through the momentary fusion of form and content. In contrast, allegory showed itself to be indelibly marked by the passage of time and the presence of death.[282]

Stuart McLean argues that the symbol is the 'preferred vehicle of romantic nationalist imaginings'[283] in which the past and present are synthesised into a 'timeless unity'. Within allegory, on the other hand, history becomes 'legible in fragmentary guise through natural forms and details of landscape',[284] most emblematically in the figure of the ruin. It is a contrast between landscape as timeless symbol of the nation and landscape as a space upon which are written the ravages of time. It is the former which characterises the rural space of Ireland and Spain's nationalist imaginings; a rigid conceptualisation of space which is challenged by the acknowledgement of time and its effects. It is through an insistence on historicity that the spatial categories of nationalist ideology begin to break down.

The constructed nature of temporal and spatial categories is inscribed into the formal structure of Almodóvar's *La mala educación*, which consists of a series of stories within stories, the ontological status of successive framing devices being destabilised through an interrogation of the relationship between the image and the real. The uncertain status of the image is established from the opening credits, the last of which, 'written and directed by Pedro Almodóvar', fades from the screen only for a new credit, 'written and directed by Enrique Goded', to take its place. Immediately the audience is thrown into confusion as to Almodóvar's authorial status by the signification of this alternative *auteur*, a confusion which is resolved as the camera pulls back to reveal that we are in fact looking at a film poster within the office of Enrique (Fele Martínez), a character in the film. Nevertheless,

20. The uncertain visual space of Fr Manolo's office

this moment of confusion establishes a recurrent formal conceit within the film, the slippage between different levels of reality occasioned by Almodóvar's manipulation of framing devices. One of the effects of this is to interrogate established categories, as the truth value of binaries such as present–past and urban–rural is challenged by a formal structure that insists upon the interpenetration and constructedness of these opposing spatial and temporal frames.

La mala educación begins as the aforementioned film director Enrique, in the midst of a creative crisis, is visited by Ignacio (Gael García Bernal), an old school-friend he hasn't seen in years, who offers him a story which he has written and suggests it may give him some ideas for a screenplay. Immediately the ontological status of the image is questioned by the confusion over Ignacio's name, as he insists that Enrique now calls him by his stage name Angel. This results in a comical interchange where Enrique repeatedly refers to his friend as Ignacio, only to be immediately corrected 'Angel', until finally telling his production assistant that 'Ignacio, before he became Angel was ... is an old school-friend of mine.' In this confusion over his name can be read a more general question about representation, an interrogation of the relationship between the symbol and the referent, captured in Enrique's corrected use of the past tense. Is the Ignacio/Angel that we see on the screen still the school-friend that Enrique knew, or does his change of name reflect some more fundamental shift in identity? Can the former school-friends Enrique and Ignacio, which at this stage the viewer can only imagine, be conceived as merely youthful versions of the figures on screen? Or has there been some sort of traumatic rupture that prevents any simple retrieval of the past and resumption of prior identities?

Of course, in my retelling of this scene I am repeating Almodóvar's own strategic withholding of information for, as we discover later, Angel is not in fact Ignacio, but his brother Juan. Thus the image which on first viewing we take for granted is subsequently undermined by narrative revelations. Once again, this is a consistent strategy within the film, which refuses any simplistic relationship between the image and the real, or indeed between the present(s) and the past(s) which the film alternatively evokes, realises or refutes.

That evening, as Ignacio sits in the distinctively modern space of his flat, a space that is largely empty except for many unpacked boxes, he begins to read Ignacio's story, 'The Visit'. Enrique begins to read in voiceover, as the camera tracks out the window. The story begins, 'ever since we started touring with the show "The Bomb", I've been waiting for this moment. Today we're playing in the town where I went to school.' The image cross-fades to a shot of a cinema building which, along with its adjacent streets, fills the screen. The dusty streets, the red clay walls of the cinema and the Moorish traces in its architecture; all clearly identify the space as rural Spain. The voiceover informs us that we won't be informed of the town's name 'so as not to promote it', thereby ensuring that its particularity is denied, instead becoming an 'everytown' image of rural Francoist Spain. Yet, already, the status of this image is questioned by the incongruity of the voiceover. For, although the words we hear are Ignacio's, the voice belongs to Enrique; the 'I' in the film is incommensurate with the 'I' of the story, thereby disturbing the viewer's own relationship to the images depicted on the screen. What is more, Ignacio/Angel/Juan has informed Enrique in the previous scene that although the story is partly based on their childhood, the part which concerns the characters as adults is fiction. Thus the image presented to us is mediated through both the fictionalising process of Ignacio's short story and the impossible subjectivity assumed by Enrique as the enunciating 'I' of the reader. In short, the timeless rural space of nationalist Spain is represented to us only for the very possibility of its existence to be thrown into question by the formal structure of the film.

Ignacio/Angel/Juan is introduced within the short story as a drag queen whom his fellow performer announces on stage as 'the authentic, the inimitable Zahara'. The designation 'authentic' can only be seen as ironic, given the multiple questions around identity that the film has invoked within its opening minutes. This irony is reinforced when we see Zahara on stage, wearing a dress with fake pubic hair and nipples stuck to the outside, miming to a backing track. The play on surfaces and gender herein serves to question the very notion of authenticity, a notion which is integral to the spatial categories at the heart of nationalism. Those categories are further challenged by the fact of Zahara's presence in this rural space. The audience is presented to us almost in tableau, a careful arrangement of parts from the middle-aged couple who are positioned in the foreground to the pair of businessmen and uniformed soldiers who sit behind them on the left and right respectively, the overall effect of which is to imply a conscious camp intrusion into the rigid space of Francoist Spain. The polite applause they offer to this transvestite cabaret suggests a queering of the rural space, which ruptures the spatial norms of nationalist ideology.

As 'The Visit' progresses, Zahara meets and sleeps with 'Enrique Serrano' (Alberto Ferreiro), Enrique's textual surrogate. Following this scene the action cuts back briefly to Enrique Goded reading the story in his house, the intrusion of this scene from an alternate level of reality serving to disrupt the coherent world of the story which we had till then been presented with. The cut heightens the sense of disruption by highlighting the fact that the Enrique within 'The Visit' and the Enrique who is reading the story are played by different actors. The question this poses for the viewer is that if the world with which we are presented is Enrique's own visualisation of Ignacio's story, suggested by the fact that his voiceover introduces the first images of 'The Visit', then why does he picture himself within the story as somebody else? The reason for this is ultimately revealed by the film, but for now it serves to further destabilise the relationship between the levels of reality which constitute *La mala educación*, provoking questions around issues of identity, subjectivity and authorship. Furthermore, it reveals one of the fundamental needs of cinema, the need to construct a visual space in order to tell a story; suggesting by extension the constructed nature of all space. If space must be constructed, as the film reveals, then it becomes prey to the functioning of ideology, a fact which nationalism attempts to deny within its own essentialised spatial representations.

Through its narrative and formal structure, the film refutes any simplistic relationship between present and past. Within 'The Visit' Zahara returns to his old school to confront Father Manolo (Daniel Giménez Cacho), blackmailing him with a short story written by Ignacio about his abuse as a child at the hands of that same priest. This introduces another framing device into the film, the story-within-a-story which Father Manolo reads and which provokes a flashback to Ignacio and Enrique's childhood in school. The veracity of these childhood images is suggested by two connecting devices; the first being the voiceover that introduces the flashback, which belongs to Ignacio as a child, and the second being the photograph that Father Manolo takes from a drawer in his office, which shows us the same child who we subsequently identify as Ignacio in the flashback. Thus we are led to believe that this is an authentic representation of the past, provoked by Father Manolo's remembrance of the events depicted in Ignacio's story. The ontological status of the photograph as bearer of visual truth connects the two timeframes in the sequence; that of Ignacio's childhood and that in which Father Manolo is remembering that childhood. The photograph of Ignacio exists as a trace from that earlier time, confirming that this is how he really looked, and by extension this is 'how things really were'.

However, the ontological status of this entire section of the film is exploded by subsequent revelations. The flashback ends with the childhood faces of Ignacio and Enrique morphing into their adult counterparts, now back in the 'real world' of Enrique's office. The apparent simplicity of this connecting device between different timeframes is complicated by the fact that, unknown to us at this time, it is Ignacio's brother Juan who is in the office with Enrique. Furthermore, as is later revealed, the entire sequence we have just witnessed was part of Enrique's film version of 'The Visit' and the children that are presented to us as Ignacio and Enrique are therefore only actors. This revelation challenges the notion of a coherent personal identity which mediates continuity between past and present. Any assumptions which the viewer has made about the characters' identities or the relationship between different spatio-temporal frames are refuted by the consistent fictionalisations which the film insists on revealing, thereby showing the inherent constructedness of both identity and space.

In the climactic scene of Almodóvar's play on narrative form, Enrique's voiceover tells us that 'I shot "The Visit" as a homage to Ignacio' while the camera tracks across the working interior of a movie camera, thereby insisting on the physicality of the film stock and recording process which allow alternative spaces to be visualised. Enrique then informs us that on the last day of filming they had a visitor, as the camera cuts to a middle-aged man stepping forward from shadows, before cutting again to the interior of Father Manolo's office. It is the same office we have seen previously, only this time a clapperboard in front of the camera reveals that it is actually a film set and what we had witnessed previously was a filmed version of Ignacio's story. The camera cuts between the action in Father Manolo's office, the film crew observing it, and the middle-aged man, who is in fact the 'real' Father

Manolo. Here Almodóvar fully reveals the constructedness of the image, confronting the viewer with the reality of the filming process as well as confronting the fictional Father Manolo, in whom we had up till now believed, with his 'real' counterpart. However even now, within this supposedly self-reflective, transparent representation of the representational process, the image continues to undermine itself. As the scene begins, Almodóvar's camera and Enrique's camera are one. The clapperboard which we see in front of the lens informs us that we are viewing the scene through Enrique's camera. As the scene progresses the shot changes frequently and the action in Father Manolo's office assumes the status of a self-contained diegetic world. However, in the 'real-time' of Enrique's filmset the camera position never changes, as revealed by several shots in which Almodóvar's camera steps outside the diegesis of the scene to reveal the film set and crew. Despite apparently revealing the truth behind the conflicting levels of reality within *La mala educación*, this scene continues to slip between those different levels. The camera does not confine us to the diegetic world of the film set, but gives us access to the filmed scene in Father Manolo's office in a manner that is not available at the moment of its filming. In doing this it sustains the imagined world of 'The Visit' at the same time as attempting to debunk it and equally disavows the possibility that the reality of Enrique's filmset is any less constructed. Such is the insistence on deconstructing all spatial representations that there is no level of reality within the film from which all other representations may be judged.

It is this insistent disruption of the relationship between form and content that allows us to read *La mala educación* as a rejection of the symbolic mode of representation characteristic of romantic nationalism. The distinction between symbolism and allegory as modes of representation was first formulated by Goethe and provides a revealing insight into the functioning of nationalist rhetoric. Symbolism posits a representational object which intrinsically expresses a universal idea beyond the capacity of language or sensory perception to articulate. Within the allegorical mode, on the other hand, the object only acquires meaning in relation to other objects as part of a systematic whole. It is instructive here to return to Goethe's original definitions as found in *Werke*:

1. Symbolism transforms appearance into an idea, the idea into an image in such a way that the idea remains always infinitely effective and unreachable in the image and remains ineffable even if uttered in all languages.

2. Allegory transforms appearance into a concept, the concept into an image, but in such a way that the concept can be grasped and can be had completely as something delimited in the image and can be expressed in it. [285]

Thus the symbol always expresses something beyond itself, a universal idea that resides within the symbolic object and yet always also exceeds it as unrepresentable. The symbol, therefore, reaches towards the eternal and the immutable, the invocation of which lies at the heart of nationalist self-legitimation. Although situated, inevitably, in the temporal reality of concrete objects, the symbolic object bears witness to 'the translucence of the eternal through and in the temporal', in the words of Samuel Taylor Coleridge.[286] As such there is a fusion of form (the symbolic object) and content (the inexpressible idea) that transcends context and temporality. If we consider Irish and Spanish nationalist discourses, we can see how the symbolic association of rural space and nation evacuated temporality and precluded analysis of either signifier or signified. As Vance Bell argues, '[the] synechdochical relationship of the symbolic object and the greater reality precipitates a hermeneutic circle in which it becomes impossible to obtain knowledge of either the symbol or the "whole" it mirrors apart from their interrelationship'.[287] Allegory, on the other hand, 'emphasizes ... a systematic wholeness while at the same time fundamentally questioning the unity of the "sign" in the direction of signifier and signified'.[288] In other words, allegory insists on the construction of meaning, on its dependence upon both an interpretative framework and an enunciating subject. Allegorical objects 'obtain a form of significance based purely on the relationship of concept and object assigned by the subject'.[289] By revealing the extent to which form is subjectively manipulated to produce a particular content, *La mala educación* illustrates 'the infinity of meaning which attaches to every representation', which Scholem posits as allegory's retort to symbolism's conjoining of form and meaning within an eternal sign.[290]

The problem with symbolism is that it is a process of mystification, a teleological assertion of a truth that is beyond the comprehension of reason. The symbiotic relationship between object and idea cannot, by definition, be prised apart; it is only by meditating upon the particular form of the object that we may understand the universal idea it expresses. This precludes the possibility that the relationship between object and idea is arbitrary or reliant on an external structure for meaning. Thus, for romantic nationalism, the rural space expresses the nation in a manner which is inexpressible in the abstractions of language. The abstract idea of nation finds its natural form in the rural, and therefore that which is not rural cannot express the nation, just as that which is not of the nation cannot truly belong to the rural. Within this formulation there is no space for contestation, the rural and the nation form a perfect hermeneutic circle from which there is no escape. However, this symbolic relationship rests on an acceptance of the fixed spatial category of the rural and its opposition to the urban space of modernity. *La mala educación* challenges nationalist symbolism, not by rationally interrogating the relationship between object and idea, but by problematising the spatial categories on which it depends, revealing the extent to which they are unreliable constructs prone to narrative manipulation. The rural space of 'The Visit' is revealed as imaginary, nothing more than the conscious construction of Enrique's camera, as is the past of Ignacio and Enrique's childhood. Yet, these were a space and time which we, the viewer, believed in until they were revealed as masquerade. We believed in them because they conformed to our idea of what the space and time of rural Francoist Spain might look like. Therefore, the possibility is suggested that our own imagination, informed by nationalism's Manichean spatiality, needs to be interrogated so that it affords greater complexity to the relationship between time and space. Interestingly, in *La mala educación*, when Enrique visits the home of Ignacio in the 'real world', outside of the various framing devices within the film, it is depicted as a distinct rural space. An on-screen caption informs us that we are in Galicia, a generally rural part of Spain, as we see Enrique's car driving through woods and across a bridge to the small village from which Ignacio comes. The bridge suggests a space cut off, a journey into the 'other'; an idea reinforced by the images of the village which we see. As Enrique stands outside Ignacio's house, he is passed by a man on a tractor, a woman carrying hay up the road and a woman dressed in black carrying a scythe. These figures pass almost in procession, and function mainly to point up the constructedness of the scene. They feel like a purposeful overstatement on Almodóvar's part, aware that in the context of the film's own deconstruction of spatial and temporal categories, such essentialised spatial representations, can no longer be sustained.

If symbolism is the fusion of signifier and signified in an eternal sign, then allegory functions like narrative as a combination of elements in time. The content, or idea, does not reside in the form of the object but in the relationship between objects, a relationship which inevitably admits temporality. The differing relationship to time of symbol and allegory is captured by Bell: 'The symbol's hermetic form/content relation

seeks to exclude both time and the natural process of decay. Allegory,
by allowing a gap to exist between form and content, embraces temporality, decay, and finally – history.'[291] Thus, if nationalist symbolism insists on the eternal symbiosis of the rural space and the nation, then
allegory problematises that relationship by admitting the process of
time. Of course the evacuation of time is always a falsity, a contradic-
tory gesture borne witness to in an Irish context by those Fáilte Ireland
brochures advertising a timeless rural Ireland while a few pages later attempting to entice inward investment by pointing out the country's
rapid industrial development. As a result of its materiality the symbol
is 'immanently historical',[292] and it is this historicity which it must deny
through a conjoining with the eternal. As a consequence, therefore, by
drawing attention to the processes of history, the essentialism of nationalist symbols can be undermined and the relationships between
space and time interrogated.

Rural space is first introduced within *La mala educación* by an image
of the cinema where Ignacio and Enrique explored their sexual attraction as boys. It is introduced by Enrique's voiceover, reading Ignacio's
text, declaring, 'I owe my best memories to the Olympo cinema, which
is now in ruins.' The camera lingers on the sign above the cinema door,
once surely grand but now a dilapidated memento of the past. The effects of time can be read on its visage. In its current manifestation, contrasted with Ignacio's memories of a happier past, it has assumed the
status of the ruin, described by Benjamin as the site where 'the events
of history shrivel up and become absorbed'.[293] The camera then tracks
down the face of the building, upon which are written the traces of
time in the layers upon layers of posters, many now in shards, advertising the films that once showed inside. Gazing at this monument to
the passing of time, Zahara declares, 'We saw Sara's first films here,
and *Breakfast at Tiffany's.'* 'Sara' is Sara Montiel, the star of such Francoist classics as *Locura de amor* (*Madness of Love*, Juan de Orduña,
1948) and *El último cuplé* (*The Last Song*, Juan de Orduña, 1957). The
reference to her here alongside the Hollywood classic *Breakfast at
Tiffany's* (Blake Edwards, 1961) constitutes a shift from the nationalist discourse which appropriated her image as a symbol of virtuous
Spanish femininity in order to reinscribe her within a discourse of international entertainment cinema in which she is merely another star.
Thus the scene destabilises the nationalist appropriation of rural space
as symbol in two ways. It displays the passing of time in the fragments
of accumulated film posters and the ruin of the cinema, and it inscribes
the national space of Francoist Spain within the international timeframe

of popular cinema, thereby refuting the timelessness of the rural space and insisting on its contextualisation in contemporary global life. It is the same contextualisation of the national space evident in Neil Jordan's *The Butcher Boy* (1997), set in small-town Ireland of the 1960s, and the declaration of one local woman discussing the impending threat of nuclear war that, 'it'll be a bitter day for this town if the world comes to an end'. In this line is captured both the narrow isolationism of nationalist thought and the inexorable passing of time, which exceeds the boundaries of the nation and lays waste to the petrified spatial categories on which it stakes its claims to truth.

SUBJECTIVITY AND NARRATIVE IN *BREAKFAST ON PLUTO*

Writing on *The Butcher Boy*, McLoone invokes the abuse suffered by its central character Francie (Eamonn Owens), and his subsequent psychosis, as a metaphor for Ireland's own relation to its traumatic past.[294] As well as exploring the relationship between abuse and psychosis at the individual level of the character, McLoone argues, the film offers an alternative reading of Francie's disturbed mind as an inevitable reaction to the social and cultural ills of twentieth-century Ireland. His troubled subjectivity is offered as the effect of two layers of social and cultural trauma. The first that McLoone outlines is 'the narrow Catholic society into which he was born, a culture riven by poverty, complacency, hypocrisy and neglect and encased in an unfeeling nationalist rhetoric'.[295] This is the world of small-town Catholic Ireland as visualised within the film and against the backdrop of which Francie commits his increasingly deranged acts. However, McLoone suggests, 'the psychosis may lie further back, in the trauma of colonial oppression, famine and emigration'. These historical events shattered the social and cultural frameworks of Irish life and disrupted the narrative of the nation. Furthermore, the loss of social and cultural autonomy as a colony saw the Irish frequently constructed as objects rather than subjects of discourse. The effects of this problematised subjectivity can be traced in the insular, overstated nationalism of Catholic Ireland, and in Francie's troubled reaction to this suffocating society. In this context, Irish history may be considered as a series of traumatic events which must be re-narrativised in order to allow a reconstitution of a troubled or denied subjectivity.

The danger of such an approach is suggested by McLean, for whom positing an event such as the famine as a national trauma that explains all Ireland's problems merely replicates the totalising narrative of nationalism.

> To write of an unproblematically given, albeit repressed, national
> past is to overlook the ways in which such a past, construed in
> precisely those terms, has itself served and continues to serve as a
> resource for the self-legitimation of the modernizing state.[296]

McLean describes this as a gesture 'of containment involving the sub-
stitution of a knowable national origin for one that potentially escapes
or exceeds configuration'.[297] However, the approach here is not to position the famine, or any other event, as the originary traumatic event
which explicates an alternative, yet equally essentialised national narrative. Rather, it is to explore the relationship between trauma, subjectivity and narrative as a means of opening up multiple approaches to
Irish history.

The relationship between trauma and subjectivity is outlined by
Susan Brison:

> Working through, or remastering, traumatic memory (in the case
> of human-inflicted trauma) involves a shift from being the object
> or medium of someone else's (the perpetrator's) speech (or other
> expressive behaviour) to being the subject of one's own.[298]

Brison describes a traumatic event as 'one in which a person feels ut-
terly helpless in the face of a force that is perceived to be life-threaten-
ing'.[299] She argues that a fundamental step in the process of recovery for
the victims of trauma is the restoration of their selfhood, their reconstitution as acting subjects. The victims of a traumatic personal event
such as rape or the collective trauma of the holocaust 'are reduced to
mere objects by their tormenters: their subjectivity is rendered useless
and viewed as worthless'.[300] This denial of the victim's subjectivity shatters a coherent sense of identity, constructed through a narrative of
remembered past and anticipated future in which one participates as
an acting subject. Therefore, the act of constructing *any* narrative becomes in this context a political gesture, asserting as it does the subject's
right to speak and fashion a reality which is comprehensible within the
subject's own terms.

If we consider the experience of colonisation as a traumatic event on
a national level, it becomes clear how Brison's model of denied subjectivity may apply. Central to the colonising process is the denigration of
the native to the status of object within a Manichean colonial discourse
which asserts the primacy of the centre. The colonised people are rendered helpless before a superior military force (although recurrent acts
of rebellion illustrate that this position is not absolute) and find themselves the objects of a political and cultural discourse in which their

subjectivity is constructed as worthless. The experience of the Great Famine also conforms to Brison's description of a traumatic event, involving a dehumanisation of its victims and a shattering of the assumed connections between remembered past and anticipated future. It is against this background of colonisation and the rupture of the famine that a new social order emerged, one which rooted an emerging native subjectivity in the structuring discourse of Catholicism.

However, even following independence, the unresolved relationship to Ireland's colonial past remained as a traumatic presence within the national culture and politic, most visibly in the continuing violence within Northern Ireland, but also in the rejection of modernity by the political and cultural hierarchy in favour of a retreat into the invented traditions of Catholic nationalism. These traditions offered a means of reconstituting a denied subjectivity within colonised Ireland. However, the inability of a national culture predicated upon these discourses to engage constructively with either modernity or history constructed an insular subjectivity that seemed to endlessly repeat the moment of its own creation. The appeal to a timeless Catholic Ireland concealed the origins of such a cultural identity in the trauma of colonisation and failed to integrate itself into an historical narrative which acknowledged the contingency of identity in the face of historical process. This was a subjectivity that could acknowledge neither the relationship to its own past nor the inevitable change effected by modernity, and one that was therefore frozen in time, like the trauma victim who experiences the traumatic event repeatedly and compulsively in the present. Or, as Kevin Whelan argues in relation to Irish revivalism, 'the only reality bequeathed by the Irish past is a treadmill of brute repetition'.[301]

It is this experience of stifling repetition and cultural stagnation that fuels Francie's psychotic destruction in *The Butcher Boy*. James M. Smith describes Francie as the hidden underside of De Valera's Ireland, an aberrance which was rendered invisible by what he calls Ireland's 'architecture of containment'.[302] This is the set of institutions and discourses within post-independence Ireland, such as the Magdalene Laundries and Industrial Schools, the purpose of which were to 'render invisible segments of the population whose very existence threatened Ireland's national imaginary'.[303] Thus, the attempt to solidify an official version of Irish culture and history was institutionally enshrined within the apparatus of the state. Against this, Smith argues, *The Butcher Boy* 'participates in the formation of a narrative that excavates the elided history of Ireland's architecture of containment'.[304] Through the medium of Francie's troubled subjectivity, and visual strategies such as the oft-cited vision of an atomic bomb detonating within the tranquil idyll of rural Ireland, the film radically disrupts the monolithic discourse of nationalist Ireland. If, ultimately, Francie's threat to society is contained through his own institutionalisation, the reappearance of his own radical vision of the Virgin Mary to the adult Francie at the end of the film suggests that the denied subjectivities and troubled pasts of Irish society cannot so easily be elided. In *Breakfast on Pluto*, adapted, like *The Butcher Boy*, from a novel by Pat McCabe, Jordan elaborates on this theme and suggests a way beyond the traumatic repetitions of Irish history. He offers us an escape through the assertion of an alternative subjectivity, one that refuses to be defined by the discourses which have dominated Irish cultural and political life.

Patrick 'Kitten' Brady (Cillian Murphy), the central character in *Breakfast on Pluto*, is characterised by an insistent refusal to be the object of another's discourse. He boldly asserts his own subjectivity at every juncture, and in doing so subverts the discourses that attempt to contain him. His position as the enunciating subject of his own narrative is inscribed into the structure of the film, which is constructed as a series of chapters from the story of his life, given coherence by his voiceover. Throughout this narrative he insists on the validity of his own experience of events, which is often radically different from the interpretations given them by the dominant discourses which surround him. As Ernst Van Alphen argues, 'the notion of experience already implies a certain degree of distance from the event; experience is the transposition of the event to the realm of the subject. Hence the experience *of* an event is already a representation of it and not the event itself'.[305] Thus subjectivity is integral to experience; it is in the relationship between subject and event that both are constructed. By repeatedly reinterpreting events within his own camp sensibility, Kitten both insists on his own integrity as an acting subject and queers the interpretive frameworks that have dominated the historical circumstances in which he finds himself.

Kitten is born into an apparently typical small Irish town, the illegitimate son of the parish priest (Liam Neeson). He is brought up by a local woman (Ruth McCabe), her husband characteristically absent, who is horrified by his increasingly transgressive behaviour. The first example we witness of this is when she arrives home to find Kitten wearing her dress and makeup. In order to reprimand him she invokes the spectre of public disgrace, claiming that she will march him up and down the street and disgrace him in front of the whole town. This public regulation of private behaviour has been a dominant feature of rural Irish life, as evidenced by both sociological research[306] and cinematic representations such as *This is My Father*. Following the devotional revolution of the nineteenth century, behaviour was strictly regulated, particularly in the realm of sexuality, by the threat of public disapproval and the moral authority of the Catholic priest. Of course, in Kitten's case, the latter authority is already undermined by his own origins, although at this time they remain unknown to him. The threat of disgrace is completely emptied of its power, however, when Kitten, on being threatened with being paraded before the town, replies with a grin, 'Promise?' By embracing his own difference and refusing to be controlled by conformity, Kitten ensures that the suffocating controls of small-town life have no power over him.

Clearly enraged by her inability to threaten Kitten, his foster-mother forces him to repeat after her 'I'm a boy and not a girl', while his foster-sister (Charlene McKenna) urges on her mother's rebuke. However, once again their anger and attempts to discipline are completely undermined by Kitten's unwillingness to accept his role as the object of their discipline. He eagerly chants after his foster-mother, repeating her phrase, 'I'm a boy and not a girl, I'm a boy and not a girl.' However, his eagerness is such that the phrase becomes ironic, illustrated by his sister's growing anger as she shouts at her mother to 'make him say it right'. Kitten's response here calls to mind de Certeau's notion of the tactic, which subverts the dominant order from within by appropriating its terms and 'mak[ing] it function in another register'.[307] By repeating the required phrase Kitten protects himself from further punishment, yet here the words assume an entirely subversive meaning, filtered as they are through his own camp subjectivity.

We see this refusal to recognise authority or become the object of someone else's discourse repeatedly through the film. In an early scene, when asked to write a story on the topic of his choosing in English class, he enrages his teacher by constructing a racy tale of his own conception involving the parish priest and his housekeeper. The teacher drags Kitten from his chair and beats him from the classroom with his rolled-up copybook. However, rather than appearing bowed by this act of discipline, he turns to the class as he is being pushed out the door and introduces himself as 'Miss Kitten'. From inside the classroom the camera tracks Kitten through the separating windows as he is beaten down the corridor, repeatedly turning to shout to his fellow students his tale of 'mis-conception'.

Even his interaction with the IRA, despite the threat of physical violence which they embody, is marked by his own queered interpretation of events. During an IRA march through the streets of his town, Kitten spots his friend (Laurence Kinlan) amongst the crowd, his face stern as he marches in regulation black beret and dark glasses. Reflected in these glasses we see Kitten approach him and inches from his face ask, 'If I volunteer Irwin, can I have pink glasses please?' Kitten's irreverent attitude undercuts the seriousness with which Irwin and his fellow volunteers clearly take themselves. Although Irwin warns him that soon he may have to take things seriously, in a veiled threat of impending violence, Kitten's queered subversion of IRA imagery nevertheless disturbs the presumption that republicanism offers the only available subject position in nationalist Ireland. It undercuts the posturing masculinity of the march and reminds us of those subjectivities that are denied within nationalism's erasure of difference, aptly captured in the identical outfits worn by the marchers, male and female alike.

Kitten's interaction with republicanism is consistently depoliticising, as he refuses to engage with nationalist political rhetoric or to adopt any of the established political positions that it offers. However, given the restrictive nature of nationalist political discourse, particularly in relation to issues of gender and sexuality, this refusal can be itself seen as a political gesture. A useful distinction to describe Kitten's position is offered by the terms 'filiation' and 'affiliation' as utilised by Whelan in his discussion of memory and politics in post-colonial Ireland.[308] He outlines the importance of constructing a space from which to speak which negotiates the distance between 'filiation (that to which we are born) and affiliation (that to which we aspire)'. As Whelan argues, if we are too close to filiation, 'we are asphyxiated by the pressure of proximity', while if we adopt too great a distance from the cultural context of that which we address, the danger is detachment 'to the point of indifference'. Kitten's rejection of the mores of small-town Ireland, his insistence on his own queer identity and his search for personal fulfilment through his idealised and exoticised mother would seem to position him 'towards the alienation of an excessive affiliation'. This allows charges of indifference to be levelled at him, and by extension the film, towards the spectre of republican violence. However Kitten is not entirely detached from the reality of this violence, as evidenced by the death of his Down's syndrome friend, Lawrence (Seamus Reilly), in a car bomb. Standing in the street, he witnesses his friend's death, the camera lingering on Kitten's face in slow-motion as he screams in anguish. His evident pain in this scene shatters the self-assured detachment which has characterised his interaction with his environment up until this point. In response to this tragedy he discards a stash of IRA guns, which have been

hidden under the floorboards of the caravan where he lives. Having previously been accused of not taking anything seriously, as he flings the
guns into the water he mutters to himself, 'serious, serious, time for
some serious spring-cleaning'. Thus he both addresses the serious reality of IRA violence by discarding the guns while in the same moment refuses to engage with the political discourse from which that violence
emerges by describing his actions as 'spring-cleaning'.

Returning to Whelan's terminology, he states that an appropriate
distance from the thing addressed creates the possibility for 'ethical witness'.[309] Thus, Kitten's interaction with the socio-cultural environment
into which he was born is defined by a kind of ethical individualism. Although repeatedly distancing himself from the terms of that culture, he
maintains an ethical stance. In this he is contrasted with his friend
Irwin, whose interpretation of reality is confined within the perspective
of republicanism and who is unable to see that it is the culture of violence, of which he is a part, that is responsible for his friend's death, regardless of whether republicans or loyalists planted the bomb. Kitten's
position as an 'ethical witness' is emphasised when the IRA discover
the fact of the missing guns and prepare to shoot him in a shallow grave
outside his caravan. When they discover that Irwin, now an IRA volunteer, is Kitten's friend, they pause in their actions. However Kitten is
impatient and urges them to hurry up, declaring, 'I've nothing left to
live for in this stupid, serious world.' Kitten refuses to assume the role
of victim and denies the IRA men power over him through his lack of
fear, instead asserting his own power to judge them and the 'stupid serious world' which they have created and which so dismays him that he
prefers death than to live in it. However, Kitten's demeanour unnerves
his would-be killers and they decide to leave him, pronouncing that
'he's not worth the bullet, the mental Nancy-boy'. To this Kitten won-
ders what the matter is with Nancy-boys 'that you can't be bothered
killing them. You kill everybody else.' Thus, in a comically subversive
turn, Kitten reinterprets a terrorist attack on himself as an issue of sexual equality, and in doing so challenges the IRA with the reality of their
own acts outside of the political discourse with which they explain
them. In removing politics, or rather replacing nationalist politics with
queer politics, one fundamental truth remains; the IRA kill people. As
an 'ethical witness', who refuses the available subject positions within
his immediate cultural milieu, he is better positioned than anyone to see
this.

As in the example above, Kitten's insistence on his own subjectivity
throughout the film reimagines established cultural tropes in radically

new ways. This is seen again when he moves to London in search of his birth-mother and encounters the other great structuring presence in Irish cultural and political life, the British state. One evening, whilst dancing in a club, Kitten is a victim of an IRA bomb, which leaves him injured. He is wrongly arrested under suspicion of being behind the explosion and interred in a police cell. This is a scene which is deeply familiar to Irish cinematic audiences from cinematic and television representations of the Guilford Four and Birmingham Six. It is the image of a wrongfully accused Irish prisoner who is physically and mentally abused by an officer of the British state until he is broken and succumbs to their will. Indeed, the recurrence of this scene could be considered a traumatic repetition of the experience of colonisation, in which the Irish were remade as objects and subjugated to a superior British power. Yet the presence of Kitten and his refusal again to assume the role of victim subverts the situation and reconstitutes the relationships between all parties.

When we first enter Kitten's cell the scene is a familiar one. We see Ian Hart's violent policeman repeatedly punch Kitten and throw him against a wall whilst his partner, Inspector Routledge (Steven Waddington), calmly appeals to Kitten to tell them what they want. The whole time Kitten carries on his own surreal monologue, describing life on Pluto. This continues until Kitten, slumped bloodily over a desk, agrees to give a statement. The officers visibly soften as Kitten leans in conspiratorially and whispers that he had been working in an IRA cell, but he was doing so undercover. An inter-title introduces Kitten's story with the heading, 'Kitten saves the world', as Kitten takes the pen and paper from the officer and begins to write. His statement begins, 'Patricia Kitten a.k.a. "Deep Throat" had penetrated the deepest recesses of the republican sphincter.' We see a leather-clad Kitten slinking up a stairway and into an IRA hideout, which resembles a parodic exaggeration of a villain's lair from a James Bond movie. The terrorists, all dressed in exactly matching green combat jacket and black balaclava, are disarmed by Kitten's anti-terrorist Coco Chanel spray, as he gracefully and rhythmically downs them one by one to the tune of Buffalo Springfield's 'For What It's Worth'. This camp and stylish reimagining of anti-terrorist activity constitutes a significant shift from the usual gritty images that have depicted such scenes in Irish and British drama. However, although this is a fantasy of Kitten's, the connection with reality is not abandoned completely and the sequence ends with a shot of the bomb's destruction in reverse, the nightclub restored and finally Kitten, dancing as he was before the bomb exploded, only this time he is cheek to

21. Kitten's camp re-imagining of 'troubles' iconography

cheek with Lawrence, his dead friend. This image of Lawrence reinforces the reality of IRA violence, and when the action cuts back to the
police cell Kitten is shown in tears as the officers look on uncertainly.

Kitten's refusal to conform to the behaviour expected by the British
officers fundamentally alters the relationship between them. They are
forced to view him as an idiosyncratic individual rather than a name-
less 'Paddy', and their attitude towards him becomes correspondingly
more humane. They begin to assume roles in Kitten's narrative, rather
than the other way around. When he mentions his mother they won-
der if she might be able to help them with their enquiries and ask him
where she lives. He whispers in Inspector Routledge's ear that he could
try 'the house that vanished'. 'The house that vanished', the other officer eagerly repeats before realising that this makes no sense. They are
slowly being incorporated into Kitten's world where, as Routledge wor-
ries, they may 'all be losing it'. The action cuts to a later moment in the
same interrogation room as Inspector Routledge enters and tenderly
picks Kitten up from the table where he is lying and carries him to a
cell. As he does so Kitten asks him if one day he came home and found
Kitten lying on the floor he would take him to the hospital. 'Of course
I would', he replies. 'So,' Kitten continues, as he gazes into the officer's face whilst lying cradled in his arms, 'if I wasn't a transvestite terrorist, would you marry me?' The relationship between Kitten and the
officers of the British state has been altered so much as to become unrecognisable within the conventions that have governed previous cultural representations. Kitten is revealed as the author of his own

personal narrative rather than merely the victim of a repressive British state apparatus. Equally, the police officers become more than merely representatives of that apparatus. They become humanised through their interaction with Kitten's strange new world and their behaviour changes accordingly. Later in the movie, Ian Hart's officer takes Kitten from the streets where he is working as a rent boy and installs him in the safety of a legal sex club. Kitten's one-time abuser now becomes his protector. Whilst this may seem a Utopian depiction which acts as an alibi for perpetrators of abuse on behalf of the British state, the focus on Kitten as the source of this representational shift allows us to consider it in a more positive light. As Whelan states, 'narrative means that it is always possible to tell it another way',[310] and it is Kitten's retelling of Irish history through his own queered narrative which constructs such representations as radical. Kitten reveals the possibility of a new Irish subjectivity which refuses to be the object of another's discourse and insists on the right to speak. His narrative suggests the development of what Whelan labels an 'ethical memory'; a relationship to the past that avoids the entropy of traumatic memory and is instead directed towards the future.[311] Kitten's story treads the line between filiation and affiliation, acknowledging the structuring forces of British colonialism and Catholic nationalism within Irish culture even as, in the same moment, it leaves them behind for a radically new subjectivity which is defined by neither.

REFLECTIVE NOSTALGIA AND THE SEARCH FOR HISTORICAL TRUTH

Soldados de Salamina was adapted from an internationally successful book of the same name and deals with the attempts of a journalist, Lola Cercas (Ariadna Gil), to uncover the exact circumstances surrounding the attempted execution and escape of the prominent Falangist writer Rafaél Sánchez Mazas (Ramon Fontseré) in the final days of the Spanish Civil War. The film jumps between present and past, between Lola's search for historical truth and the various complementary, as well as conflicting, representations of historical time which her research produces. It utilises flashback, newsreel footage, newspaper clippings, documentary-style camera work and a naturalistic depiction of Lola's personal narrative in present-day Spain. Although the film is based on factual events, the combined effect of its form and content is to challenge any simplistic concept of historical truth in favour of a form of knowledge which is always subjective and provisional and which acknowledges the interrelationship between past and present and the impossibility of stepping outside historical time. In doing so it opens up the possibility of multiple histories and the recovery of those voices that have been silenced within official narratives.

Lola's historical enquiry begins when she is commissioned by the editor of a newspaper to write an article on the Spanish Civil War. She is led to the story of Sánchez Mazas rather fortuitously, when a book she is using for research falls off her desk and opens on a picture of the Republican poet Antonio Machado, who died shortly after the war while in exile in France. Her article constructs the two writers' stories as a parallel. Machado, the Republican, is visited at his grave by his Nationalist brother; Sánchez Mazas, having escaped from a firing squad, is saved from recapture and death by a Republican soldier who sees him hiding in a bush but does not tell his commander. Lola questions what went through the mind of both; the brother at the grave of his sibling and sworn political enemy, and the soldier who rejected the dictates of war in a moment of shared humanity; pondering that 'in both may lie some essential secret of the Spanish Civil War'. Her historical journey becomes an attempt to answer that question; to arrive at an understanding of what causes a nation to tear itself apart, but equally to understand what holds a nation together, what bonds survive the self-destruction of civil war, and if there is, finally, a common humanity, a shared past, upon which an alternative, inclusive nation can be built.

Any Utopian notion of the ease with which an alternative, inclusive history may be established is shattered, however, by the responses Lola receives to her article: alternatively enraged at her equation of the Republican hero Machado with a fascist, and contemptuous of another article on national reconciliation. In Spain, as in Ireland, history can clearly not be relegated to a politically neutral past. The strength of *Soldados de Salamina* is in the manner in which it engages with history, not as a set of empirically given facts, but as a battleground of interpretation. History, in this understanding, requires intervention in order to fashion a narrative upon which can be built a vision of the present and the future. It is a vision of history which is determinedly political, which consciously engages with the past to create meaning in the present. The danger in this is the risk of slipping into essentialism, as is evident in the nationalist historiographies of twentieth-century Ireland and Spain, in which the intervention is denied and a singular version of history asserted as pre-given truth. To this end, *Soldados* makes its own claims on history while avoiding the dangers of essentialism by refusing to reveal any prediscursive past which can settle all questions of interpretation.

The central character, Lola, is a fictionalised (and in the process feminised) version of Javier Cercas, the author of the book on which the film is based. At the start of the film she is depicted as 'a writer who cannot write', sitting at her computer staring at a blank screen. Following the publication of her article she is drawn into the story of Sánchez Mazas and through her investigations into this historical incident she slowly re-engages with the process of storytelling. The relationship between the fictional and the 'real' is often uncertain in the film, with certain characters playing themselves yet interacting with the fictional Lola, while actual newsreel footage of Franco and José Antonio Primó de Rivera (founder of the Falange) is interspersed with fictional newsreel clips and dramatisations of historical events. The range of historical evidence in the film is presented to the viewer through the figure of Lola, who must sift through these often competing discourses in order to impose form and meaning on the past. The historical sources Lola discovers include a book written by another Nationalist, who escaped the firing squad with Sánchez Mazas, called '*Yo fui asesinado por los rojos* (*I was assassinated by the reds*)', and a diary that Sánchez Mazas kept while hiding out in the forest. They also include interviews with the son of Sánchez Mazas and the 'forest friends', three Republican deserters who gave him food and lodgings in the days after his escape. These men all play themselves in the film and their interviews with Lola are filmed by hand-held camera, giving the footage the *verité* tone of documentary. Yet, the fact that these 'real' images are incorporated into Lola's fictionalised story problematises the whole notion of truth in the film. This intertwining of 'truth' and fiction is continued in the depiction of the civil war, which includes both Nationalist newsreels from the war front, dramatisations of Sánchez Mazas' story and even one newsreel which is doctored in the style of *Forrest Gump* so as to depict the actor playing Sánchez Mazas being sworn in as a government minister by Franco himself. The dramatisations of the past are provoked within the film by the testimonials of the 'forest friends' or by the accounts which Lola reads, the action frequently intercutting between the historical dramatisation and shots of Lola reading or interviewing in the present. Thus, these images are dramatic recreations of inevitably partial accounts of historical events. This partiality is made explicit in a scene where shots of Lola reading Sánchez Mazas' diary are intercut with images of his escape through the forest, until a close-up of Lola turning the pages of the diary reveal the next page to be torn out, abruptly halting the recreation. The missing page of the diary captures the inevitably incomplete and imperfect knowledge of the past, which is all that Lola can hope to attain. Similarly, the combination of fictional and documentary imagery in the film's recreation of the past disturb the notion

22. Verité camerawork captures the interaction between fiction and the 'real'

of film-as-document and force us to question any understanding of the past as pre-given and certifiable.

Central to the film's exploration of the past is the distinction between memory and history. Whelan defines this distinction as that between a spontaneous, collective and encompassing memory, and the professional discipline of history, which defines the self-knowledge of society within the nation-state.[312] He quotes Pierre Nora's phrase that 'history is perpetually suspicious of memory and its true mission is to annihilate it',[313] a phrase which carries particular resonance for a society in which official Francoist history silenced the memories of the civil war defeated. This loss of memory within society is evocatively captured in the figure of Lola's father (Luis Cuenca), who suffers from senile dementia. Whilst visiting him in his old folks' home, Lola reads to him her article on Sánchez Mazas. The article begins with a description of pre-war Madrid as a Utopian space of artistic ferment, while newsreel footage shows us streets teeming with people and motor cars. However, the article continues, 'all that changed with the start of the war'. Suddenly, the footage alters in tone, the bustling urban crowds are replaced by shots of people pointing to the sky and scurrying for cover. A bomb explodes, filling the screen with rubble. The scene cuts back to the present and a close-up of Lola's father, his weary eyes and intravenous tube presenting a picture of a feeble old man as he asks, 'What war?' Later, after his death, we see a photograph of him taken when he was a soldier during the civil war. His lack of memory of this event, in which he partook, suggests the enforced cultural amnesia under Franco which denied any public space for the remembrances of those who fought on the Republican side. His death makes all the more evident the urgency of recovering lost memories in the face of 'the annihilating force of time and its erosion of traces'.[314]

In a reverse of Nora's description, the film asserts memory as the riposte to the totalising narrative of history. The relationship to the past which the film proposes is partial, purposeful and embodied in the subjects who sustain the past into the present. In this respect it is significant that in the shift from book to film the protagonist has become a woman. The film insists on Lola's sexuality, on her embodiedness as a woman. In an early scene she meets a student, Gastón (Diego Luna), in a stairway of the university where she teaches writing. After briefly discussing her class she takes her leave. As she climbs the stairs the camera cuts to Gastón staring after her and then to a reverse shot showing the object of his gaze, lingering on her legs as they ascend the steps. Here she is clearly depicted as a sexual figure, an object of desire for her student. This insistence on her sexuality belies the possibility of a detached observer of history. Lola is both a feeling, experiencing subject and the locus of the film's historical explorations. The position from which she narrates history, defined by her femininity amongst other things, is acknowledged rather than concealed by the film. When she is first commissioned to write an article on the civil war and responds less than enthusiastically, her editor comments 'You women are all the same. No interest in the past.' However, it is not a lack of interest in the past but the phallocentric historical narratives that have interpreted it which have excluded women from engaging fully with that past. Through the figure of Lola the film explicitly addresses that exclusion and seeks to reinscribe elided memories into the construction of an inclusive national past.

As argued above, the knowledge of the past that *Soldados de Salamina* proposes is always partial and provisional. It rejects the comprehensive for the fleeting and the contingent. It cherishes the historical trace; the torn diary and the memories of old men. Its approach is characteristic of what Svetlana Boym labels 'reflective nostalgia'.[315] Boym outlines two contrasting relationships to the past which occur within cultures, 'restorative' and 'reflective' nostalgia. Restorative nostalgia is concerned with the recreation of a lost time and is characteristic of nationalist movements and their focus on 'the return to origins'.[316] Reflective nostalgia, on the other hand, does not attempt to recreate the past but seeks fragments of the past in the present which '[open] up a multitude of potentialities, nonteleological possibilities of historic development'.[317] As Boym declares, it is an approach to the past which cherishes details and 'shattered fragments of memory'.[318] It is captured in the repeatedly imagined details of the film. Again and again we see the same shots of Sánchez Mazas stumbling through the forest or coming face to face with his would-be executioner, isolated fragments of the past built up through their retelling in the present. When Lola visits the site where the Nationalists were executed, the action cuts repeatedly between her present-day exploration of this space and the historical events which it contained. As she pushes through the forest, the film cuts to Sánchez Mazas making the same journey. The visual juxtaposition of these two historical times within the same space creates a sense of an historical trace persisting from the past to the present. There is an official memorial at the spot to remember 'those who fell for God and country', but it is not the official version of history which dominates, it is the personal relationship of Lola to these events. She almost seems to re-experience them herself as she struggles through the trees, an impression which is heightened when she is shot at by hunters in the forest, the sound of gun shot and dogs barking echoing the sense of approaching danger which Sánchez Mazas must have felt all those years before. Again, the historical perspective is insistently embodied in the present in the figure of Lola, whose search for the fragments of the past opens up the multitude of possibilities which history contains.

Whelan discusses memory in terms of restoring 'openness' to the past, as a potentially radical force which 'keeps alive the memory of suffering and defeat against the obliterative force of the victor's narrative'.[319] It is the possibility of uncovering this radical memory which represents the culmination of Lola's journey. Her search for the soldier who saved Sánchez Mazas from death takes her to a retirement home in France to meet a man named Miralles (Joan Dalmau), who was present at Collell, where the incident took place. However, when she questions him on it his response is pointed. 'You don't really care about Sánchez Mazas,' he accuses, 'you're looking for a hero.' Yet, he goes on, 'it's the heroes who don't survive'. He lists the friends who went to war with him, 'the García Sagués boys, Miguel Cardós, Gobí Baldrich, Pipo Canal, Fatty Odena, Santi Brugada, Jordi Gudayal. All dead.' These names speak of the memories that have been lost to time and the losses that have been denied by history. It is this denial which Miralles rails against. 'No one remembers them,' he declares, 'and not one miserable street, of one miserable village, in one shitty country will be named after them.' This is the 'obliterative' effect of the victor's narrative; these are the denied subjectivities of memorialised history.

Through Miralles the film reads their name into the records and asserts the existence of an alternative, untold past. David Lloyd argues that within the framework of historicism 'pasts that envisaged different futures are detached from any life to come, are fixed in their distinction, furnishing only debris – remnants, whose excavation proves only the inevitability of their passing, their fundamental incapacity to blend into the onward flow of history'.[320] These dead soldiers are the debris of a totalising historicism, the aim of which was to legitimise the Francoist Spanish nation-state. *Soldados de Salamina* seeks to excavate these fragments and to connect them with a lived present, to reinstate history as a radical force in contemporary Spain.

This returns us to de Certeau's metaphor of the bridge, and the idea that the exteriority that we cross the bridge to find is ultimately something which exists within. Lola seeks in the past, in the story of Sánchez Mazas and the soldier who saved his life, the 'essential secret' of the Spanish Civil War. Yet, what she discovers is that in trying to tell that story she can only tell the story of herself. History contains no essential truths, its value must be fought over in the present. The act of storytelling is an assertion of values, it is an ethical act as '[that which] we consider *communicable* and *memorable* is also what we consider valuable'.[321] If the historical narratives which are contained within the film are partial and contestable, this does not imply that all history is arbitrary. Rather, it emphasises the necessity of what Richard Kearney calls 'the criteria of justice' in the construction of historical narrative.[322] It is not any hidden secret contained within the past which Lola discovers, but her own 'criteria of justice', which can give form to that past. When Lola first attempts to write the story of Sánchez Mazas, it becomes a dry attempt at historical reconstruction. As her friend Conchi remarks on reading it, 'I don't know what you think or why you wrote it. I don't see you.' It is her encounter with Miralles and his invocation of all those dead friends which provides shape to her history. However, the history which this creates can only be a subjective one, a conscious engagement with the past which seeks to forge from it an ethical narrative. As Lola steps into a taxi outside Miralles' retirement home, she turns to the old man and describes the soldier who saved Sánchez Mazas one last time. She lifts her face to him and entreats, 'it was you wasn't it'. Miralles pauses, his weathered face filling the screen, before replying with a curt 'no' and sending the taxi on its way. We do not know if he is telling the truth, his denial emphasising that the totality of the past will always remain unknowable. Yet, as Miralles has pointed out, Lola's search for this totality is a futile one, as so many voices from the past are now silent.

As the taxi pulls away it seems that Lola's journey is complete. She turns to gaze out the rear window at Miralles retreating into the distance, tears rolling down her face as she promises, 'I won't forget you, I won't forget you, I won't let them forget you.' She has learned that her duty to history is not to recreate but to remember, to cherish the lost fragments of the past obliterated by the passing of time and the reductive narratives of historicism. She opens her notebook and begins, this time with the story of herself: 'the first time I heard of Rafaél Sánchez Mazas I was just a writer who couldn't write …' For Lola, the past is no longer something external, which can be discovered, but something which must be related to from the present. *Soldados de Salamina* insists that to speak of the present is to silently invoke the past, and that in order to address the past we must first establish our own ethical position in the present.

CONCLUSION

The three films examined in detail within this chapter each contribute in their own way towards a more complex understanding of the relationship between the past and the present in Irish and Spanish culture. Through their form and content they suggest ways of retelling the past which can break down the fixed spatial and temporal categories of nationalist culture, as well as exploring ways in which the past can be renarratised and made a radical force in the present. They advocate an ethical position which critiques the enforced silences and acknowledges the denied subjectivities of nationalist historiographies. Taken as a whole, they suggest that the national past should not be abandoned as the repository of a backward traditionalism, but that progressive currents should be sought, upon which a cultural identity can be built.

Conclusion

The aim of this book has been to establish ways in which the framework of national culture continues to be useful as a means of interpreting Irish and Spanish cinema. The move towards a less explicitly political cinema within Ireland and Spain in the 1990s, and the lessening of concern with markers of national identity within these films, has challenged this view. Nevertheless, this book has established connections between representations of modern life within recent Irish and Spanish film and cultural concerns which emerge from a specifically national context. It has established certain shared characteristics within Irish and Spanish culture and traced these in the films which have been produced within Ireland and Spain since 1992, analysing how these characteristics have marked Irish and Spanish representations of modernity as different. The key cultural feature in this respect has been the speed of the modernising process which has occurred within both countries, wherein a previously dominant Catholic nationalist ideology has rapidly lost its cultural power. The devaluation of the national culture as a repository of discredited traditionalism has left Irish and Spanish culture particularly open to the transnational cultural forces which structure modern life. The effects on the representational strategies of recent Irish and Spanish cinema of this interaction between a problematic national past and the process of modernisation have been the focus of this book.

By examining the interactions between national history and 'transnational' modernity within Irish and Spanish films, this book has explored the ways in which that history continues to mark the contemporary cultures of both countries. The comparative approach allows us to make connections between two European countries which, although in many ways dissimilar, shared a dominant Catholic ethos and a peripheral status within twentieth-century Europe. The advantage of this is that it avoids the tendency to see Ireland and Spain's historical and cultural developments as *sui generis*, while still registering that which makes those countries unique in a European environment. Certain historical features have been shared by both: the intertwining of church and state;

the dominance of a cultural nationalism rooted in a romanticised vision of rural life; the comparatively late shift towards urban modernity; the experience of civil war. The genesis of these features was quite different in each country. Ireland's political and cultural development cannot be understood without acknowledging the transformative impact of British colonisation on the country, while Spain's reactionary Catholic nationalism was in many ways a product of her own decline as a colonial power. Thus, each country experienced colonisation from different sides of the power divide. Nevertheless, despite their differences, the twentieth century saw Ireland and Spain sharing many cultural, political and economic features which marked their relationship to European modernity as distinctive. By tracing the impact of these historical features in recent cinema, we have registered the ways in which they continue to mark both countries' relationship to modernity. Such an approach allows us to address the effects of Ireland's colonial experience while tracing its trajectory within a European process of modernisation. Similarly, it opens up the debates within Spanish cultural and film studies surrounding the legacy of Francoism and suggests productive routes of analysis which may allow a revaluation of the relationship between past and present. In short, the aim of this book has been to develop an analysis of Irish and Spanish cinematic culture which registers the local while critically engaging with issues of identity within the transnational economic and cultural context of global modernity.

Notes

INTRODUCTION

1. Mette Hjort, 'Themes of Nation' in Mette Hjort and Scott MacKenzie (eds), *Cinema and Nation* (London and New York: Routledge, 2000), p.105.

CHAPTER 1: THE COMPARATIVE APPROACH

2. Kevin Rockett, 'History, Politics and Irish Cinema' in Kevin Rockett, Luke Gibbons and John Hill, *Cinema and Ireland* (London: Routledge, 1988), pp.8–9.
3. Lance Pettitt, *Screening Ireland: Film and Television Representation* (Manchester: Manchester University Press, 2000), p.33.
4. Ibid., p.35.
5. Kevin Rockett, *Irish Film Censorship: a Cultural Journey from Silent Cinema to Internet Pornography* (Dublin: Four Courts Press, 2004), p.65.
6. Pettitt, *Screening Ireland*, p.38.
7. Ruth Barton, *Irish National Cinema* (London and New York: Routledge, 2004), p.46.
8. Rockett, 'History, Politics and Irish Cinema', p.129.
9. Martin McLoone, *Irish Film: The Emergence of a Contemporary Cinema* (London: British Film Institute, 2000), pp.134–5.
10. Peter William Evans, 'Cifesa: Cinema and Authoritarian Aesthetics' in Helen Graham and Jo Labanyi (eds), *Spanish Cultural Studies – an Introduction: The Struggle for Modernity* (Oxford: Oxford University Press, 1995), pp.215.
11. Marsha Kinder, *Blood Cinema: The Reconstruction of National Identity in Spain* (Berkeley: University of California Press, 1993), p.19.
12. Ibid., p.27.
13. Ibid., p.42.
14. M. Tierney, 'Minister for Transport, Gerry Stembridge', *Film West*, 43, 2001, p.16.
15. Barton, *Irish National Cinema*, p.112.
16. Luke Gibbons, *Transformations in Irish Culture* (Cork: Cork University Press in association with Field Day, 1996), p.117.
17. Pettitt, *Screening Ireland*, p.276.
18. Ibid., pp.269–71.
19. McLoone, *Irish Film*, pp.185–6.
20. Ibid., pp.176–83.
21. Ibid., pp.168.
22. Barry Jordan and Rikki Morgan-Tamosunas, *Contemporary Spanish Cinema* (Manchester: Manchester University Press, 1998), p.114.
23. Mark Allinson, *Spanish Labyrinth: The Films of Pedro Almodóvar* (London: I.B.Tauris, 2001).
24. Martin McLoone, 'Music Hall Dope and British Propaganda? Cultural Identity and Early Broadcasting in Ireland', *Historical Journal of Film, Television and Radio*, 20, 3, 2000, p.313.
25. Peter Besas, *Behind the Spanish Lens: Spanish Cinema under Fascism and Democracy* (Denver, CO: Arden, 1985), p.100.
26. Frances Lannon, 'The Social Praxis and Cultural Politics of Spanish Catholicism' in Graham and Labanyi (eds), *Spanish Cultural Studies – an Introduction*, p.42.
27. Enric Ucelay da Cal, 'The Nationalisms of the Periphery: Culture and Politics in the Construction of National Identity' in Graham and Labanyi (eds), *Spanish Cultural Studies – an Introduction*, p.32.

28. Mike Richards, '"Terror and Progress": Industrialization, Modernity and the Making of Francoism' in Graham and Labanyi (eds), *Spanish Cultural Studies – an Introduction*, p.176.
29. Diarmaid Ferriter, *The Transformation of Ireland 1900–2000* (London: Profile Books, 2004), p.337.
30. Tom Inglis, *Moral Monopoly: The Catholic Church in Modern Irish Society* (Dublin: Gill and Macmillan, 1987), p.245.
31. Ibid., p.143.
32. Roy Foster, *Modern Ireland 1600–1972* (London: Allen Lane, 1989), p.573.
33. Ferriter, *Transformation of Ireland 1900–2000*, p.376.
34. Ibid., p.408.
35. Helen Graham and Jo Labanyi, 'Democracy and Europeanization: Continuity and Change' in Graham and Labanyi (eds), *Spanish Cultural Studies – an Introduction*, p.312.
36. Ferriter, *Transformation of Ireland 1900–2000*, p.536.
37. Foster, *Modern Ireland 1600–1972*, pp.579–80.
38. Lannon, 'Social Praxis and Cultural Politics of Spanish Catholicism', p.43.
39. Sebastian Balfour, 'Myth of National Identity' in Graham and Labanyi (eds), *Spanish Cultural Studies – an Introduction*, pp.25–31.
40. Ferriter, *Transformation of Ireland 1900–2000*, p.418.
41. Ibid., pp.417–18.
42. Herbert Rutledge Southworth, 'The Falange: An Analysis of Spain's Fascist Heritage' in Paul Preston (ed.), *Spain in Crisis* (Sussex: Harvester Press, 1976), p.1.
43. Ibid.
44. Ibid., p.14.
45. Stanley Payne, 'Spanish Fascism', *Salmagundi*, 76–77, fall 1987–winter 1988, pp.101–12.
46. Kinder, *Blood Cinema*, p.72.
47. Joan Esteban, 'The Economic Policy of Francoism: An Interpretation' in Preston (ed.), *Spain in Crisis*, pp.89–90.
48. Luke Gibbons, 'Romanticism, Realism and Irish Cinema' in Rockett, Gibbons and Hill, *Cinema and Ireland*, p.194.
49. Ibid., p.204.
50. Ibid., p.211.
51. Gibbons, *Transformations in Irish Culture*, p.172.
52. José F. Colmeiro, 'Exorcising Exoticism: Carmen and the Construction of Oriental Spain', *Comparative Literature*, 54, 2, 2002, p.127.
53. Román Gubern, '1930–1936: II Republic' in A. Martinez Torres (ed.), *Spanish Cinema 1896–1983* (Madrid: Minesterio de Cultura, 1986), pp.32–45.
54. Colmeiro, 'Exorcising Exoticism', p.130.
55. Marvin D'Lugo, *Carlos Saura: The Practice of Seeing* (Princeton, NJ : Princeton University Press, 1991), p.203.
56. Colmeiro, 'Exorcising Exoticism', p.129.
57. Balfour, 'Myth of National Identity', p.31.
58. Pettitt, *Screening Ireland*, p.89.
59. Barton, *Irish National Cinema*, p.42.
60. Ibid., p.44.
61. Declan Kiberd, *Inventing Ireland* (London: Jonathan Cape, 1995), p.381.
62. John Hill, 'Images of Violence' in Rockett, Gibbons and Hill, *Cinema and Ireland*, p.153.
63. Ibid., p.166.
64. Kiberd, *Inventing Ireland*, p.406.
65. Kinder, *Blood Cinema*, pp.197–274.
66. Ibid., p.218.
67. Timothy Mitchell, *Passional Culture: Emotion, Religion, and Society in Southern Spain* (Philadelphia: University of Pennsylvania Press, 1990).
68. Debbie Ging, 'The Lad from New Ireland: Marginalised, Disaffected and Criminal Masculinities in Contemporary Irish Cinema', *Film and Film Culture*, 3, 2004, pp.122–32.
69. Ibid., p.124.
70. Barton, *Irish National Cinema*, p.127.
71. Jordan and Morgan-Tamosunas, *Contemporary Spanish Cinema*, pp.140–1.
72. Barton, *Irish National Cinema*, p.114.
73. Kiberd, *Inventing Ireland*, p.101.

74. Gibbons, *Transformations in Irish Culture*, p.112.
75. Ibid., p.116.
76. Luke Gibbons, 'On the Beach', *Artforum*, October 1992, p.13.
77. Elizabeth Butler-Cullingford, *Ireland's Others: Gender and Ethnicity in Irish Literature and Popular Culture* (Cork: Cork University Press in association with Field Day, 2001), p.6.
78. Helen Graham, 'Gender and the State: Women in the 1940s' in Graham and Labanyi (eds), *Spanish Cultural Studies – an Introduction*, p.184.
79. Kinder, *Blood Cinema*, p.232.
80. Lesley Heins Walker, 'What Did I Do to Deserve This? The Mother in the Films of Pedro Almodóvar' in Jenaro Talens and Santos Zunzunequi (eds), *Modes of Representation in Spanish Cinema* (Minneapolis: University of Minnesota Press, 1998), p.274.
81. Paul Julian Smith, 'Eloy de la Iglesia's Cinema of Transition', in Talens and Zunzunequi (eds), *Modes of Representation in Spanish Cinema*, p.241.
82. Marvin D'Lugo, 'Almodóvar's City of Desire' in Kathleen Vernon and Barbara Morris (eds), *The Films of Pedro Almodóvar* (Westport CT: Greenwood Press, 1995), p.126.
83. Ibid.
84. Esteban, 'Economic Policy of Francoism', p.86.
85. Raymond Carr, *Modern Spain 1875–1980* (Oxford: Oxford University Press, 1980), pp.156–9.
86. D'Lugo, 'Almodóvar's City of Desire', p.126.
87. Jordan and Morgan-Tamasunas, *Contemporary Spanish Cinema*, p.46.
88. Rockett, 'History, Politics and Irish Cinema', p.31.
89. McLoone, *Irish Film*, p.201.
90. Ibid., pp.38–44.
91. Ibid., p.53.
92. Barton, *Irish National Cinema*, p.45.
93. McLoone, *Irish Film*, p.202.
94. Ibid., p.203.

CHAPTER 2: POWER AND PATRIARCHY

95. McLoone, *Irish Film*, p.176.
96. Inglis, *Moral Monopoly*, p.184.
97. Gibbons, *Transformations in Irish Culture*, p.131.
98. Kiberd, *Inventing Ireland*, p.388.
99. Ibid., p.380.
100. Ibid., pp.380–3.
101. Richard Kearney, *Postnationalist Ireland: Politics, Culture, Philosophy* (London and New York: Routledge, 1997), p.119.
102. Ibid.
103. Angela Martin, 'Death of a Nation: Transnationalism, Bodies and Abortion in late Twenti-eth-Century Ireland' in Tamar Mayer (ed.), *Gender Ironies of Nationalism: Sexing the Nation* (London and New York: Routledge, 2000), p.75.
104. Kearney, *Postnationalist Ireland*, p.119.
105. Inglis, *Moral Monopoly*, p.189.
106. Kiberd, *Inventing Ireland*, p.389.
107. Ibid.
108. Ibid., p.380.
109. Fintan O'Toole, 'In the Land of the Emerald Tiger', *Irish Times*, 28 December 1996.
110. Inglis, *Moral Monopoly*, p.137.
111. Virginia Higginbotham, *Spanish Film under Franco* (Austin: University of Texas Press, 1988), p.20.
112. Kinder, *Blood Cinema*, p.143.
113. Jesús González-Requena, '*Vida en Sombras*: The Recusado's Shadow' in Talens and Zunzunequi (eds), *Modes of Representation in Spanish Cinema*, p.87.
114. Ibid., p.86.
115. Ibid., p.90.
116. Kinder, *Blood Cinema*, p.144.

117. Izvetan Todorov, *The Conquest of America*, trans. Richard Howard (New York: Harper & Row, 1984), p.143.
118. Ibid., p.144.
119. Ibid.
120. Southworth, 'The Falange: An Analysis of Spain's Fascist Heritage', p.15.
121. Carr, *Modern Spain 1875–1980*, p.165.
122. Kinder, *Blood Cinema*, p.142.
123. Alun Kenwood, 'Art, Propaganda, Commitment: Hispanic Literature and the War' in Alun Kenwood (ed.), *The Spanish Civil War: A Cultural and Historical Reader* (Providence, RI: Berg, 1993), p.36.
124. Kenwood (ed.), *Spanish Civil War: A Cultural and Historical Reader*.
125. Kinder, *Blood Cinema*, p.150.
126. Todorov, *Conquest of America*, p.143.
127. Stephen Tropicano, 'Out of the Cinematic Closet: Homosexuality in the Films of Eloy de la Iglesia' in Marsha Kinder (ed.), *Refiguring Spain* (Durham, NC: Duke University Press, 1997), p.161.
128. Kinder, *Blood Cinema*, p.60.
129. González-Requena, 'Vida en Sombras: The Recusado's Shadow', p.85.
130. Gwynne Edwards, *Indecent Exposures* (London: Marian Boyars, 1995), p.194.
131. Michel Foucault, *Power: Essential Works of Michel Foucault 1954–1984*, ed. James D. Faubion (Harmondsworth: Penguin, 2000), p.340.
132. Ibid., p.341.
133. Michel Foucault, *Discipline and Punish: The Birth of the Prison*, trans. Alan Sheridan (London: Allen Lane, 1977), pp.176–7.
134. Kiberd, *Inventing Ireland*, p.389.
135. Ibid., p.406.
136. Graham, 'Gender and the State: Women in the 1940s', p.184.
137. Jean Baudrillard, *Simulacra and Simulation* (Ann Arbor: University of Michigan Press, 1994), p.44.
138. Kiberd, *Inventing Ireland*, p.390.
139. Mitchell, *Passional Culture*, p.37.
140. Kiberd, *Inventing Ireland*, p.381.
141. McLoone, *Irish Film*, p.179.
142. Geraldine Moane, 'Colonialism and the Celtic Tiger: Legacies of History and the Quest for Vision' in Peadar Kirby, Luke Gibbons and Michael Cronin (eds), *Reinventing Ireland: Culture, Society and the Global Economy* (London: Pluto Press, 2002), pp.109–23.
143. Chris Perriam, 'Alejandro Amenábar's *Abre los ojos/Open Your Eyes* (1997)' in Antonio Lázaro Reboll and Andrew Willis (eds), *Spanish Popular Cinema* (Manchester: Manchester University Press, 2004), p.214.
144. Ibid., p.210.

CHAPTER 3: FEMININITY, SEXUALITY AND SPACE

145. Martin, 'Transnationalism, Bodies and Abortion in late Twentieth-Century Ireland', p.77.
146. Barton, *Irish National Cinema*, p.113.
147. Martin, 'Transnationalism, Bodies and Abortion in late Twentieth-Century Ireland', p.75.
148. J.J. Lee, 'Women and the Church since the Famine' in Alan Hayes and Diane Urquhart (eds), *The Irish Women's History Reader* (London and New York: Routledge, 2001), p.133.
149. Rosemary Cullen Owens, *A Social History of Women in Ireland 1870–1970* (Dublin: Gill and Macmillan, 2005), p.171.
150. Ibid., p.165.
151. Ibid., p.166.
152. Dympna McLoughlin, 'Women and Sexuality in Nineteenth-Century Ireland' in Hayes and Urquhart (eds), *Irish Women's History Reader*, p.81.
153. Cullen Owens, *Social History of Women in Ireland 1870–1970*, p.169.
154. Maryann Valiulis, 'Neither Feminist nor Flapper: the Ecclesiastical Construction of the Ideal Irish Woman' in Hayes and Urquhart (eds), *Irish Women's History Reader*, p.155.
155. McLoughlin, 'Women and Sexuality in Nineteenth-Century Ireland', p.85.

156. Lee, 'Women and the Church since the Famine', p.135.
157. Joanna Bourke, 'The Best of all Home-Rulers: The Economic Power of Women in Ireland 1880–1914' in Hayes and Urquhart (eds), *Irish Women's History Reader*, p.203.
158. McLoughlin, 'Women and Sexuality in Nineteenth-Century Ireland', p.82.
159. Balfour, 'Myth of National Identity', p.30.
160. Ibid.
161. Helen Graham, 'Women and Social Change' in Graham and Labanyi (eds), *Spanish Cultural Studies – an Introduction*, p.104.
162. Heins Walker, 'Mother in the Films of Pedro Almodóvar', p.276.
163. John Hooper, *The New Spaniards* (Harmondsworth: Penguin, 1995), p.165.
164. Ibid.
165. Graham, 'Gender and the State: Women in the 1940s', p.184.
166. Ibid.
167. Kinder, *Blood Cinema*, p.198.
168. Ibid., p.188.
169. Gibbons, *Transformations in Irish Culture*, p.130.
170. Maria Luddy, 'Women and Politics in Nineteenth-Century Ireland' in Hayes and Urquhart (eds), *Irish Women's History Reader*, pp.30–2.
171. Graham, 'Women and Social Change', p.102.
172. Cullen Owens, *Social History of Women in Ireland 1870–1970*, p.111.
173. Ibid., p.123.
174. Mary Clancy, 'Aspects of Women's Contributions to the Oireachtas Debate in the Irish Free State 1922–1937' in Maria Luddy and C. Murphy (eds), *Women Surviving: Studies in Irish Women's History in the Nineteenth and Twentieth Centuries* (Dublin: Poolbeg, 1990), pp.206–32.
175. Graham, 'Women and Social Change', p.104.
176. Butler-Cullingford, *Ireland's Others*, p.5.
177. Jordan and Morgan-Tamosunas, *Contemporary Spanish Cinema*, p.132.
178. Peter William Evans, '*Furtivos*: My Mother, My Lover' in Peter William Evans (ed.), *Spanish Cinema: The Auteurist Tradition* (Oxford: Oxford University Press, 1999), p.118.
179. María José Gámez Fuentes, 'Women in Spanish Cinema: "Raiders of the Missing Mother"', *Cineaste*, 29, 1, 2003, p.39.
180. Evans, '*Furtivos*: My Mother, My Lover', p.126.
181. Ibid., p.122.
182. Jordan and Morgan-Tamosunas, *Contemporary Spanish Cinema*, p.132.
183. Kiberd, *Inventing Ireland*, p.381.
184. McLoone, *Irish Film*, p.172.
185. Ibid., p.178.
186. Barton, *Irish National Cinema*, p.120.
187. Candyce Leonard, '*Solas* and the Unbearable Condition of Loneliness in the Late 1990s' in Lázaro Reboll and Willis (eds), *Spanish Popular Cinema*, p.225.
188. Inglis, *Moral Monopoly*, p.142.
189. Kiberd, *Inventing Ireland*, pp.395–407.
190. Carol Pateman, *The Disorder of Women: Democracy, Feminism and Political Theory* (Cambridge, MA: Polity Press, 1989), p.43.
191. Janet Wolff, 'The Invisible *Flâneuse*: Women and the Literature of Modernity' in Andrew Benjamin (ed.), *The Problems of Modernity: Adorno and Benjamin* (London and New York: Routledge, 1989), p.152.
192. James MacPherson, 'Ireland Begins in the Home: Women, Irish National Identity and the Domestic Sphere in the Irish Homestead 1896–1912', *Eire/Ireland*, fall/winter 2001.
193. Margaret Ward, 'Marginality and Militancy: Cumann na mBan 1914–1936' in Hayes and Urquhart (eds), *Irish Women's History Reader*, p.59.
194. Graham, 'Gender and the State: Women in the 1940s', p.189.
195. Jo Labanyi, 'Feminizing the Nation: Women, Subordination and Subversion in Post-Civil War Spanish Cinema' in Ulrike Sieglohr (ed.), *Heroines Without Heroes: Reconstructing Female and National Identities in European Cinema 1945–1951* (London: Cassell, 2000), p.164.
196. Valiulis, 'Neither Feminist nor Flapper', p.156.
197. Griselda Pollock, *Vision and Difference: Femininity, Feminism and Histories of Art* (London and New York: Routledge, 1988), p.69.

198. Ibid., p.71.
199. Ibid., p.67.
200. Ibid., p.69.
201. Elizabeth Wilson, 'Into the Labyrinth' in Linda McDowell and Joanne P. Sharp (eds), *Space, Gender, Knowledge: Feminist Readings* (London and New York: Edward Arnold, 1997), p.280.
202. Daniel Kowalsky, 'Rated S: Softcore Pornography and the Spanish Transition to Democracy 1977–1982' in Lázaro Reboll and Willis (eds), *Spanish Popular Cinema*, p.193.
203. Marsha Kinder, 'Refiguring Socialist Spain: An Introduction' in Kinder (ed.), *Refiguring Spain*, p.3.
204. Ricardo Roque-Baldovinos, 'Jose Luis García-Sánchez's "*Pasdoble*"' in Talens and Zunzunequi (eds), *Modes of Representation in Spanish Cinema*, p.260.
205. Pettitt, *Screening Ireland*, p.272.
206. Smith, 'Eloy de la Iglesia's Cinema of Transition', p.225.
207. Paul Julian Smith, *Laws of Desire: Questions of Homosexuality in Spanish Writing and Film 1960–1990* (Oxford: Clarendon Press, 1992), p.168.

CHAPTER 4: THE CITY SPACE

208. David Clarke, 'Introduction: Previewing the Cinematic City' in David Clarke (ed.), *The Cinematic City* (London and New York: Routledge, 1997), p.4.
209. Raymond Williams, *The Country and the City* (London: Chatto & Windus, 1973), p.150.
210. Ibid., p.241.
211. Felizitas Lenz-Romeiss, *The City – New Town or Home Town*, trans. Edith Küstner and J.A. Underwood (London: Pall Mall, 1973), p.53.
212. David Pinder, 'Ghostly Footsteps: Voices, Memories and Walks in the City', *Ecumene* 8, 1, 2001, p.2.
213. Scott MacDonald, *The Garden in the Machine* (Berkeley and Los Angeles: University of California Press, 2001), p.189.
214. Antonio Sanchez, 'Barcelona's Magic Mirror: Narcissism or the Rediscovery of Public Space and Collective Identity' in Jo Labanyi (ed.), *Constructing Identity in Contemporary Spain* (Oxford: Oxford University Press, 2000), p.304.
215. Edward Soja, *Postmodern Geographies* (London and New York: Verso, 1989), p.126.
216. Ibid., p.127.
217. MacDonald, *Garden in the Machine*, p.218.
218. Mark Shiel, 'Cinema and the City in History and Theory' in Mark Shiel and Tony Fitzmaurice (eds), *Cinema and the City* (Oxford: Blackwell, 2001), p.2.
219. MacDonald, *Garden in the Machine*, p.153.
220. Helmut Weihsmann, 'The City in Twilight: Charting the Genre of the "City Film" 1900–1930' in Francois Penz and Maureen Thomas (eds), *Cinema and Architecture: Méliès, Mallet-Stevens, Multimedia* (London: British Film Institute, 1997), p.23.
221. Henri Lefebvre, *The Production of Space*, trans. Donald Nicholson-Smith (Oxford: Blackwell, 1991), p.21.
222. Ibid.
223. Jill Forbes, *Les Enfants du Paradis* (London: British Film Institute, 1997), p.21.
224. Susan Hayward, 'The City as Narrative: Corporeal Paris in Contemporary French Cinema (1950s–1990s)' in Myrto Konstantarakos (ed.), *Spaces in European Cinema* (Exeter and Portland, OR: Intellect, 2000), p.23.
225. Lefebvre, *Production of Space*, p.225.
226. Ibid., p.220.
227. Paul Julian Smith, *The Moderns* (Oxford: Oxford University Press, 2000), p.113.
228. Colm Lincoln, 'City of Culture: Dublin and the Discovery of Urban Heritage' in Barbara O'-Connor and Michael Cronin (eds), *Tourism in Ireland* (Cork: Cork University Press, 1993), p.211.
229. Hayward, 'City as Narrative', p.30.
230. Smith, *The Moderns*, p.124.
231. Kevin Rockett, '(Mis-)Representing the Irish Urban Landscape' in Shiel and Fitzmaurice (eds), *Cinema and the City*, p.225.

232. Soja, *Postmodern Geographies*, p.234.
233. Ibid.
234. Lincoln, 'City of Culture: Dublin and the Discovery of Urban Heritage', p.219.
235. Ibid., p.212.
236. Terry Eagleton, 'Nationalism: Irony and Commitment' in Seamus Deane (ed.), *Nationalism, Colonialism and Literature* (Minneapolis: University of Minnesota Press, 1988), p.36.
237. Fintan O'Toole, 'Myth that Lets Dublin 4 Evade its Responsibility' *Irish Times*, 27 May 1992.
238. Deborah Parsons, 'Fiesta Culture in Madrid Posters 1935–1955' in Jo Labanyi (ed.), *Constructing Identity in Contemporary Spain* (Oxford: Oxford University Press, 2000), p.180.
239. Ibid., p.195.
240. Ibid., pp.183–5.
241. Martin McLoone, *Film, Media and Popular Culture in Ireland* (Dublin and Portland, OR: Irish Academic Press, 2007), p.37.
242. David Bass, 'Insiders and Outsiders: Latent Urban Thinking in Movies of Modern Rome' in Penz and Thomas (eds), *Cinema and Architecture*, p.85.
243. Ibid., p.86.
244. Ibid., p.88.
245. Ibid.
246. Ibid., p.91.
247. Jeff Hoplans, 'A Mapping of Cinematic Places: Icons, Ideology and the Power of (Mis)representation' in Stuart C. Aitken and Leo E. Zohn (eds), *Place, Power, Situation and Spectacle: A Geography of Film* (Maryland and London: Rowman & Littlefield, 1994), p.50.
248. Michel de Certeau, *The Practice of Everyday Life*, trans. Steven Rendall (Berkeley and London: University of California Press, 1988), p.117.
249. Ewa Mazierska and Laura Rascaroli, *From Moscow to Madrid: Postmodern Cities, European Cinema* (London and New York: I.B. Tauris, 2003), p.18.
250. Kevin Lynch, *The Image of the City* (Massachusetts: MIT Press, 1960).
251. Rockett, '(Mis-)Representing the Irish Urban Landscape', p.218.
252. D'Lugo, 'Almodóvar's City of Desire', p.125.
253. De Certeau, *Practice of Everyday Life*, p.103.
254. Ibid.
255. bell hooks, 'Homeplace: a Site of Resistance' in bell hooks (ed.), *Yearning: Race, Gender, and Cultural Politics* (Boston: South End Press, 1991), pp.41–50.
256. De Certeau, *Practice of Everyday Life*, p.xix.
257. Ibid., p.37.
258. Ibid.
259. Ibid., p.29.
260. Desmond Bell, 'Ireland Without Frontiers? The Challenge of the Communications Revolution' in Richard Kearney (ed.), *Across the Frontiers: Ireland in the 1990s* (Dublin: Wolfhound Press, 1988), pp.228–229.
261. De Certeau, *Practice of Everyday Life*, p.95.
262. David Harvey, *The Condition of Postmodernity: an Enquiry into the Origins of Cultural Change* (Oxford: Blackwell, 1989), p.117.
263. Soja, *Postmodern Geographies*, p.246.
264. Linda Hutcheon, 'Circling the Downspout of Empire' in Bill Ashcroft, Gareth Griffiths and Helen Tiffin (eds), *The Post-Colonial Studies Reader* (London and New York: Routledge, 1995), pp.130–1.
265. Sanchez, 'Barcelona's Magic Mirror', p.301.
266. Shiel, 'Cinema and the City', pp.11–12.
267. Smith, *The Moderns*, p.129.
268. Hayward, 'City as Narrative', p.33.
269. Manuel Castells, 'European Cities, the Informational Society, and the Global Economy' in Richard T. Le Gates and Frederic Stout (eds), *The City Reader* (London and New York: Routledge, 1996), p.495.
270. De Certeau, *Practice of Everyday Life*, p.29.

CHAPTER 5: THE NATIONAL PAST

271. Conor McCarthy, *Modernisation: Crisis and Culture in Ireland 1969–1992* (Dublin: Four Courts Press, 2000), p.30.
272. Clare Carroll, 'Introduction: The Nation and Postcolonial Theory' in Clare Carroll and Patricia King (eds), *Ireland and Postcolonial Theory* (Cork: Cork University Press, 2003), pp.10–11.
273. De Certeau, *Practice of Everyday Life*, pp.128–9.
274. Fintan O'Toole, *The Ex-Isle of Erin: Images of Global Ireland* (Dublin: New Ireland Books, 1997), p.16.
275. Ernest Gellner, *Nations and Nationalism* (Oxford: Blackwell, 1983).
276. Ryuzo Uchida, 'Memory and the Transformation of Social Experience in Modern Japan', *Media, Culture and Society*, 21, 1999, p.212.
277. Harry Harootunian, 'Shadowing History', *Cultural Studies*, 18, 2/3, 2004, p.184.
278. De Certeau, *Practice of Everyday Life*, pp.128–9.
279. Paul Connerton, *How Societies Remember* (Cambridge: Cambridge University Press, 1989), p.26.
280. Kenwood (ed), *Spanish Civil War: A Cultural and Historical Reader*, pp.158–9.
281. Inglis, *Moral Monopoly*, p.100.
282. Stuart McLean, *The Event and its Terrors: Ireland, Famine, Modernity* (Stanford: Stanford University Press, 2004), p.14.
283. Ibid., p.29.
284. Ibid., p.14.
285. Rainer Nägelle, *Theatre, Theory, Speculation: Walter Benjamin and Scenes of Modernity* (Baltimore, MD: Johns Hopkins University Press, 1991), p.88.
286. Samuel Taylor Coleridge, 'The Statesman's Manual', reprinted in Hazard Adams and Leroy Searle, *Critical Theory since Plato* (New York: Harcourt Brace Jovanovich, 1971), p.468.
287. Vance Bell, 'Falling into Time: The Historicity of the Symbol', *Other Voices*, 1, 1, 1997, http://www.othervoices.org
288. Ibid.
289. Ibid.
290. Gershom Scholem, *Major Trends in Jewish Mysticism* (New York: Schocken Books, 1946), p.26.
291. Bell, 'Falling into Time: The Historicity of the Symbol'.
292. Ibid.
293. Walter Benjamin, *The Origin of German Tragic Drama*, trans. John Osborne (London and New York: Verso, 1977), p.179.
294. McLoone, *Irish Film*, pp.213–23.
295. Ibid., p.221.
296. McLean, *Ireland, Famine, Modernity*, p.156.
297. Ibid.
298. Susan J. Brison, 'Trauma Narratives and the Remaking of the Self' in Mieke Bal, Jonathon Crewe and Leo Spitzer (eds), *Acts of Memory: Cultural Recall in the Present* (Hanover, NH: University Press of New England, 1999), p.39.
299. Ibid., p.40.
300. Ibid., p.41.
301. Kevin Whelan, 'Between Filiation and Affiliation: The Politics of Postcolonial Memory' in Carroll and King (eds), *Ireland and Postcolonial Theory*, p.100.
302. James M. Smith, 'Remembering Ireland's Architecture of Containment: "Telling" Stories in *The Butcher Boy* and *States of Fear*' *Eire/Ireland*, fall/winter 2001.
303. Ibid.
304. Ibid.
305. Ernst Van Alphen, 'Symptoms of Discursivity: Experience, Memory and Trauma' in Bal, Crewe and Spitzer (eds), *Cultural Recall in the Present*, p.27.
306. Inglis, *Moral Monopoly*.
307. De Certeau, *Practice of Everyday Life*, p.32.
308. Whelan, 'Between Filiation and Affiliation: The Politics of Postcolonial Memory', pp.107–8.
309. Ibid., p.108.

310. Ibid., p.93.
311. Ibid.
312. Ibid., p.97.
313. Ibid.
314. Ibid., p.93.
315. Svetlana Boym, *The Future of Nostalgia* (New York: Basic Books, 2001).
316. Ibid., p.xviii.
317. Ibid., p.50.
318. Ibid.., p.49.
319. Whelan, 'Between Filiation and Affiliation: The Politics of Postcolonial Memory', p.93.
320. David Lloyd, 'After History: Historicism and Irish Postcolonial Studies' in Carroll and King (eds), *Ireland and Postcolonial Theory*, p.46.
321. Richard Kearney, *On Stories* (London and New York: Routledge, 2002), p.154.
322. Ibid., pp.146–7.

Bibliography

Allinson, Mark, *Spanish Labyrinth: The Films of Pedro Almodóvar* (London: I.B. Tauris, 2001)

Balfour, Sebastian, 'Myth of National Identity' in Helen Graham and Jo Labanyi (eds), *Spanish Cultural Studies – an Introduction: The Struggle for Modernity* (Oxford: Oxford University Press, 1995), pp.25–31

Barton, Ruth, *Irish National Cinema* (London and New York: Routledge, 2004)

'Introduction' in Ruth Barton and Harvey O'Brien (eds), *Keeping it Real: Irish Film and Television* (London: Wallflower Press, 2004), pp.1–5

Bass, David, 'Insiders and Outsiders: Latent Urban Thinking in Movies of Modern Rome' in Francois Penz and Maureen Thomas (eds), *Cinema and Architecture: Méliès, Mallet-Stevens, Multimedia* (London: British Film Institute, 1997), pp.84–101

Baudrillard, Jean, *Simulacra and Simulation* (Ann Arbor: University of Michigan Press, 1994)

Bell, Desmond, 'Ireland Without Frontiers? The Challenge of the Communications Revolution' in Richard Kearney (ed.), *Across the Frontiers: Ireland in the 1990s* (Dublin: Wolfhound Press, 1988), pp.219–30

Bell, Vance, 'Falling into Time: The Historicity of the Symbol', *Other Voices*, 1, 1 (1997), accessed on 5 April 2006 at http://www.othervoices.org

Benjamin, Walter, *The Origin of German Tragic Drama*, trans. John Osborne (London and New York: Verso, 1977)

Besas, Peter, *Behind the Spanish Lens: Spanish Cinema under Fascism and Democracy* (Denver, CO: Arden, 1985)

Bew, Paul, 'The National Question, Land and "Revisionism": Some Reflections' in D. George Boyce and Alan O'Day (eds), *Modern Irish History: Revisionism and the Revisionist Controversy* (London and New York: Routledge, 1996), pp.90–9

Bourke, Joanna, 'The Best of all Home-Rulers: The Economic Power of Women in Ireland 1880–1914' in Alan Hayes and Diane Urquhart (eds), *The Irish Women's History Reader* (London and New York: Routledge, 2001), pp.203–8

Boym, Svetlana, *The Future of Nostalgia* (New York: Basic Books, 2001)

Bradshaw, Brendan, 'Nationalism and Historical Scholarship in Modern Ireland', *Irish Historical Studies*, 26, 1/4 (1989), pp.329–51

Brison, Susan J., 'Trauma Narratives and the Remaking of the Self' in Mieke Bal, Jonathon Crewe and Leo Spitzer (eds), *Acts of Memory: Cultural Recall in the Present* (Hanover, NH: University Press of New England, 1999), pp.39–54

Butler-Cullingford, Elizabeth, *Ireland's Others: Gender and Ethnicity in Irish Literature and Popular Culture* (Cork: Cork University Press in association with Field Day, 2001)

Carr, Raymond, *Modern Spain 1875–1980* (Oxford: Oxford University Press, 1980)

Carroll, Clare, 'Introduction: The Nation and Postcolonial Theory' in Irish Studies in Clare Carroll and Patricia King (eds), *Ireland and Postcolonial Theory* (Cork: Cork University Press, 2003), pp.1–15

Castells, Manuel, 'European Cities, the Informational Society, and the Global Economy' in Richard T. Le Gates and Frederic Stout (eds), *The City Reader* (London and New York: Routledge, 1996), pp.494–8

Clancy, Mary, 'Aspects of Women's Contributions to the Oireachtas Debate in the Irish Free State 1922–1937' in Maria Luddy and C. Murphy (eds), *Women Surviving: Studies in Irish Women's History in the Nineteenth and Twentieth Centuries* (Dublin: Poolbeg, 1990), pp.206–32

Clarke, David, 'Introduction: Previewing the Cinematic City' in David Clarke (ed.), *The Cinematic City* (London and New York: Routledge, 1997), pp.1–18

Cleary, Joe, 'Misplaced Ideas?: Colonialism, Location, and Dislocation in Irish Studies' in Clare Carroll and Patricia King (eds), *Ireland and Postcolonial Theory* (Cork: Cork University Press, 2003), pp.16–45

Coleridge, Samuel Taylor, 'The Statesman's Manual', reprinted in Hazard Adams and Leroy Searle, *Critical Theory since Plato* (New York: Harcourt Brace Jovanovich, 1971), p.468

Colmeiro, José F., 'Exorcising Exoticism: Carmen and the Construction of Oriental Spain', *Comparative Literature*, 54, 2 (2002), pp.127–44

Connerton, Paul, *How Societies Remember* (Cambridge: Cambridge

University Press, 1989)

Connolly, S.J., 'Eighteenth Century Ireland' in D. George Boyce and Alan O'Day (eds), *Modern Irish History: Revisionism and the Revisionist Controversy* (London and New York: Routledge, 1996), pp.15–33

Crotty, Raymond, *Irish Agricultural Production: Its Volume and Structure* (Cork: Cork University Press, 1966)

Cullen, L.M., *An Economic History of Ireland since 1660* (London: Batsford, 1972)

Cullen Owens, Rosemary, *A Social History of Women in Ireland 1870–1970* (Dublin: Gill and Macmillan, 2005)

De Certeau, Michel, *The Practice of Everyday Life*, trans. Steven Rendall (Berkeley and London: University of California Press, 1988)

Deleuze, Gilles, *Cinema 2: The Time-Image*, trans. Hugh Tomlinson and Roberta Galeta (London: Athlone Press, 1989)

D'Lugo, Marvin, *Carlos Saura: The Practice of Seeing* (Princeton, NJ: Princeton University Press, 1991)

'Almodóvar's City of Desire' in Kathleen Vernon and Barbara Morris (eds), *The Films of Pedro Almodóvar* (Westport CT: Greenwood Press, 1995), pp.125–44

Eagleton, Terry, 'Nationalism: Irony and Commitment' in Seamus Deane (ed.), *Nationalism, Colonialism and Literature* (Minneapolis: University of Minnesota Press, 1988), pp.23–42

Edwards, Gwynne, *Indecent Exposures* (London: Marian Boyars, 1995)

Esteban, Joan, 'The Economic Policy of Francoism: An Interpretation' in Paul Preston (ed.), *Spain in Crisis* (Sussex: Harvester Press, 1976), pp.82–100

Evans, Peter William, 'Cifesa: Cinema and Authoritarian Aesthetics' in Helen Graham and Jo Labanyi (eds), *Spanish Cultural Studies – an Introduction: The Struggle for Modernity* (Oxford: Oxford University Press, 1995), pp.215–22

'*Furtivos*: My Mother, My Lover' in Peter William Evans (ed.), *Spanish Cinema: The Auteurist Tradition* (Oxford: Oxford University Press, 1999), pp.115–27

Ferriter, Diarmaid, *The Transformation of Ireland 1900–2000* (London: Profile Books, 2004)

Forbes, Jill, *Les Enfants du Paradis* (London: British Film Institute, 1997)

Foster, Roy, *Modern Ireland 1600–1972* (London: Allen Lane, 1989)

Foucault, Michel, *Discipline and Punish: The Birth of the Prison*, trans. Alan Sheridan (London: Allen Lane, 1977)

Power: Essential Works of Michel Foucault 1954–1984, ed. James D. Faubion (Harmondsworth: Penguin, 2000)

Gámez Fuentes, María José, 'Women in Spanish Cinema: "Raiders of the Missing Mother"', *Cineaste*, 29, 1 (2003), pp.38–43

Gellner, Ernest, *Nations and Nationalism* (Oxford: Blackwell, 1983)

Gibbons, Luke, 'Romanticism, Realism and Irish Cinema' in Kevin Rockett, Luke Gibbons and John Hill, *Cinema and Ireland* (London: Routledge, 1988), pp.194–257

'On the Beach', *Artforum* (October 1992), p.13

Transformations in Irish Culture (Cork: Cork University Press in association with Field Day, 1996)

Ging, Debbie, 'The Lad from New Ireland: Marginalised, Disaffected and Criminal Masculinities in Contemporary Irish Cinema', *Film and Film Culture*, 3 (2004), pp.122–32

Girard, René, *Violence and the Sacred*, trans. Patrick Gregory (Baltimore, MD: Johns Hopkins University Press, 1977)

González-Requena, Jesús, '*Vida en Sombras*: The Recusado's Shadow' in Jenaro Talens and Santos Zunzunequi (eds), *Modes of Representation in Spanish Cinema* (Minneapolis: University of Minnesota Press, 1998), pp.81–103

Gordon, Colin (ed.), *Power/Knowledge: Selected Interviews and Other Writings 1972–1977. Michel Foucault* (New York: Pantheon, 1980)

Graham, Helen, 'Gender and the State: Women in the 1940s' in Helen Graham and Jo Labanyi (eds), *Spanish Cultural Studies – an Introduction: The Struggle for Modernity* (Oxford: Oxford University Press, 1995), pp.183–95

'Women and Social Change' in Helen Graham and Jo Labanyi (eds), *Spanish Cultural Studies – an Introduction: The Struggle for Modernity* (Oxford: Oxford University Press, 1995), pp.99–115

Graham, Helen and Labanyi, Jo, 'Democracy and Europeanization: Continuity and Change' in Helen Graham and Jo Labanyi (eds), *Spanish Cultural Studies – an Introduction: The Struggle for Modernity* (Oxford: Oxford University Press, 1995), pp.311–13

Gubern, Román, '1930–1936: II Republic' in A. Martinez Torres (ed.), *Spanish Cinema 1896–1983* (Madrid: Minesterio de Cultura, 1986), pp.32–45

Harootunian, Harry, 'Shadowing History', *Cultural Studies*, 18, 2/3 (2004), pp.181–200

Harvey, David, *The Condition of Postmodernity: an Enquiry into the Origins of Cultural Change* (Oxford: Blackwell, 1989)

Hayward, Susan, 'The City as Narrative: Corporeal Paris in Contemporary French Cinema (1950s–1990s)' in Myrto Konstantarakos (ed.), *Spaces in European Cinema* (Exeter and Portland, OR: Intellect, 2000), pp.23–34

Heins Walker, Lesley, 'What Did I Do to Deserve This? The Mother in the Films of Pedro Almodóvar' in Jenaro Talens and Santos Zunzunegui (eds), *Modes of Representation in Spanish Cinema* (Minneapolis: University of Minnesota Press, 1998), pp.273–88

Higginbotham, Virginia, *Spanish Film Under Franco* (Austin: University of Texas Press, 1988)

Hill, John, 'Images of Violence' in Kevin Rockett, Luke Gibbons and John Hill, *Cinema and Ireland* (London: Routledge, 1988), pp.147–93

Hjort, Mette, 'Themes of Nation' in Mette Hjort and Scott Mackenzie (eds), *Cinema and Nation* (London and New York: Routledge, 2000), pp.103–18

hooks, bell, 'Homeplace: a Site of Resistance' in bell hooks (ed.), *Yearning: Race, Gender, and Cultural Politics* (Boston: South End Press, 1991), pp.41–50

Hooper, John, *The New Spaniards* (Harmondsworth: Penguin, 1995)

Hoplans, Jeff, 'A Mapping of Cinematic Places: Icons, Ideology and the Power of (Mis)representation' in Stuart C. Aitken and Leo E. Zohn (eds), *Place, Power, Situation and Spectacle: A Geography of Film* (Maryland and London: Rowman & Littlefield, 1994), pp.47–68

Hutcheon, Linda, 'Circling the Downspout of Empire' in Bill Ashcroft, Gareth Griffiths and Helen Tiffin (eds), *The Post-Colonial Studies Reader* (London and New York: Routledge, 1995)

Hutchinson, John, 'Irish Nationalism' in D. George Boyce and Alan O'Day (eds), *Modern Irish History: Revisionism and the Revisionist Controversy* (London and New York: Routledge, 1996), pp.100–19

Inglis, Tom, *Moral Monopoly: The Catholic Church in Modern Irish Society* (Dublin: Gill and Macmillan, 1987)

Jordan, Barry and Morgan-Tamosunas, Rikki, *Contemporary Spanish Cinema* (Manchester: Manchester University Press, 1998)

Kearney, Richard, *Postnationalist Ireland: Politics, Culture, Philosophy* (London and New York: Routledge, 1997)

On Stories (London and New York: Routledge, 2002)

Kenwood, Alun, 'Art, Propaganda, Commitment: Hispanic Literature and the War' in Alun Kenwood (ed.), *The Spanish Civil War: A Cultural and Historical Reader* (Providence, RI: Berg, 1993), pp.27–38

Kenwood, Alun (ed.), *The Spanish Civil War: A Cultural and Historical Reader* (Providence, RI: Berg, 1993)

Kiberd, Declan, *Inventing Ireland* (London: Jonathan Cape, 1995)

Kinder, Marsha, *Blood Cinema: The Reconstruction of National Identity in Spain* (Berkeley: University of California Press, 1993)

'Refiguring Socialist Spain: An Introduction' in Marsha Kinder (ed.), *Refiguring Spain: Cinema/Media/Representation* (Durham, NC and London: Duke University Press, 1997), pp.1–32

Kowalsky, Daniel, 'Rated S: Softcore Pornography and the Spanish Transition to Democracy 1977–1982' in Antonio Lázaro Reboll and Andrew Willis (eds), *Spanish Popular Cinema* (Manchester: Manchester University Press, 2004), pp.188–208

Labanyi, Jo, 'Feminizing the Nation: Women, Subordination and Subversion in Post-Civil War Spanish Cinema' in Ulrike Sieglohr (ed.), *Heroines Without Heroes: Reconstructing Female and National Identities in European Cinema 1945–1951* (London: Cassell, 2000), pp.163–82

Lannon, Frances, 'The Social Praxis and Cultural Politics of Spanish Catholicism' in Helen Graham and Jo Labanyi (eds), *Spanish Cultural Studies – an Introduction: The Struggle for Modernity* (Oxford: Oxford University Press, 1995), pp.40–4

Lee, J.J., 'Women and the Church since the Famine' in Alan Hayes and Diane Urquhart (eds), *The Irish Women's History Reader* (London and New York: Routledge, 2001), pp.133–8

Lefebvre, Henri, *The Production of Space*, trans. Donald Nicholson-Smith (Oxford: Blackwell, 1991)

Lenz-Romeiss, Felizitas, *The City – New Town or Home Town*, trans. Edith Küstner and J.A. Underwood (London: Pall Mall, 1973)

Leonard, Candyce, '*Solas* and the Unbearable Condition of Loneliness in the Late 1990s' in Antonio Lázaro Reboll and Andrew Willis (eds), *Spanish Popular Cinema* (Manchester: Manchester University Press, 2004), pp.222–36

Lincoln, Colm, 'City of Culture: Dublin and the Discovery of Urban Heritage' in Barbara O'Connor and Michael Cronin (eds), *Tourism in Ireland* (Cork: Cork University Press, 1993), pp.203–30

Lloyd, David, 'After History: Historicism and Irish Postcolonial Studies' in Clare Carroll and Patricia King (eds), *Ireland and Postcolonial Theory* (Cork: Cork University Press, 2003), pp.46–62

Luddy, Maria, 'Women and Politics in Nineteenth-Century Ireland' in Alan Hayes and Diane Urquhart (eds), *The Irish Women's History Reader* (London and New York: Routledge, 2001), pp.29–36

Lynch, Kevin, *The Image of the City* (Massachusetts: MIT Press, 1960)

MacDonald, Scott, *The Garden in the Machine* (Berkeley and Los Angeles: University of California Press, 2001)

MacPherson, James, 'Ireland Begins in the Home: Women, Irish National Identity and the Domestic Sphere in the Irish Homestead 1896–1912', *Eire/Ireland* (fall/winter 2001), accessed on 26 June 2006 at http//www.findarticles.com

Mahoney, Elisabeth, 'Citizens of its Hiding Place: Gender and Urban Space in Irish Women's Poetry' in Scott Brewster *et al.* (eds), *Ireland in Proximity: History, Gender, Space* (London and New York: Routledge, 1999), pp.145–56

Martin, Angela, 'Death of a Nation: Transnationalism, Bodies and Abortion in late Twentieth-Century Ireland' in Tamar Mayer (ed.), *Gender Ironies of Nationalism: Sexing the Nation* (London and New York: Routledge, 2000), pp.65–88

Mazierska, Ewa and Rascaroli, Laura, *From Moscow to Madrid: Postmodern Cities, European Cinema* (London and New York: I.B. Tauris, 2003)

McCarthy, Conor, *Modernisation: Crisis and Culture in Ireland 1969–1992* (Dublin: Four Courts Press, 2000)

McLean, Stuart, *The Event and its Terrors: Ireland, Famine, Modernity* (Stanford, CA: Stanford University Press, 2004)

McLoone, Martin, *Irish Film: The Emergence of a Contemporary Cinema* (London: British Film Institute, 2000)

'Music Hall Dope and British Propaganda? Cultural Identity and Early Broadcasting in Ireland', *Historical Journal of Film, Television and Radio*, 20, 3 (2000), pp.301–15

Film, Media and Popular Culture in Ireland (Dublin and Portland, OR: Irish Academic Press, 2007)

McLoughlin, Dympna, 'Women and Sexuality in Nineteenth-Century Ireland' in Alan Hayes and Diane Urquhart (eds), *The Irish Women's History Reader* (London and New York: Routledge, 2001), pp.81–6

Mitchell, Timothy, *Passional Culture: Emotion, Religion, and Society in Southern Spain* (Philadelphia: University of Pennsylvania Press, 1990)

Moane, Geraldine, 'Colonialism and the Celtic Tiger: Legacies of History and the Quest for Vision' in Peadar Kirby, Luke Gibbons and Michael Cronin (eds), *Reinventing Ireland: Culture, Society and the Global Economy* (London: Pluto Press, 2002), pp.109–23

Morgan, Rikki, 'Female Subjectivity in *Gary Cooper que estás in los cielos*' in Peter William Evans (ed.), *Spanish Cinema: The Auteurist Tradition* (Oxford: Oxford University Press, 1999), pp.176–93

Morris, Brian, 'What We Talk About When We Talk About "Walking in the City"', *Cultural Studies*, 18, 5 (2004), pp.675–97

Nägelle, Rainer, *Theatre, Theory, Speculation: Walter Benjamin and Scenes of Modernity* (Baltimore, MD: Johns Hopkins University Press, 1991)

Nowell-Smith, Geoffrey, 'Minnelli and Melodrama' in Bill Nichols (ed.), *Movies and Methods II* (Berkeley, Los Angeles and London: University of California Press, 1985), pp.190–4

O'Connell, Díog, 'Characters that "Say and Do" versus Characters that "See and Hear": *Accelerator* and *Disco Pigs*', *Film and Film Culture*, 3 (2004), pp.114–21

'*The Boy from Mercury*: Educating Emotionally through Universal Story-telling' in Ruth Barton and Harvey O'Brien (eds), *Keeping it Real: Irish Film and Television* (London: Wallflower Press, 2004), pp.121–31

O'Toole, Fintan, 'Myth that Lets Dublin 4 Evade its Responsibility', *Irish Times*, 27 May 1992

'In the Land of the Emerald Tiger', *Irish Times*, 28 December 1996

The Ex-Isle of Erin: Images of Global Ireland (Dublin: New Ireland Books, 1997)

Packenham, Thomas and Packenham, Valerie (eds) *Dublin: A Traveller's Companion* (New York: Atheneum, 1988)

Parsons, Deborah, 'Fiesta Culture in Madrid Posters 1935–1955' in Jo Labanyi (ed.), *Constructing Identity in Contemporary Spain* (Oxford: Oxford University Press, 2000), pp.178–205

Pateman, Carol, *The Disorder of Women: Democracy, Feminism and Political Theory* (Cambridge, MA: Polity Press, 1989)

Payne, Stanley, 'Spanish Fascism', *Salmagundi*, 76–77 (fall 1987–winter 1988), pp.101–12

Perriam, Chris, 'Alejandro Amenábar's *Abre los ojos/Open Your Eyes* (1997)' in Antonio Lázaro Reboll and Andrew Willis (eds), *Spanish Popular Cinema* (Manchester: Manchester University Press, 2004), pp.209–21

Pettitt, Lance, 'Pigs and Provos, Prostitutes and Prejudice' in Eibhear Walshe (ed.), *Sex, Nation and Dissent in Irish Writing* (Cork: Cork University Press, 1997), pp.252–84

Screening Ireland: Film and Television Representation (Manchester: Manchester University Press, 2000)

Pinder, David, 'Ghostly Footsteps: Voices, Memories and Walks in the City', *Ecumene* 8, 1 (2001), pp.1–19

Pollock, Griselda, *Vision and Difference: Femininity, Feminism and Histories of Art* (London and New York: Routledge, 1988)

Porter, Robert, *Ideology: Contemporary Social, Political and Cultural Theory* (Aberystwyth: University of Wales Press, 2006)

Richards, Mike, '"Terror and Progress": Industrialization, Modernity and the Making of Francoism' in Helen Graham and Jo Labanyi (eds), *Spanish Cultural Studies – an Introduction: The Struggle for Modernity* (Oxford: Oxford University Press, 1995), pp.173–82

Rockett, Kevin, 'History, Politics and Irish Cinema' in Kevin Rockett, Luke Gibbons and John Hill, *Cinema and Ireland* (London: Routledge, 1988), pp.3–146

'(Mis-)Representing the Irish Urban Landscape' in Mark Shiel and Tony Fitzmaurice (eds), *Cinema and the City* (Oxford: Blackwell, 2001), pp.217–28

Irish Film Censorship: a Cultural Journey from Silent Cinema to Internet Pornography (Dublin: Four Courts Press, 2004)

Roque-Baldovinos, Ricardo, 'Jose Luis García-Sánchez's "Pasdoble"' in Jenaro Talens and Santos Zunzunequi (eds), *Modes of Representation in Spanish Cinema* (Minneapolis: University of Minnesota Press, 1998), pp.253–63

Ruse, Joseph, 'Power/Knowledge' in Gary Cutting (ed.), *The Cambridge Companion to Foucault* (Cambridge: Cambridge University Press, 1994), pp.92–114

Said, Edward, *Culture and Imperialism* (London: Vintage, 1994)

Sanchez, Antonio, 'Barcelona's Magic Mirror: Narcissism or the Rediscovery of Public Space and Collective Identity' in Jo Labanyi (ed.), *Constructing Identity in Contemporary Spain* (Oxford: Oxford University Press, 2000), pp.294–310

Scholem, Gershom, *Major Trends in Jewish Mysticism* (New York: Schocken Books, 1946)

Shiel, Mark, 'Cinema and the City in History and Theory' in Mark Shiel and Tony Fitzmaurice (eds), *Cinema and the City* (Oxford: Blackwell, 2001), pp.1–18

Smith, James M., 'Remembering Ireland's Architecture of Containment: "Telling" Stories in *The Butcher Boy* and *States of Fear*', *Eire/Ireland* (fall/winter 2001), accessed on 10 March 2006 at http//www.findarticles.com

Smith, Paul Julian (1992) *Laws of Desire: Questions of Homosexuality in Spanish Writing and Film 1960–1990* (Oxford: Clarendon Press, 1992)

'Eloy de la Iglesia's Cinema of Transition', in Jenaro Talens and Santos Zunzunequi (eds), *Modes of Representation in Spanish Cinema* (Minneapolis: University of Minnesota Press, 1998), pp.216–52

The Moderns (Oxford: Oxford University Press, 2000)

Soja, Edward, *Postmodern Geographies* (London and New York: Verso, 1989)

Southworth, Herbert Rutledge, 'The Falange: An Analysis of Spain's Fascist Heritage' in Paul Preston (ed.), *Spain in Crisis* (Sussex: Harvester Press, 1976), pp.1–22

Tierney, M., 'Minister for Transport, Gerry Stembridge', *Film West*, 43 (2001), pp.14–17

Todorov, Tzvetan, *The Conquest of America*, trans. Richard Howard (New York: Harper & Row, 1984)

Triana-Toribio, Núria, *Spanish National Cinema* (London and New York: Routledge, 2003)

Tropicano, Stephen (1997) 'Out of the Cinematic Closet: Homosexuality in the Films of Eloy de la Iglesia' in Marsha Kinder (ed.), *Refiguring Spain* (Durham, NC: Duke University Press, 1997), pp.157–77

Ucelay da Cal, Enric, 'The Nationalisms of the Periphery: Culture and Politics in the Construction of National Identity' in Helen Graham and Jo Labanyi (eds), *Spanish Cultural Studies – an Introduction: The Struggle for Modernity* (Oxford: Oxford University Press, 1995), pp.32–9

Uchida, Ryuzo, 'Memory and the Transformation of Social Experience in Modern Japan', *Media, Culture and Society*, 21 (1999), pp.205–19

Valiulis, Maryann (2001) 'Neither Feminist nor Flapper: the Ecclesiastical Construction of the Ideal Irish Woman' in Alan Hayes and Diane Urquhart (eds), *The Irish Women's History Reader* (London and New York: Routledge, 2001), pp.152–8

Van Alphen, Ernst, 'Symptoms of Discursivity: Experience, Memory and Trauma' in Mieke Bal, Jonathon Crewe and Leo Spitzer (eds), *Acts of Memory: Cultural Recall in the Present* (Hanover, NH: University Press of New England, 1999), pp.24–37

Vernon, Kathleen M., 'Scripting a Social Imaginary: Hollywood in/and Spanish Cinema' in Jenaro Talens and Santos Zunzunequi (eds), *Modes of Representation in Spanish Cinema* (Minneapolis: University of Minnesota Press, 1998), pp.319–29

Vernon, Kathleen and Morris, Barbara, 'Introduction: Pedro Almodóvar, Postmodern Auteur' in Kathleen Vernon and Barbara Morris (eds), *The films of Pedro Almodóvar* (Westport CT: Greenwood Press, 1995), pp.1–23

Ward, Margaret, 'Marginality and Militancy: Cumann na mBan

1914–1936' in Alan Hayes and Diane Urquhart (eds), *The Irish Women's History Reader* (London and New York: Routledge, 2001), pp.58–63

Weihsmann, Helmut, 'The City in Twilight: Charting the Genre of the "City Film" 1900–1930' in Francois Penz and Maureen Thomas (eds), *Cinema and Architecture: Méliès, Mallet-Stevens, Multimedia* (London: British Film Institute, 1997), pp.8–27

Whelan, Kevin, 'Between Filiation and Affiliation: The Politics of Post-colonial Memory' in Clare Carroll and Patricia King (eds), *Ireland and Postcolonial Theory* (Cork: Cork University Press, 2003), pp.92–108

Willemen, Paul and Pines, Jim, *Questions of Third Cinema* (London: British Film Institute, 1989)

Williams, Raymond, *The Country and the City* (London: Chatto & Windus, 1973)

Wilson, Elizabeth, 'Into the Labyrinth' in Linda McDowell and Joanne P. Sharp (eds), *Space, Gender, Knowledge: Feminist Readings* (London and New York: Edward Arnold, 1997), pp. 277–84

Wolff, Janet, 'The Invisible *Flâneuse*: Women and the Literature of Modernity' in Andrew Benjamin (ed.), *The Problems of Modernity: Adorno and Benjamin* (London and New York: Routledge, 1989), pp.141–56

Filmography

About Adam (Gerry Stembridge, Ireland/GB/US, 2000)
Abre los ojos (Open your Eyes, Alejandro Amenábar, Spain/France/Italy, 1997)
Accelerator (Vinny Murphy, Ireland/GB, 2000)
Adam and Paul (Leonard Abrahamson, Ireland, 2004)
Agnes Browne (Anjelica Huston, Ireland/US, 1999)
Ailsa (Paddy Breathnach, Ireland, 1994)
Alba de América (Dawn of America, Juan de Orduña, Spain, 1951)
A Mother's Love's a Blessing (Charlie McCarthy, Ireland, 1994)
Anne Devlin (Pat Murphy, Ireland/GB, 1984)
A Terrible Beauty (Tay Garnett, GB/US, 1960)
Ballroom of Romance (Pat O'Connor, GB, 1982)
Barrio (Neighbourhood, Fernando León de Aranoa, Spain/Portugal, 1998)
Berlin, Symphony of a City (Walter Ruttman, Germany/France, 1927)
Bicycle Thieves (Vittorio De Sica, Italy, 1948)
Bienvenido Mr Marshall (Welcome Mr Marshall, Luis García Berlanga, Spain, 1952)
Breakfast at Tiffany's (Blake Edwards, US, 1961)
Breakfast on Pluto (Neil Jordan, Ireland/GB, 2006)
Calle Mayor (Main Street, Juan Antonio Bardem, Spain, 1956)
Camada negra (Black Brood, Manuel Gutiérrez Aragón, Spain, 1977)
Caoineadh Airt Uí Laoire (Lament for Art O'Leary, Bob Quinn, Ireland, 1975)
Caricias (Caresses, Ventura Pons, Spain, 1998)
Carne trémula (Live Flesh, Pedro Almodóvar, Spain/France, 1997)
Country (Kevin Liddy, Ireland/GB, 2000)
Cowboys and Angels (David Gleeson, Ireland/GB/Germany, 2003)
Crush Proof (Paul Tickell, Ireland/GB/Germany/Netherlands, 1996)
Cuando todo esté in orden (When Everything is in Order, César Martínez Herrada, Spain, 2002)
Dias contados (Running Out of Time, Imanol Uribe, Spain, 1994)

Disco Pigs (Kirsten Sheridan, Ireland/GB, 2000)

Do the Right Thing (Spike Lee, US, 1989)

Driftwood (Ronan O'Leary, Ireland/GB, 1996)

El corazón del bosque (The Heart of the Forest, Manuel Gutiérrez Aragón, Spain, 1979)

El dia de la bestia (The Day of the Beast, Alex de la Iglesia, Spain, 1995)

El espíritu de la colmena (The Spirit of the Beehive, Víctor Erice, Spain, 1973)

El otro lado de la cama (The Other Side of the Bed, Emilio Martínez Lázaro, Spain 2002)

El último cuplé (The Last Song, Juan de Orduña, Spain, 1957)

Far and Away (Ron Howard, US, 1992)

Furtivos (Poachers, José Luis Borau, Spain, 1975)

Gary Cooper, que estás en los Cielos (Gary Cooper, who Art in Heaven, Pilar Miró, Spain, 1980)

Gidget Goes to Rome (Paul Wendkos, US, 1963)

Goldfish Memory (Elizabeth Gill, Ireland, 2003)

Guiltrip (Gerry Stembridge, Ireland/France/Italy, 1995)

¡Harka! (Carlos Arévalo, Spain, 1941)

Home for Christmas (Charlie McCarthy, Ireland, 2002)

Huevos de oro (Golden Balls, Bigas Luna, Spain/Italy/France, 1993)

Hush-a-Bye-Baby (Margo Harkin, GB, 1989)

Intermission (John Crowley, Ireland/GB, 2003)

Into the West (Mike Newell, Ireland/GB/US, 1992)

Irish Destiny (George Dewhurst, Ireland, 1926)

Irma La Douce (Billy Wilder, US, 1963)

Jamón Jamón (Ham Ham, Bigas Luna, Spain, 1992)

Kathleen Manourveen (Norman Lee, GB, 1937)

Kilometre Zero (Kilometre Zero, Yolanda García Serrano and Juan Luis Iborra, Iraq/France, 2000)

Korea (Cathal Black, GB, 1995)

La gran familia (The Big Family, Fernando Palacios, Spain, 1962)

La Haine (Mattieu Kassovitz, France/US, 1995)

La mala educación (Bad Education, Pedro Almodóvar, Spain, 2004)

La orilla (The Border, Luis Lucía, Spain, 1971)

Last Days in Dublin (Lance Daly, Ireland, 2001)

Last of the High Kings (David Keating, Ireland/Denmark, 1996)

La vida que te espera (Your Next Life, Manuel Gutiérrez Aragón, Spain, 2004)

Locura de amor (Madness of Love, Juan de Orduña, Spain, 1948)

Los lunes al sol (Mondays in the Sun, Fernando León de Aranoa,

Spain/Italy, 2002)

Los últimos de Filipinas (Last Stand in the Philippines, Antonio Román, Spain, 1945)

Maeve (Pat Murphy, Ireland/GB, 1981)

Man of Aran (Robert Flaherty, GB, 1934)

Mapmaker (Johnny Gogan, Ireland/GB, 2001)

Michael Collins (Neil Jordan, Ireland/GB/US, 1996)

Mise Éire (George Morrison, Ireland, 1959)

Morena Clara (Clara, the Brunette, Florián Rey, Spain, 1936)

Muerte de un ciclista (Death of a Cyclist, Juan Antonio Bardem, Spain, 1955)

Mujeres al borde de un ataque de nervios (Women on the Verge of a Nervous Breakdown, Pedro Almodóvar, Spain, 1988)

My Left Foot (Jim Sheridan, Ireland/GB, 1989)

Nobleza Baturra (Rustic Chivalry, Juan de Orduña, Spain, 1965)

Odd Man Out (Carol Reed, GB, 1947)

Opera prima (Opera Cousin, Fernando Trueba, Spain/France, 1980)

Ordinary Decent Criminal (Thaddeus O'Sullivan, Ireland/GB/Germany/US, 2000)

Our Boys (Cathal Black, Ireland, 1982)

Ourselves Alone (Brian Desmond Hurst, UK, 1936)

Pete's Meteor (Joe O'Byrne, Ireland, 1998)

Poitín (Bob Quinn, Ireland, 1978)

Posición avanzada (Advanced Position, Pedro Lazaga, Spain, 1965)

Rat (Steve Barron, GB/US, 2000)

Raza (Race, José Luis Sáenz de Heredia, Spain, 1941)

Reefer and the Model (Joe Comerford, Ireland, 1988)

Roman Holiday (William Wyler, US, 1953)

Ryan's Daughter (David Lean, UK, 1970)

Saoirse? (George Morrison, Ireland, 1961)

Secretos del corazón (Secrets of the Heart, Montxo Armendáriz, Spain/Portugal/France, 1997)

Shake Hands with the Devil (Michael Anderson, Ireland/GB, 1959)

Silencio roto (Broken Silence, Montxo Armendáriz, Spain, 2001)

Snakes and Ladders (Trish McAdam, Ireland/Germany/GB, 1996)

Solas (Alone, Benito Zambrano, Spain, 1999)

Soldados de Salamina (Soldiers of Salamis, David Trueba, Spain, 2003)

Spaghetti Slow (Valerio Jalongo, Ireland/Italy, 1997)

Surcos (Furrows, José Antonio Nieves Conde, Spain, 1950)

Tesis (Thesis, Alejandro Amenábar, Spain, 1996)

The Boy from Mercury (Martin Duffy, Ireland/GB/France, 1996)

The Butcher Boy (Neil Jordan, Ireland/USA, 1997)

The Courier (Frank Deasy, Ireland/GB, 1987)

The Dawn (Tom Cooper, Ireland, 1936)

The Fifth Province (Frank Stapleton, Ireland/GB/Germany, 1997)

The General (John Boorman Ireland/GB, 1998)

The Informer (John Ford, US, 1935)

The Last Bus Home (Johnny Gogan, Ireland, 1997)

The Luck of the Irish (Donovan Pedelty, Ireland, 1935)

The Quiet Man (John Ford, US, 1952)

The Rocky Road to Dublin (Peter Lennon, Ireland, 1968)

The Snapper (Stephen Frears, Ireland/GB, 1993)

The Sun, the Moon and the Stars (Geraldine Creed, Ireland/Germany, 1996)

This is My Father (Paul Quinn, Ireland/Canada, 1998)

Todo sobre mi madre (All About my Mother, Pedro Almodóvar, Spain/France, 1999)

Torrente: el brazo tonto de la ley (Torrente: the Stupid Arm of the Law, Santiago Segura, Spain, 1998)

Viridiana (Luis Buñuel, Spain/Mexico, 1961)

When Love Came to Gavin Burke (Fred O'Donovan, GB, 1917)

Index